SOUTH AFRICA AT 10

SOUTH AFRICA AT 10

Perspectives by political, business and civil leaders

WORLD ECONOMIC FORUM

Human & Rousseau
Cape Town Pretoria

All rights strictly reserved.
First published in 2004 by Human & Rousseau,
40 Heerengracht, Cape Town
Cover design by Abdul Amien
Typography by Etienne van Duyker
Typeset in 10.5 on 13.25 pt Palatino, Trajan and Helvetica
by Alinea Studio, 120 Bree Street, Cape Town
Printed and bound by Paarl Print,
Oosterland Street, Paarl, South Africa

Softcover edition: ISBN 0 7981 4460 2
Hardcover edition: ISBN 0 7981 4483 1

No part of this book may be reproduced or transmitted in
any form or by any means, electronic or mechanical,
or by photocopying, recording of microfilming,
or stored in any retrieval system, without the
written permission of the publisher

ACKNOWLEDGEMENTS

I would like to thank the people who have worked with me on this project. First and foremost, Seán Cleary, whom I met in Namibia on my first trip to that country and who, over the years, has become a friend and mentor, as well as an advisor to the World Economic Forum. He encouraged me to transform the idea of this book into reality and provided the strategic guidance to make it happen.

Linette Viljoen of Human & Rousseau deserves a special mention for her dedication, well beyond the course of any conceivable duty, to the realisation of the project. Richard Steyn once again demonstrated his exceptional editing skills and great understanding of South Africa's recent history. All our authors, of course, merit the greatest of thanks for delivering their insights into this decade with clarity and grace, and on time. A special word of gratitude is due to the Nelson Mandela Foundation and Ross Calder for allowing us to incorporate the evocative words and images crafted by South Africa's first democratically elected President, and to Bertie Lubner for having facilitated this co-operation.

Many thanks to my assistant at the World Economic Forum, Paula Verholen, who kept Seán and me focused on our tasks; also to Nadine Bonard, Senior Regional Manager for Africa and Haiko Alfeld, Director for Africa at the Forum, for sharing their passion for Africa with me. I also wish to thank Chris Liebenberg, former chairman of Nedcor and Nelson Mandela's first finance minister, for having been a constant guide as I came to know South Africa.

A friendly salute to all those leaders in South Africa whom I have had the privilege of knowing. As always in these circumstances, they are too many to be listed, but they know who they are. Together we worked, laughed, shared moments of grave concern, and of happiness. Above all, we built relationships of trust and learned from one another. You gave me the opportunity of living through a fascinating journey!

My deepest respect is due to Professor Klaus Schwab, Founder and Executive Chairman of the World Economic Forum, for having entrusted me with the responsibility of working for Africa through the Forum. And, of course, a loving thought to my wife Lisa, who has endured so many of my absences as I travelled through Africa and the world.

Frédéric Sicre

ABBREVIATIONS USED

ABC: Audit Bureau of Circulation
ADSL: Asymmetric digital subscriber line
AGOA: African Growth and Opportunity Act
ANC: African National Congress
ART: Antiretroviral therapy
AWB: Afrikaner Weerstandsbeweging
BEE: Black Economic Empowerment
BEECom: Black Economic Empowerment Commission
CBM: Consultative Business Movement
CBO: Community-based organisation
CODESA: Convention for a Democratic South Africa
COSATU: Confederation of South African Trade Unions
CPIX: Consumer price index
CRB: China Resource Breweries
CSI: Corporate social investment
DRM: Digital radio mondiale
DTI: Department of Trade and Industry
DVD: Digital video disc
EU: European Union
FCC: Federal Communications Commission
GATT: General Agreement on Traffic and Trade
GEAR: Growth, Employment and Redistribution
GEIS: General Export Incentive Scheme
GSM: Global System for Mobile Communications
ICASA: Independent Communications Authority of South Africa
IDC: Industrial Corporation
IFP: Inkatha Freedom Party
IMF: International Monetary Fund
IT: Information technology
JSE: Johannesburg Stock Exchange

LAN: Local area network
MDDA: Media Development and Diversity Agency
MDM: Mass Democratic Movement
NAB: National Association of Broadcasters
NASA: Newspaper Association of South Africa
NEPAD: New Partnership for Africa's Development
NGO: Non-government organisation
NOFP: Net open foreign currency position
NPO: Not-for-profit organisation
NP: National Party
NFVF: National Film and Video Foundation
OECD: Organisation for Economic Co-operation and Development
Ofcom: Office of Communications
PAC: Pan Africanist Congress
RDP Reconstruction and Development Programme
RISA: Record Industry of South Africa
SAA: South African Airways
SAB: South African Breweries
SABC: South African Broadcasting Corporation
SADC: Southern African Development Co-ordination
SADCC: Southern African Development Co-ordination Conference
SAFACT: South African Federation Against Copyright Theft
SAMRO: South African Music Rights Organisation
SANEF: South African National Editors' Forum
SARS: South African Revenue Services
SAVANT: South African Technology Vanguard
SME: Small and medium enterprise
SMME: Small, medium and micro enterprise
SMS: Short message service
SNO: Second network operator
SOE: State-owned enterprise
SPV: Special Purpose Vehicle
TRC: Truth and Reconciliation Commission
WAP: Wireless application protocol
WASP: Wireless application service providers
WEF: World Economic Forum
WSIS: World Summit on Information Society
WTO: World Trade Organisation
XML: Extensible mark-up language

CONTENTS

Preface: South Africa, making the difference   11
   President Thabo Mbeki

Introduction   15
   Frédéric Sicre

A Touch of Mandela   23
   Nelson Mandela

Civil Society: The role of business and the
   churches in facilitating the transition   29
   Neal Chapman and Peter Wrighton

South Africa's Transition from Financial Sanctions
   to a Choice Emerging Market   45
   Tito Mboweni

From Local to Global in One Decade   59
   Graham Mackay

Black Empowerment: Myths and realities   72
   Cyril Ramaphosa

The Role of Women in a Democratic South Africa   85
   Wendy Luhabe

Confronting the HIV/AIDS Pandemic in
   South Africa: The challenge for business   97
   Sir Mark Moody-Stuart

ICT in South Africa: Recollections of an
    extraordinary decade   107
Jeremy Ord

The Role of Technology in Meeting
    Development Challenges   123
Jay Naidoo

A Democratic South Africa: Three perspectives on
    the role of culture and the contribution of
    entertainment and the media   139
Koos Bekker, Anant Singh and Peter Sullivan

Philanthropy in South Africa: A feel-good factor
    or a net contributor to social upliftment?   172
Bertie Lubner

Recovering the Soul of the South African Nation   187
Willie Esterhuyse

New Partnership for Africa's Development
    (NEPAD)   197
Reuel Khoza

The Next Ten Years   211
Clem Sunter

Index   221

PREFACE:
SOUTH AFRICA, MAKING THE DIFFERENCE

Only the churlish would deny that something immensely encouraging has been going on in South Africa over the last ten years. The past was marked by oppression, racism, conflict and instability, and a continuously deepening economic crisis.

This has changed to the current reality of freedom, dedication to non-racialism and demonstrable stability, and robust economic recovery. Now we have a South Africa where yesterday's oppressors and the oppressed work as partners.

Though many problems inherited from the past still remain to be solved, there is an enduring optimism in the air, even among those who still await the socioeconomic fruits of our freedom.

The story of the last ten years is the story of sustained progress away from a South Africa that had isolated itself in an embittered racist laager, towards a South Africa now fit and able to play a positive role in the wider world.

Surely, all this is common cause. But a seasoned analytical readership such as members of the World Economic Forum will seek explanations beyond generalisations and congratulatory remarks.

It will want to be empowered by this book and other research, to make informed decisions as participants in a country that is growing and an economy that is expanding as never before. Unlike a magician's show, in which too much understanding spoils the illusion, our changing South Africa is, in its fundamentals, a comprehensible and straightforward place.

It is a country now reaping the benefits of the firm building blocks put in place after 1994. In this book you will find some of the voices of those active in our economic and technological transformation. These voices intend to clarify rather than mystify.

The economic history of South Africa over the last decade is one of a sustained, successful and continuing struggle to overcome the legacy of a social system that had condemned our country to a permanent and deepening political, economic and social crisis.

The establishment of a stable democratic system has created the conditions for us to tackle our socioeconomic development challenges. Through hard work and correct policies, we have succeeded in correcting the macroeconomic imbalances that meant high inflation and interest rates, an unmanageable budget deficit and negative growth rates.

We have taken down the barriers that isolated our economy, which rendered it internationally uncompetitive. The process of modernising and restructuring the economy has increased the importance of new sectors, proportionately reducing our dependence on the production and export of raw materials.

This, in turn, has freed the country from the balance of payments constraint, which made it impossible to maintain high and sustained rates of growth without having to slow down the economy, and to reduce the volume of imports occasioned by higher growth.

As demonstrated by the rapid expansion in the export of motor vehicles and motor vehicle components, our economy has shown its capacity to produce goods that can compete successfully in the global markets. This is also confirmed by the rapid expansion of back-office operations in our country, which handle business information on behalf of international customers.

Our bilateral trade and development agreement with the EU, as well as the US's AGOA, have also facilitated our access to international markets. In addition to what will be achieved through the WTO Doha Development Round, access will also be improved by the conclusion of trade agreements with Mercosur, the USA, and, later, India and China.

This will further improve our attractiveness as a production base from which to export into the world markets, as has happened with regard to motor vehicles and vehicle components.

Gradually, we are also overcoming the constraint to investment and growth resulting from the shortage of skilled workers. This is being addressed through a vigorous skills- and human resource development programme.

Prudent management of our public finances and the relative health of our economy have also given us the possibility of confronting the serious challenge of poverty, deliberately created by the previous system of white privilege and domination.

What we have managed to do has given hope to, and improved the quality of life of, millions of our people, making a critical contribution to the stability we need both to consolidate the democratic system and attend to our development challenges.

In the period ahead, we will continue to focus on the task of eradicating poverty, which is also directly related to the objective of addressing the racial imbalances and inequalities that are part of our legacy. The sustained effort to eradicate the legacy of racism, which is critical to our success as a country, must and will also include further progress towards the achievement of broad-based black economic empowerment.

Because of everything we have done in the last decade, the latest available Article IV Report of the IMF commended our government for its sound macroeconomic management and the implementation of structural policies, which it said had increased the efficiency of the economy and its resilience to external shocks.

While agreeing with the government's expenditures on social policy, skills development and economic services, the report commended the government for its strong record of fiscal discipline, which had kept long-term interest rates low, ensured a competitive exchange rate and revived confidence in our economy.

South Africa's next decade will unfold from a script written by and for South Africans, within a country eager to embrace the continent and the wider world beyond. In this time of great violence and geopolitical challenges, South Africa remains equipped to support the international rule of law in the quest for African and world peace and prosperity.

Having been the beneficiaries of the global movement against South African *apartheid*, we now hope to play a continuing but responsible role in the international movement against global *apartheid*, and in the push for fair economic relations among a peaceable community of nations.

In particular, we will continue to contribute to the achievement of the African Renaissance, entailing the construction of our continent as one of democracy, peace, prosperity and mutually advantageous co-operation among all Africans. We will strive to improve the effectiveness of the African Union and NEPAD, the New Partnership for Africa's Development.

In a world troubled, among other things, by violence throughout the Middle East and international terrorism, we will continue to work with other nations to strengthen the multilateral system, emphasising the importance of the dialogue of civilisations rather than the clash of these civilisations.

We are confident that, in the period ahead, we will score new victories in the effort to build a nonracial and non-sexist South Africa. We will make fresh advances towards the eradication of poverty and underdevelopment and towards prosperity for all. We will continue to contribute to the renewal of Africa, and towards a better world of democracy, stability and shared prosperity.

All these positive developments will position our country among those that will help to make a real difference in the context of the exciting and challenging world now unfolding at the beginning of the 21st century.

President Thabo Mbeki

INTRODUCTION

"South Africa would not be where it is today if it were not for the World Economic Forum", said Nelson Rolihlahla Mandela in January 1999 as he bade farewell to the twelve hundred chief executives and members at the annual meeting of the Forum in Davos that year.

The political transformation of South Africa a decade ago has often been called a "miracle". The epithet acknowledges that few observers of South Africa's travails at the end of the 1980s expected an inclusive democracy to emerge from the death-throes of apartheid, leading to an economic revival and a new sense of patriotism. While the award of the Nobel Peace Prize to Nelson Mandela and F W de Klerk recorded the extraordinary contribution of leadership, foresight and vision that both had made in enabling a largely peaceful transition, other unsung heroes contributed to the making of South Africa's unique success story. Many stories are still untold!

Cyril Ramaphosa and Roelf Meyer are rightly celebrated for their joint role as midwives to a new Constitution; Archbishop Desmond Tutu's contribution to the birth of a "rainbow nation" is widely recognised, but the parts played by Thabo Mbeki, Jacob Zuma and Constand Viljoen in mitigating and managing the fears of the Afrikaner right, and the exceptional role of Zuma and his Inkatha Freedom Party counterpart, Frank Mdlalose, in quieting tensions among the *amaZulu* in the lead-up to the first democratic elections, are less well known. Many in the Christian churches and other faith communities and some leading members of the South African business community also played exemplary roles in smoothing the path.

History has properly bestowed an iconic status on Nelson Mandela; he is a living legend whose ability to transcend the injustices heaped on him, seems superhuman. Who else could have visited Betsie Verwoerd, the widow of apartheid's architect, in her whites-only enclave of Orania, when she was unable to attend his luncheon for the widows of deceased South African leaders, including those of John Vorster and Steve Biko? Who else could have invited to lunch the man who had prosecuted him, called in court for the death sentence and led to his incarceration for 27 years?

Mandela's contribution to national reconciliation in the five years after he became President in 1994, is unparalleled. F W de Klerk's courage in embarking on his own version of *glasnost* has earned him a place in history. But South Africa's political path might well have taken a different turn if a number of South African business leaders and their counterparts in the churches, including Desmond Tutu and Frank Chikane, had not played an active mediatory role, with the support of political leaders like Thabo Mbeki, Roelf Meyer, Frank Mdlalose, Jacob Zuma and Zach de Beer, during the difficult years leading up to the elections in 1994.

The origin of this book, *South Africa at 10*, lies in my desire to pay tribute to the leaders in South Africa's business community who played a crucial role in enabling their country to achieve democracy in 1994, and to celebrate its progress a decade later. I sought, when conceiving this book, to embed their contributions in a wider social context and to look forward as well as backward. As President Thabo Mbeki notes in his Preface, "Only the churlish would deny that something immensely encouraging has been going on in South Africa over the last ten years." As he also notes, however, "a seasoned analytical readership . . . will seek explanations beyond generalisations and congratulatory remarks."

When Klaus Schwab created the World Economic Forum in 1971, he founded it on the belief that business had a duty to engage in *"improving the state of the world"*, nationally, regionally and globally. Today, it is widely recognised that the private sector has the resources and skills needed to help governments address the challenges they face. Whether these are securing the rule of law, promoting good governance and sound macroeconomic policy, or lifting communities out of poverty and fighting crime, business cannot be a bystander. The South African experience shows that when business and civil society leaders engage constructively, the chances of success are multiplied.

The task of righting the wrongs of apartheid in South Africa and uplifting its disadvantaged citizens will still be a long one. But the foundation that has been laid in the past decade is sound, as the essays by the authors in this book make clear. South Africa's success is due to leading South Africans from many parts of society, with different experiences and skill-sets, being able to find common cause in building an enlightened polity, underpinned by an increasingly strong economy. It was this common purpose and their collective determination to achieve success that has allowed South Africa to play a disproportionately influential role, not only in Africa, but in the global community.

The World Economic Forum was able to play a modest role in facilitating South Africa's passage and I was especially privileged to spend a fascinating decade at the heart of the process. As a young 26-year-old project manager at the Forum, I was given a bone to chew on called "Africa". At that time people spoke of the "lost continent" and one global business leader made clear his level of interest in Africa by saying to me "I thought the Atlantic and Indian oceans had swallowed it up". I wondered what I could do to get our members, the one thousand foremost companies in the world, to engage with this continent. Little did I know that only six months after I was hired, Nelson Mandela, freed from prison, would be on his way to capture their interest for me!

In 1990, Sandton was a shadow of its present self. Jan Smuts International Airport in Johannesburg was small by international standards – it looked truly provincial. Most of the planes on the tarmac bore SAA's orange tailfin, emblazoned with the flying Springbok. I still wonder whether, on my first trip to the country, my suitcases accompanied me, or I them. They were filled with 70 kilograms of Forum brochures and Swiss chocolates. Although a few leading South African companies had joined the Forum and a few CEOs had been to Davos, nobody from the Forum had visited South Africa and here I was, new to the job and to the continent.

Our members welcomed me with open arms and organised meetings with a most impressive array of their peers, who did not yet know the Forum. My first business dinner was organised in the Sandton Sun Hotel by Basil Landau of Gencor, who invited the Director-General of Foreign Affairs, Leo 'Rusty' Evans and Donald Gordon of Liberty Life. It was the first business dinner I had hosted and I appreciated Basil's quiet advice on the selection of wines and on procedure.

Before every appointment I was nervous, not knowing what to

expect, but was quickly put at ease by the enthusiasm of my hosts. As I walked into Bertie Lubner's office, his first words were "It's about time the Forum sent someone down here to see us!" The CEOs and chairmen of South Africa's major corporations immediately recognised that the Forum could help them walk the nation down the dangerous but essential path that President F W de Klerk had chosen on 2 February 1990.

I returned to Geneva with empty suitcases, thinking that South African business leaders either truly needed us, or were simply very friendly people. I was soon to realise that both were true and came to feel increasingly optimistic about South Africa's chances of success, if these private sector leaders were determined to play a meaningful role.

My visit that year to Namibia (which had just achieved independence), was unforgettable. The members of Sam Nujoma's first government were moving into their offices and most of my meetings took place amidst movers and boxes. The buzz in the air was palpable and presaged what was to come in South Africa on a much larger scale. I travelled to Lusaka in Zambia to seek ANC party economists in the exile camps. Accompanied by armed bodyguards we drove amidst shacks down dirt roads looking for Max Sisulu. I must confess that I failed to find him and only met him years later!

I did meet with members of the government of President Robert Mugabe, then clearly the leader of the Frontline States, to discuss our desire to help bring the region together now that decisive change had come to South Africa. These meetings were facilitated by the late minister of finance, Bernard Chidzero, whose son I had known since our high school days together in Geneva. We encouraged the Zimbabweans to accept that the process beginning in South Africa required them to think about transforming the SADCC into an inclusive regional bloc, in which a democratic South Africa could play a vital role.

After the return of the ANC leaders from exile, our focus shifted to South Africa itself. I visited Shell House regularly, building relationships with Tito Mboweni, Thabo Mbeki and Trevor Manuel, discussing over coffee and my Swiss chocolates ways in which we could help build a new future for the nation.

We discussed with South Africa's business leaders how best to offer our politically neutral platform to promote discussion about the economic policies that would best serve a democratic South Africa in a rapidly changing global environment. The ANC's alliance with the South African Communist Party and COSATU (the Confederation of South African Trade Unions) worried many in the business community. The fall of the Berlin Wall in 1989 and the implosion of the Soviet Union in 1991 seemed to make it clear that political and economic liberalism, characterised by market-driven systems, would define the decade.

The Forum's offices in Geneva were the location for the first inclusive meeting between South Africa's political parties and leading representatives of its business community. Discussions centred on which path to take, one emphasising the creation of wealth and the other the redistribution of wealth. This was the launch-pad of what became known as the Thabo Mbeki/Barend du Plessis Road Show, which took these two leaders around the world to foster international support. A picture of Conservative Party member Koos van der Merwe sitting next to Thabo Mbeki with a broad smile on his face was to create havoc in parliament shortly thereafter. Global business executives participating in this meeting still recall Chief Buthelezi drawing his genealogical tree on a napkin, at their request, and explaining the greatness of the Zulu. The Forum was building bridges between former enemies and developing an international support network for South Africa at the highest level.

On 2 February 1992, exactly two years to the day after President De Klerk had unbanned the liberation movements and freed Nelson Mandela, De Klerk, Mandela and Buthelezi appeared together on an international platform at our annual meeting in Davos. This was a milestone in South Africa's history. The opening of Parliament had been delayed to allow the three leaders to gather in the Swiss Alps, symbolising their common determination to succeed. Klaus Schwab deserves tremendous credit for his shuttle diplomacy in the last days before the meeting, without which this historic event would not have taken place.

My first meeting with Madiba to prepare for this had been organised by Neal Chapman and Peter Wrighton, who had invited him and Cyril Ramaphosa to lunch at the Premier Group's head office in Killarney. Before lunch we planned to show the two ANC leaders a video of the annual meeting at Davos. As I entered the theatre, Madiba greeted me with his famous smile and asked me warmly to sit next to him. Those who have been blessed with encounters with this man will know the awe and admiration that overwhelmed me. During lunch we answered the many questions the ANC leaders had about the World Economic Forum, many of which were tinged with suspicion about our motives in requesting Madiba's presence in Davos. Neal, Peter and I worked mightily to dispel their fears and we ended the lunch on a note of mutual trust and a desire to work together.

The tremendous efforts of South Africa's business leaders to prepare the historic meeting of the three leaders in Davos are well described by Neal and Peter in their chapter in this book. It was a remarkable success: After a meeting with Chinese Premier Li Peng, Madiba changed his mind on the merits of nationalising the commanding heights of the South African economy!

In May 1993, the Forum brought together its global membership on South African soil for the first time, in the Mount Nelson Hotel in Cape Town. Eight other southern African countries participated officially, a remarkable circumstance before the 1994 elections. This exemplified our role in providing common platforms for the region's business and political leaders to meet, thus breaking down the walls of the past.

Robert Mugabe made his first trip to South Africa in 52 years to attend our 1994 Southern Africa Summit, held once again in Cape Town. The Mount Nelson was becoming too small for the community of international leaders from business, government and academia who wanted to contribute to South Africa's development through the Forum, so we moved our yearly summit in 1995 to Gallagher Estates and in 1996 to the Cape Sun in Cape Town.

These summits gave hope to leaders from all sectors of society in South Africa and the region that a brighter, more prosperous future was possible. None of us will forget the pride in the voice of the SAA pilot who announced to the passengers after take-off that the World Economic Forum team was on board, making its way to Cape Town for our first summit in the country. F W de Klerk later called it "an historic event".

Nor shall we forget visiting Ministers Trevor Manuel and Tito Mboweni in their new ministerial offices a few weeks after the first democratic election in 1994. Long gone were the days of cramped offices in Shell House! My Swiss chocolates and I were received with broad smiles and accolades; I shared in their joy and celebrated the fact that they had "made it". Ministers Manuel and Mboweni, along with many others, had indeed made history, and I feel privileged and humbled to have been given the opportunity by Klaus Schwab to be a part of that journey.

After 1994, the World Economic Forum used the platform of a democratic South Africa to initiate broader discussions between the public and private sectors in Zimbabwe, Tanzania, Kenya, Mozambique, Namibia, and Zambia. We have organised summits in South Africa, Namibia, Zimbabwe and, in 2004, Mozambique. Africans from all SADC countries and many other states on the continent – from government, business and civil society – have been able to meet, share views and discuss their concerns and aspirations.

In some cases elsewhere in Africa, we have been the catalyst that enabled business leaders to meet for the first time with their governments to discuss economic policy and regional integration. We created the *Africa Competiveness Report* as a tool to help them develop objective benchmarks to measure and encourage progress.

In 1998, we were the privileged partner of the newly elected President Thabo Mbeki in presenting his new government to the international business community.

In January 2001, in Davos, President Mbeki and other African leaders launched the New Partnership for Africa's Development (NEPAD). In 2002, the Southern Africa Summit was transformed into an *Africa Economic Summit*, which became the platform from which hundreds of leading companies and business organisations active in Africa committed to playing a key supporting role in making the NEPAD a reality.

We have been privileged to work with NEPAD Business Groups established in six African countries, and the NEPAD Secretariat in doing this. The South African NEPAD Business Group, chaired by Reuel Khoza, has developed four documents to give effect to the commitment of its members. These are two Business Covenants – on Corporate Governance and the Elimination of Corruption and Bribery – and two Business Declarations – on Corporate Responsibility and Accounting and Audit Practices respectively.

The World Economic Forum is a business-centred organisation representing the one thousand leading global companies that are *committed to improving the state of the world*. It is a multi-stakeholder platform for the collective efforts of global business, national governments, multilateral organisations and civil society bodies to address the myriad challenges of constructive coexistence on our shared planet. We are delighted that our South African membership is increasingly reflective of the new reality in South Africa. Members and good friends like Patrice Motsepe are testimony that South Africa continues to produce great success stories, even though the path to eradicating the legacy of apartheid will be a long one.

This book celebrates the contribution of business to South Africa's transformation. While the Forum has been privileged to make important contributions in several parts of the world in the 33 years of our existence, I have rarely encountered such a determined and engaged group of people as those I met in South Africa. Our world in the 21st century is replete with national, regional and global challenges. Business leaders can, and do, play vital roles when they set their minds to it and show leadership beyond the limits of their balance sheets. Business leaders in South Africa have given the global community an encouraging lesson. Can this be replicated elsewhere on the African continent and indeed, the world? I am sure it can, and that is what the World Economic Forum will continue to strive for.

Frédéric Sicre
Managing Director, World Economic Forum, Switzerland

A TOUCH OF MANDELA

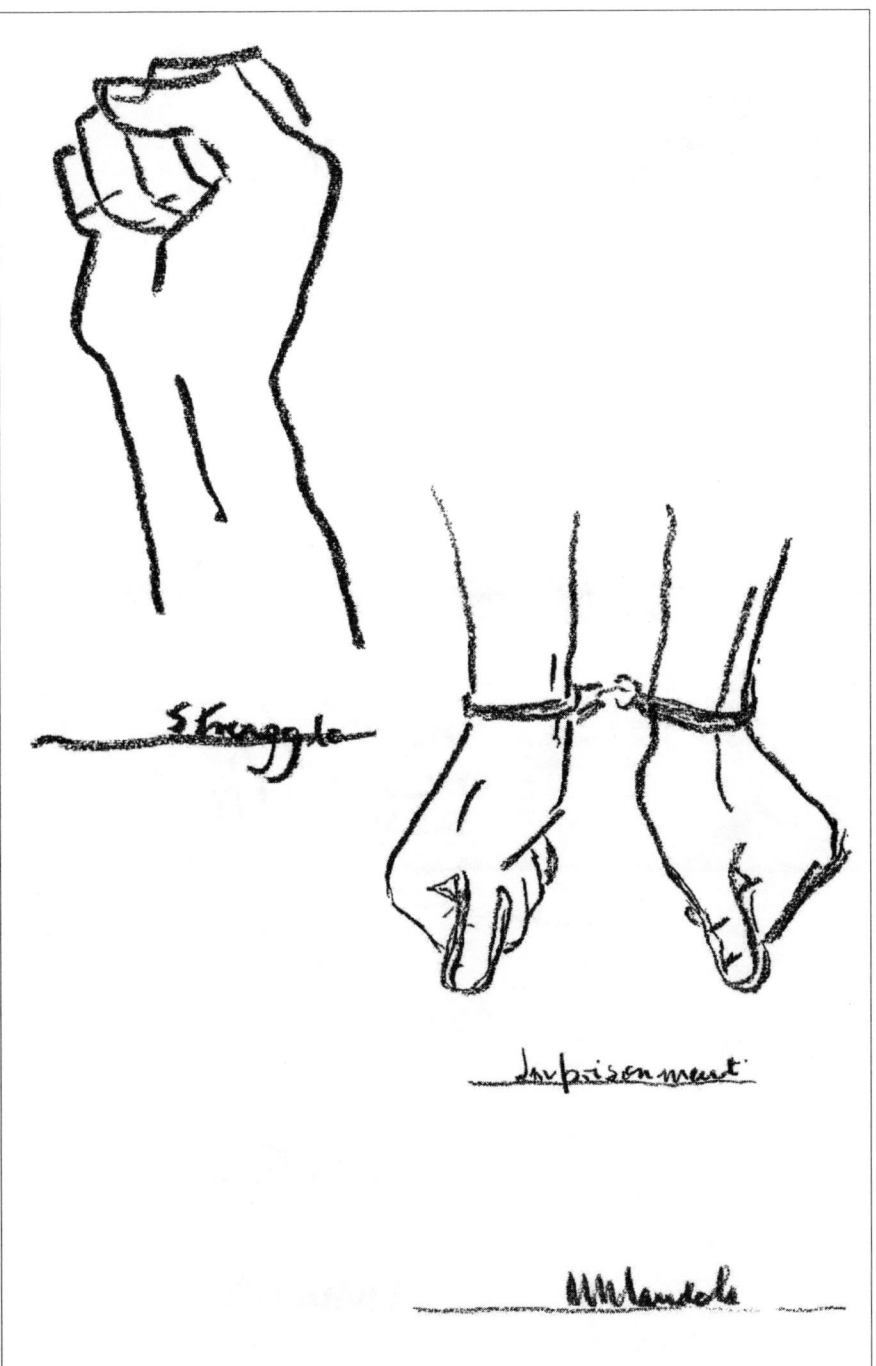

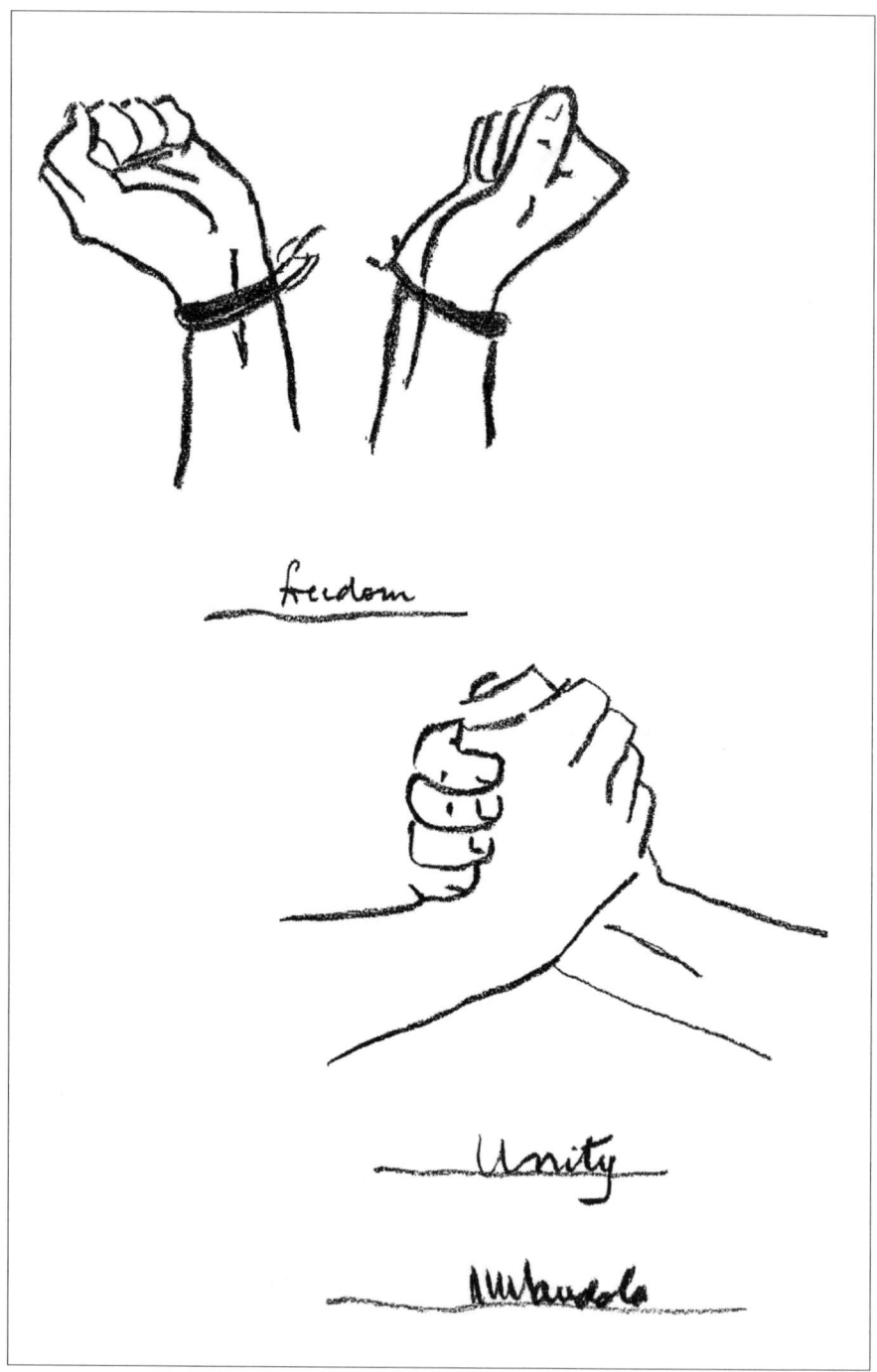

A touch of Mandela

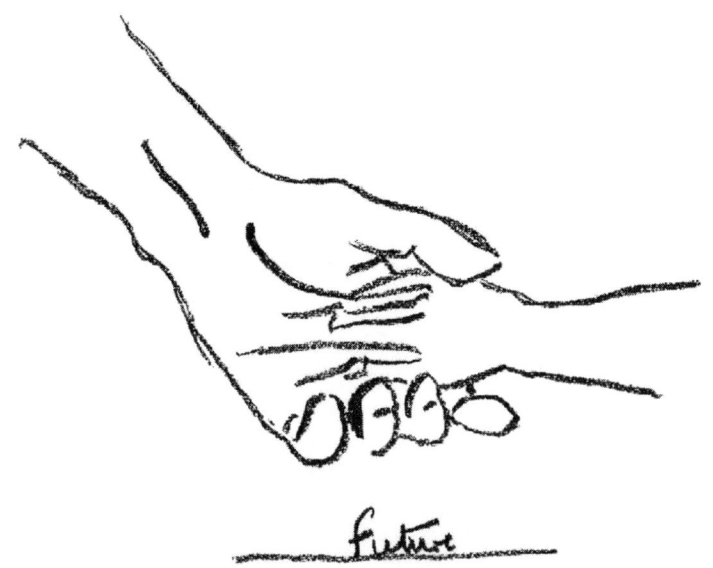

Future

These sketches are not so much about my life as they are about my own country. I draw hands because they are powerful instruments, hands can hurt or heal, punish or uplift. They can also be bound but a quest for righteousness can never be repressed. In time, we broke loose the shackles of injustice, we joined hands across social divides and national boundaries, between continents and over oceans. And now we look to the future, knowing that even if age makes us wiser, guides it is the youth that reminds us of love, of trust, and the value of life.

25.7.2001   NMandela

CIVIL SOCIETY: THE ROLE OF BUSINESS AND THE CHURCHES IN FACILITATING THE TRANSITION

On 2nd February 1992, Nelson Mandela, president of the African National Congress, and Frederik ("F W") de Klerk, president of South Africa, entered the plenary hall in Davos to address the World Economic Forum, setting the seal on a remarkable initiative undertaken by Professor Klaus Schwab, founder and president of the WEF. The importance of the occasion, and its contribution to the political and economic development of South Africa over the following ten years, cannot be overemphasised.

Over a thousand delegates in the hall were held in breathless thrall as Presidents De Klerk and Mandela described the momentous developments of the past months – and their hopes and dreams for a "new" South Africa. They also listened to addresses given by the leader of the KwaZulu Legislative Assembly, Mangosuthu Buthelezi; Jay Naidoo, secretary-general of COSATU, the trade union movement; and John Hall, chair of the Peace Committee.

For millions of television viewers around the world, the spectacle was riveting. The South African president, whose government had held Nelson Mandela captive for 27 years before releasing him, and Mandela himself were sharing a public platform – and a mission.

In the days preceding the plenary, Mandela had used the opportunity to meet many of the world leaders present to discuss and debate ANC strategies and policies. Subsequently, he made no secret of the impact these discussions were to have on the way in which the ANC was to govern. Great men possess the humility to admit to mistakes, and "Madiba" delighted in describing how his stated aim of nationalising mines and banks in order to give ownership to the people was met with polite disapproval on virtually every occasion. China's leader, Chairman Li Peng, visiting Davos for the first time, asked Professor Schwab to facilitate a private luncheon with Nelson Mandela. Reporting on the encounter, Mandela said that Comrade Li Peng had made it perfectly clear that his country's experience was such as to suggest that nationalisation would be an error. Coming from China, that message probably made more of an impression than any other. And the market economy in South Africa today owes much to these debates.

SETTING THE STAGE

Klaus Schwab's vision, prescience and courage had become manifest some three years earlier, when planning and networking for a Southern Africa Forum in Geneva began. The forum's importance was profound, as it was to set the stage for the Davos meeting. It also encouraged interest in the highest circles and brought about an international awareness of the huge task facing the key participants inside and outside South Africa. The role played by Frédéric Sicre, then a project manager and today managing director of the WEF, was key to its success. He visited South Africa on numerous occasions, won the trust of the contending parties and paved the way for both Geneva encounters and the Davos meeting. Recollecting his experiences, he recalls particularly his sense of awe on meeting Nelson Mandela for the first time.

The first of the Geneva conferences was held in early October 1990 and brought many of the ANC leaders, including their head of international affairs Thabo Mbeki, Tito Mboweni, Popo Molefe, Eric Molobi and Moss Ngoasheng – some of whom were in exile and all of whom were to play key roles in what lay ahead – together with the leader of the KwaZulu Legislative Assembly, Mangosuthu Buthelezi, South Africa's minister of finance, Barend du Plessis, and senior representatives from South African and world business – some 200 in all. Judge Jan Steyn took the chair.

The second Geneva conference was held in the following October. Its theme was "Opportunities for Growth and Development in a Southern Africa in Transition".

South Africa's Consultative Business Movement, which will be discussed in some detail later, assisted the WEF in organising the participation of a number of key delegates to ensure that both conferences had wide political representation.

The subjects selected for debate in Geneva were wide-ranging, and focused sharply on the key issues facing South Africa, as the following examples illustrate:

- How best can the international business community help South Africa help itself?
- How can South Africa become a meaningful player in the regional and global economy?
- Will the SA economy become the catalyst for regional development with regard to the creation and distribution of wealth and black economic empowerment?
- What about a new constitution; the prerequisites for an effective transition; security?

As can be readily seen, the WEF – with unerring precision – selected matters that would dominate discussions in the months ahead.

Trevor Manuel and Tito Mboweni made significant contributions to the various debates and clearly found the full Davos meetings of inestimable value. In due course, as minister of finance and governor of the reserve bank respectively, they were to guide South Africa to levels of fiscal and monetary discipline of the highest standards.

THE IMPORTANCE OF DAVOS

Annual meetings of the WEF in Davos have no equal in importance on the business calendar. Delegates include up to a thousand of the world's most powerful chief executives, twenty to thirty heads of state and leading authorities on a host of economic and business issues. In giving the stage to Nelson Mandela and F W de Klerk, Klaus Schwab and the international community made a major contribution to the miracle of South Africa's transformation. In turn the dignity, presence and gravitas of the two leaders created an indelible impression. The stage had been set for the nail-biting months of negotiation that were to come.

The WEF went on to arrange other country forums in southern Africa, each playing an important consolidating role. To these meetings came up to seventeen African presidents, joined by hundreds of WEF members worldwide, as well as most of the key participators in Southern Africa. The meetings were held in Johannesburg, Cape Town and Harare, and Nelson Mandela took part in all of them. In 1999, he made the following comment in the closing session, "South Africa could not have achieved what it has, were it not for the World Economic Forum."

THE EARLIER YEARS

Over a period of some years prior to Geneva and Davos, a series of initiatives and meetings – inspired by events and conditions within South Africa – had combined to create a climate which was to help make the WEF's initiative workable.

The mid-eighties had found the country in a state of emergency, riven by deep distrust on all sides. Soweto had not recovered from the 1976 riots when police had opened fire on children, and political violence was rife. The security police were hounding, torturing and arresting activists, some of whom died in captivity, while others simply disappeared.

The National Party's oppressive propaganda machine had done its work to great effect. It seemed at the time that P W Botha and his securocrats would remain in power for years to come. Polarisation was the word most used to describe relationships between the unenfranchised millions and the government and business sectors – business was perceived to be part of the government of the day. The international community responded to the internal repression by calling up loans, introducing boycotts and trade embargos and by withdrawing their products and businesses. The future looked bleak, and the fear of escalating violence was growing.

Then, in 1985, Anglo American's chief executive Gavin Relly, made arguably the boldest and most significant move to date, by taking a party of businessmen with him to talk to the ANC in Lusaka. On his return, he went on national television and referred to the ANC members as "my fellow South Africans". This courageous initiative, which rocked the establishment, opened new avenues of thought on many fronts.

In 1986, Chris Ball (FNB) Zach de Beer (Anglo) Neal Chapman (Southern Life), Mervyn King (Tradego), Anton Mostert (former judge) Mike Sander (AECI) and Chris van Wyk (Trust Bank) began meeting. Their primary concern was that, in this nightmarish climate, South African society might polarise irrevocably if something were not done. In January 1987, Christo Nel (of PG Bison) was asked to facilitate contact with the leadership of disenfranchised South Africa. The problem was that most were in hiding, or in jail.

Two journalists, Miranda and Roger Harris, used their connections to introduce Christo Nel to Azhar Cachalia, Murphy Morobe, who was on the run and in hiding, and Albertina Sisulu. It was decided that the Harris home would be the meeting place, and Christo Nel would be called whenever one of the leaders became available. Many of the latter – especially youth leaders – were underground and on the security forces' wanted list.

When confidence had grown to the point where business leaders were permitted to attend, Winnie Mandela joined Albertina Sisulu in a cross-examination exercise to satisfy themselves that the business representatives were not informants or government agents. These arrangements soon had to be changed when the Harris home was put under surveillance. After one late-night meeting, a businessman was followed and two nights later his home was attacked with gunfire. Within the same fortnight, Christo Nel was pulled off the road by hooded gunmen, who fired at him as he stood beside his car. In July 1987, Murphy Morobe and Valli Moosa, members of the group, were detained under the state of emergency in force at the time.

MEETING WITH THE ANC IN DAKAR

In mid-1987, Van Zyl Slabbert and Alex Boraine arranged a meeting of sixty Afrikaners with the ANC in Dakar. They also, together with Michael Cassidy, a Christian leader who had been teaching organisational skills to angry young activists in Natal, founded the Independent Democratic Association of South Africa (IDASA), which engaged in quiet, steady bridge-building work. The three operated on the assumption that people wanted to be able to talk to one another, notwithstanding the divides, and during 1987–94 the bridges they built spanned the full political spectrum. They tackled the sacred cows of ethnicity, military power and a "volkstaat". In Michael Cassidy's book *A Witness Forever* he wrote, "I think we were a vehicle needed by God and by that moment in history."

The Dakar conference was a watershed. The cream of Afrikaner intellectuals, academics, business people and clergy had overturned the accepted norms of association to meet with the banned ANC leadership. Once again something had happened that both shook the establishment and opened new prospects for negotiation. The circle of those questioning the status quo was gradually widening.

Christo Nel was among those at Dakar, as was Ds. (minister) Theuns Eloff, later to play a vital role. Nel's meetings with ANC leaders, including Thabo Mbeki, Steve Tshwete and Tito Mboweni, led to the establishment of a foundation and ground rules for contact and liaison.

ANC SUPPORT FOR THE BUSINESS INITIATIVE

By February 1988, almost all the leaders with whom the early group of businessmen had met were in jail, banned or had been served restriction orders. However, it proved possible to meet with the Delmas treason trialists, in particular Popo Molefe and Patrick Lekoto, and these two sent out a message of support for business's efforts to overcome the polarisation of society in South Africa. Meetings with Jay Naidoo, the secretary-general of the trade union movement COSATU, and Sydney Mufamadi followed, and after a further meeting in Lusaka, Steve Tshwete and Tito Mboweni were charged with ensuring continuity of contact and progress. Mboweni spelled out the rules of survival: publish no documents; do not write down names or structures; seek no publicity; and keep your heads below the parapet – we do not want you shot, arrested or restrained!

Between April and August 1988, literally hundreds of meetings were held, leading to the encounter at Broederstroom, when forty business leaders and academics met forty representatives of the then Mass Democratic Movement (MDM) and the community. In his opening remarks, Azhar Cachalia – who co-facilitated the meeting – turned to someone and said, "You know that in terms of my restriction order I am not allowed to address a meeting. In even being here, we are all breaking the law. So I'll talk to you alone and leave it to the rest to decide whether they want to listen or not!" The nervous laughter reflected the tension of people stretching out across the chasm that divided our society. The discussions that followed were open and emotional. The MDM was organised, clear and united, but business – forty individuals feeling their way into uncharted waters – was not.

Nevertheless the Consultative Business Movement (CBM) was established and the MDM accepted that it needed to develop contact with this small group of willing if uncertain business people, who realised they had to make a leap of faith. By December, the CBM had a dozen members and had set itself the target of signing up one hundred chief executives in the coming months.

ANC AND CBM MEET IN HARARE

Then followed the first official meeting of the ANC in exile with a CBM delegation. The ANC team was led by Thabo Mbeki and included Tito Mboweni, Aziz and Essop Pahad and Steve Tshwete. The CBM was led by Murray Hofmeyr and Peter Wrighton, who wrote, "Such were the preconceptions that the nervous business delegation fully expected to meet a group of AK-47-toting terrorists, while the ANC expected a group of "fat cats" in thrall to the apartheid government. By the end of the weekend, after covering a full agenda together with the inevitable conversations in the corridors and over the dinner table, a close rapport had been reached. With tears in the eyes of both delegations, the ANC members returned into exile and the business leaders to their home country and the disapproving finger of President Botha."

By now both sides had given the stamp of approval to the widening and intensifying of contacts.

CBM ACQUIRES A BASE, AND A GOVERNING BODY

In June 1987, Leon Cohen of PG Bison offered to house the CBM's first part-time staff members – Christo Nel, and Rosemary Grealy, who had already been detained without trial. PG Bison later became a secure base and, as staff numbers grew, it generously expanded the CBM's quarters.

The CBM had to be informal and mobile to be able to cope with the challenges that lay ahead. A governing group was formed, comprising 25 businessmen who were willing and able to give time and energy to the process. Mike Sander took the chair, and in due course this arrangement was changed to a "Chairco", consisting of Murray Hofmeyr and Neal Chapman, who met between meetings of the governing body in order to give the executive team guidance and direction. Regional offices were established in the provinces, and in the first months and years the focus was placed on meetings, workshops and the building of relationships.

THE UNBANNING OF THE ANC AND ITS ALLIES

On 2nd February 1990, President De Klerk announced the unbanning of the ANC, the Communist Party and the PAC. Those attending the

WEF meeting in Davos at the time will always remember the jubilation and sheer joy that followed the news.

A meeting with the ANC in Harare in March followed, and the CBM's work entered a new and wider phase. In May, there were meetings with directors-general in the civil service, a series of meetings with individual ministers on specific issues, and briefings by deputy minister Roelf Meyer, who was to prove a tower of strength. In March 1991, the CBM leadership met with the South African cabinet and in May with Chief Minister Buthelezi and his cabinet in Ulundi. Later that year Chief Buthelezi addressed a joint meeting of the CBM and his own party in Johannesburg. Meetings with the PAC of Azania in Harare, and the Azanian People's Organisation (AZAPO), were followed by meetings with the parties to the right of government, the Conservative Party of General Viljoen, as well as the Afrikaner-Weerstandsbeweging (resistance movement), of Eugene Terre'Blanche. The latter refused to attend – evoking a reaction that varied from disappointment to relief. Constructive relations with COSATU were already in place.

BUSINESS ORGANISATIONS AND THE DIPLOMATIC CORPS

Formal business organisations such as the South African Chamber of Commerce, the Afrikaanse Handelsinstituut, the National African Chamber of Commerce, the Black Management Forum, Planact and the Urban Foundation all became involved in the continuous consultative process. And special mention needs be made of the diplomatic corps. Led by the United States and the United Kingdom, ambassadors would meet at short notice when crises arose, and briefing sessions were seldom attended by fewer than twenty of them. Theuns Eloff and Debra Marsden, supported by CBM members, kept the diplomats constantly in the picture and on many occasions this led to helpful words being whispered in influential ears in many parts of the world.

THE CARLTON CONFERENCE OF MAY 1990

Once Nelson Mandela was released and the exiles were able to return to South Africa, it became possible for the wider business community to engage, and on 23rd May 1990 some 350 business leaders met

Mandela, supported by a forty-person-strong ANC delegation, including many who later became cabinet ministers or provincial premiers. Many of the ANC's delegation were making their first visit to SA after as long as thirty years in exile – and emotions ran high.

Following thoughtful introductions by Gavin Relly and Nelson Mandela, uplifting rhetoric gave way to deeper debate on the nature of a mixed economy. In his closing comments, Murray Hofmeyr remarked on the congruence that had developed during the day, observing that both economic growth and measures to correct the imbalances of the past were needed.

ADDRESSING THE CRISIS OF VIOLENCE AND THE NATIONAL PEACE PROCESS

More than a year after the unbanning of the ANC and other organisations, the negotiating process had progressed no further than the signing of a few agreements between the ANC and the government. Violence had been resumed, and anger was mounting on all sides. In an attempt to address these problems, the De Klerk government publicly called a meeting of "everyone interested" to discuss ways to stem the escalating violence. Unfortunately, prior consultation had been inadequate – to put it mildly – and the ANC denounced "this unilateral initiative" and announced that it would hold its own meeting.

This left the government, the Inkatha Freedom Party (IFP) and the homeland leaders on one side staring across the divide at the ANC, the civic movements and COSATU. Great was the chasm and deep the suspicion on both sides.

A dramatic gesture was needed and it came from church leaders. Frank Chikane, general secretary of the SA Council of Churches and Prof. Louw Alberts, chair of the Rustenburg church leaders' committee, made contact with Theuns Eloff, who had succeeded Christo Nel at the CBM, to see what could be done. Eloff was a *dominee* (minister) of the Dutch Reformed Church who had been forced to resign by his congregation following his attendance at the Dakar Conference. At the conclusion of his farewell service, members of his church had filed past Ds. and Mrs Eloff without so much as a handshake!

John Hall and others from CBM's membership took up the initiative, along with Frank Chikane, Louw Alberts, Beyers Naudé, Brigalia Bam, Johan Heyns and Ray McCauley – as well as COSATU leader

Jay Naidoo. Urgent shuttle diplomacy and the credibility of those involved resulted in an undertaking that no firm decisions would be taken at the meeting and the ANC and its allies would engage in the process at a later time.

THE PEACE ACCORD

This gave birth to the Peace Committee, chaired by the highly capable and respected John Hall. The Peace Committee, Archbishop Tutu, Frank Chikane and Bobby Godsell moved the process along towards the establishment of the National Peace Accord.

Michael Cassidy, who was chairman of the SA Council of Churches at the time recalls, "Although church and business seemed strange bedfellows, it was felt that they constituted the poles of non-political power in the country. Therefore, it made a tremendous amount of sense for them, with their collective bargaining power, to play a role in influencing the politicians. Because, first, you did not publicly defy the church very easily and, second, with business you had to keep on the ball. So, together, we had a powerful leverage over the politicians."

The Accord was signed in September 1991, amid all the pomp and ceremony that it deserved. Archbishop Tutu opened proceedings with a typically heartfelt prayer in front of all the leaders – Mandela, De Klerk, Buthelezi, Zulu king Goodwill Zwelithini, – as well as Ken Owen of the *Sunday Times*, Aggrey Klaaste of the *Sowetan*, and 26 political parties. All parties signed the Accord, as did trade unions, religious and financial institutions. Fittingly, Michael Cassidy's Africa Enterprise – Christian and philanthropic – headed the list by virtue of its alphabetical precedence.

Over the next two years the Accord played the key role in negotiating a way out of many ugly and threatening situations, with John Hall's courage, charm and ever-present sense of humour being so often the saving grace.

Said Methodist bishop Stanley Mogoba, deputy chairman of the National Peace Committee, "the work of the Peace Accord was crucial in that it brought various political groups together at a time when they did not want to be together. It took a lot of time to create a rapport between members of the IFP, ANC, Communist Party, COSATU, government and all the homelands governments. But I think we managed to get them used to one another, so much so that in the end they were pushing the whole peace thing forward themselves"

The Accord gave birth to the Peace Secretariat, which employed literally thousands of peace monitors throughout the country and at all potential trouble spots – major and minor. The monitors' presence at rallies and riots calmed situations that so often threatened to escalate into violent confrontation. The secretariat was led by Antonie Gildenhuys, who played a key role in setting up provincial and community peace committees.

John Hall later said, ". . . we saw divine intervention in the Peace Accord itself and the positive influence of the church on the process the whole time. It is amazing how many people remember their roles as peace monitors and to this day come up to me with 'do you remember' comments."

And of course Archbishop Tutu was an ever-present source of inspiration – during the years of the struggle, throughout the drama and trauma of the negotiation process and then as the guiding light during the reconciliation hearings.

THE CONSTITUTIONAL NEGOTIATIONS AND THE ELECTION (DECEMBER 1991–MAY 1994)

It was in the constitutional field that CBM made its most valuable and best-known contributions. When the NP, the ANC and others agreed towards the end of 1991 to pursue multilateral negotiations, the CBM was approached to render what was called "process and secretariat services". Having established its acceptability as an intermediary with all parties, the CBM appointed Theuns Eloff – the embodiment of these qualities – to assemble the team to carry out and lead the intermediation. And so CBM's formal involvement with the constitutional negotiation process began with CODESA 1 in December 1991, and CODESA 2 in the following year. As confidence and trust in the CBM grew, its role moved quietly from providing secretarial services to facilitating backroom negotiations and shuttle diplomacy.

In June 1992, the CODESA negotiations deadlocked following the dark days of Boipatong, when a wholesale slaughter of sleeping people aroused anger and suspicions of a third force on the far-right seeking to destabilise the process. Neal Chapman led the twenty-strong CBM delegation answering Nelson Mandela's summons the morning after the tragedy, and will never forget Madiba's hour-long tirade of accusations against the government and its allies, during which he never once broke their eye-to-eye contact. The twenty ANC delegates included their legendary chairman, Oliver Tambo.

The Bisho shootings shortly thereafter added to the tensions and the CBM's discussions with members of the SA cabinet became strained. Conflict had intensified on all fronts, with KwaZulu-Natal being especially violent. Hostilities spilled over onto the Reef and surrounding townships. Right-wingers had become well nigh hysterical as they watched the white right being marginalised, and the prospect of a nonracial democracy looming. On the 25th March, they invaded the World Trade Centre outside Johannesburg where the constitutional talks were being held, crashing an armoured vehicle through plate glass walls of the building.

Theuns Eloff described his experience of the attack, "We knew about the march of the AWB, and there were numerous discussions with police, all of us insisting there should not be any guns, etc. Then the police backed down before AWB threats. So they did bring their guns. I was in the planning committee meeting when we heard that AWB operatives had broken through the gate. Bodyguards whisked the politicians away. I went outside and there were armed young policeman lined up against the glass wall, some trembling with fear. Hundreds of AWB guys were running towards them with shotguns. I realised that if anybody shot there would be a bloodbath. General Constand Viljoen tried to get his people to stand back. But just then this armoured vehicle came through the glass wall with Eugene Terre'Blanche walking just behind it, having rather expeditiously climbed off the vehicle shortly before it went through the glass!

"I tried to stop the armoured vehicle by standing in front of it inside the hall. In fact it had to stop, otherwise it would have run me over. The AWB wanted to go into the Negotiating Council, where some of the delegates, especially the African delegates, were still present.

"We and the police tried to keep them on the ground floor, but there were too many of them. They overpowered us and burst into the Negotiating Council. By that stage everyone had left, and I was the only one there and they just took over . . . After a while they dispersed. They had wanted to show they were not going to be dictated to. They were in a strange mood combining anger with something almost festive. Oh well! There you go with politics, South Africa-style."

In March 1993, the ANC and the NP government signed a Record of Understanding, and the CBM was asked by the parties to render administration services to the multiparty negotiating process. Theuns Eloff was concerned that those negotiating lacked an appreciation of the options that were open, and the consequences of choices before the parties. CBM asked Clive Menell (Anglovaal), one of its most sagacious members, to chair a workshop involving international and local experts. This resulted in a report entitled "Constitutional Options and their implications for Good Government and a Sound Economy". According to the technical committee at CODESA, the report played a major role and was a point of constant reference.

During the negotiations, the CBM leadership was constantly called upon to help through shuttle diplomacy whenever sticking points surfaced and threatened to cause another breakdown. Roelf Meyer in the NP, Joe Slovo, Cyril Ramaphosa and Valli Moosa in the ANC, Musa Myeni in the IFP, in addition to the various party leaders, were wondrously helpful and would meet at any time of day or night. On one occasion in early 1994, CBM acted quietly behind the scenes to get the ANC and government to agree to implement changes wanted by the IFP – notwithstanding the IFP's absence from the negotiations.

The absence of the Inkatha Freedom Party (IFP) from the process, and its refusal to participate until a mere few days before the election, could have had dire consequences for a peaceful transition to democracy. Without a large part of the Zulu nation voting, the election was in danger of being labelled a sham – with ensuing chaos and violence inevitable. The CBM, religious leaders and other parties tried desperately to persuade Buthelezi to come in, but to no avail. The election date had been set, the ballot papers printed (without the name of the IFP appearing) and deep despondency descended. The churches held mass prayer meetings and, in the last ditch, the CBM proposed that Henry Kissinger, Washington Okumu and Lord Peter Carrington should attempt to mediate between the two sides. Sponsorship by their respective governments was arranged, but after cooling their heels for four days at the Carlton Hotel, the mediators were not able to persuade the ANC and IFP even to agree on the terms to be mediated. Frustrated and disappointed, Kissinger and Carrington departed, while Washington Okumu stayed on to attend to other business. On learning, however, that Chief Buthelezi was visiting Johannesburg for a meeting and flying home to KwaZulu on the same day from a small airport called Lanseria, Okumu dashed to the airport hoping to cadge a lift and to try and persuade Buthelezi for the last time to come into the election process. He arrived at Lanseria only to see the plane disappearing over the horizon. And then what many have described as "divine intervention" occurred. The pilot found that his compass was defective and returned to Lanseria to have it checked, giving Okumu the opportunity he needed. The compass, incidentally, was later found not to be faulty.

The two men, devout Christians, prayed together and Okumu begged Buthelezi to change his mind at the eleventh hour and so save the country from disaster. Buthelezi agreed, and Okumu asked the CBM to arrange urgent meetings with Mandela and De Klerk to convey his decision. Michael Spicer and CBM's Colin Coleman made the arrangements and Anglo American put a jet at their disposal to collect Okumu from Durban and fly him to Cape Town, where Nelson Mandela was electioneering. Murray Hofmeyr flew in from Knysna and he, together with Washington Okumu persuaded the ANC leader that Mangosuthu Buthelezi was now on board.

This happened late on a Sunday night, and it was agreed that if Cyril Ramaphosa and F W de Klerk – both in Johannesburg – could also be persuaded, Nelson Mandela would return to Pretoria and sign a new agreement. Okumu and Coleman put the wording together and the agreement was duly signed the next day, enabling the overprinting of ballot papers to include the IFP, to go ahead.

South Africa and the world breathed a sigh of relief.

VOTER EDUCATION

In the background, the international business community and the churches had been playing a vital role to ensure a free and fair election. The South Africa Free Elections Fund (SAFE) came about from a chance meeting between Nelson Mandela and Tony O'Reilly, CEO of HJ Heinz & company. Mandela had mentioned that millions of voters would not be able to participate knowledgeably as they had had no experience of democracy, and that voter education was an urgent priority. O'Reilly and a powerful body of liberal American leaders set about raising an astonishing $8 million to help local fundraising efforts. One of them, Theodore C Sorenson said, "I am not asking you to give to charity, I am asking you to participate in history."

Rev. Dr Beyers Naudé, chairman of the Ecumenical Assistance Trust, set up a local committee and Loraine Braithwaite, a young American lawyer, headed up a team on the ground dedicated to assisting in the education of an estimated 12 million first-time voters. But with less than six weeks to go, it was discovered that a huge number of voters had still to receive the requisite documents, and the Department of Home Affairs was proving to be hopelessly inadequate. SAFE and the Independent Electoral Commission pooled resources and launched a massive campaign which included chartering Boeing jets to fly out specialised photographic equipment to issue Temporary Voter Cards – all in all a truly amazing contribution of money, time and support on the part of the American business community and one of many contributions to the successful holding of South Africa's first free and fair election on 27th April 1994.

SOME FINAL THOUGHTS ON THE TRANSITION

- The inauguration ceremony will live forever in the memories of those who were there in person or in front of television sets or their radios.
- Even criminals downed tools and South Africa enjoyed a day of peace and goodwill.
- No one can claim a special role in the unfolding of the pathway to the new South Africa; countless numbers did their bit. All felt and still feel privileged and truly blessed to have had a role in the drama of transition.
- Never in history has control of a country passed peacefully from minority to majority rule. Nowhere in the modern world have businessmen given so generously of their time to matters outside the confines of their company or industry.
- Church leaders rendered unto political issues precious advice, counselling, wisdom and their prayers. And to great effect.
- South Africa found that it was blessed by strong and determined men and women of ability and wisdom at the helm of the key parties.

- That the World Economic Forum, which caters for those who lead the most powerful organisations and makes no bones about the need to focus on macro-issues, should have seen its way to bring a small country at the foot of sub-Saharan Africa into its limelight, is in itself a wonderful thing.
- That the CBM should have been blessed with a team of young executives, paid modestly and denied publicity, is another small miracle. Christo Nel, Theuns Eloff, Colin Coleman, Debra Marsden, Andrew Feinstein, Bruce Robertson and Renee Alberts are just some of them . . .
- A "confluence of influences" best describes the role that the civics, churches, business and individuals played in bringing about the "miracle".

Neal Chapman
Former Chairperson, Southern Life Association Ltd, South Africa
Peter Wrighton
Chairperson, Africa Resources Ltd

SOUTH AFRICA'S TRANSITION FROM FINANCIAL SANCTIONS TO A CHOICE EMERGING MARKET

INTRODUCTION

When the first fully democratically elected South African government came to power in 1994, the country was to a large extent isolated from the rest of the world economically. Economic sanctions, disinvestment, the withdrawal of other capital and the declaration of a partial debt standstill from September 1985, had forced the authorities to pursue an inward-oriented policy that had a severe impact on domestic economic performance. As a consequence, living standards deteriorated, economic growth was constrained, unemployment rose, productivity growth slowed and economic management became less effective.

The refusal of foreign creditors to roll over short-term credit facilities of domestic borrowers led to a shortage of foreign exchange and a confidence crisis in 1985. Despite the standstill on the repayment of foreign debt, capital continued to flow out of the country. At first this consisted mainly of short-term capital that was not affected by the standstill arrangements. Blocking this capital would have jeopardised trade flows. Later the capital outflows also comprised amounts which became payable in terms of the various standstill agreements. From the beginning of 1985 to 1993 the net financial outflow from South Africa amounted to about R45 billion, or 11 per cent of gross domestic fixed investment.

As a result of this outflow, the South African authorities were forced to generate current account surpluses, the gold and other foreign reserves of the country remained at low levels, and domestic savings had to be used to finance the withdrawal of capital. The balance of payments constraint effectively limited policy options. Although the forced repayment of loans improved the overall foreign debt position of the country, the policy of constrained domestic expansion called for huge sacrifices by the South African population and continued to affect the domestic economy for a long time after 1994.

One of the long-lasting impacts that the liquidity crisis of 1985 had on the functioning of the South African Reserve Bank was that plans to withdraw from the forward market had to be abandoned. From 1983, an approach of gradually reducing the oversold forward book was pursued. With the introduction of the debt standstill and the inability of the South African government to raise foreign capital, the Reserve Bank again began to provide forward cover to the private sector to ensure that the latter made use of trade credits provided by non-residents. This led to a large oversold forward book of the Reserve Bank, with an exchange rate risk for the South African government that had a negative effect on the perceptions of foreign investors. The closing down of this oversold forward book became a major challenge for the authorities in the ensuing years.

GLOBAL INTEGRATION

Even before the new government came to power, many countries started to normalise trade relations with South Africa when it became apparent that the political transition would be negotiated in a peaceful manner. Economic and financial sanctions were suspended. However, debtors in South Africa had to continue making repayments on debt affected by the standstill arrangements for a number of years. The standstill only ended on 15th August 2001 when the final repayment on the affected debt was made. In the meantime, the South African government started raising funds again on international capital markets from 1995, and non-residents resumed investing in private entities in the country.

This normalisation of international relations allowed the newly elected democratic government to gradually reintegrate the domestic economy into the global environment. High priority was given to the reform of trade policy in this process.

The trade regime at the beginning of the 1990s was characterised by three interrelated strategies, namely the promotion of domestic industries through import substitution, the development of specific industries to attain self-sufficiency such as Sasol and Armscor, and the promotion of mineral beneficiation. South Africa's industries therefore became heavily protected by formula, specific and *ad valorem* duties and surcharges. High tariff levels were complemented by quotas that limited the quantity of imports. The tariff structure was extremely complicated. Overall the strategies pursued by the authorities resulted in a complex discretionary regime with an anti-export bias.

After the transition in 1994, government became committed to a policy of import liberalisation, and agreed to import tariff reductions to levels even lower than that required by GATT, i.e. the predecessor of the World Trade Organisation. Key aspects of the trade reform included:
1. A five-year tariff reduction and rationalisation programme in which both the tariff lines as well as rates were significantly decreased.
2. A lowering of tariffs and subsidies on agricultural products and the conversion of all quantitative restrictions on agricultural imports to *ad valorem* rates.
3. An increase in the number of binding rates applicable to industries as well as in the percentage of zero tariff lines to total tariff lines.
4. A phasing out of the export subsidy scheme applicable at that time, which was called the "General Export Incentive Scheme (GEIS)".

As a result of these changes to the tariff regime, the number of tariff categories were reduced from over one hundred (100) to only six (6) and the average weighted import duties on manufactured goods to the total value of manufacturing imports decreased from 14.0 per cent in 1994 to 4.7 per cent in 2002. Several free-trade agreements were also signed to dismantle trade barriers and gain increased market access.

In addition to these measures undertaken for the promotion of competition, industrial policy was adjusted to enhance the competitiveness of manufacturing enterprises in export markets. In particular more emphasis was placed on supply-side measures, rather than demand-side measures, such as expensive export support programmes. These measures included incentives for large investments of a strategic nature and for small and medium enterprise development; training grants to firms investing in the promotion of skills; the development of industrial development zones; improved access to finance; and support for investments in economic infrastructure.

A new Competition Act was passed in Parliament in 1998 to create a greater spread of ownership in enterprises, expand opportunities for South African participation in world markets and provide consumers with competitive prices and product choices. The Act further focuses on preventing any form of anti-competitive conduct by a firm or a group of firms arising from agreements. Institutions were established in terms of the Act to ensure that these objectives are achieved and to monitor implementation and adherence to the law.

A further step to reintegrate the South African economy into the world economy was the gradual dismantling of exchange controls. Very restrictive exchange controls were applicable in 1994. These controls were principally applied to outward capital movements. Any outward transfer of funds other than normal trade-related transactions by residents was subject to approval by the Exchange Control authorities. Some trade-related transactions were also subjected to quantitative limits to ensure that capital transfers were not disguised as current payments.

Control over the outward repatriation of funds by non-residents was based on the financial rand system. Any proceeds from the sale of South African assets by non-residents had to be held by local authorised banks in an account designated "financial rand". In cases where non-residents wished to exchange these financial rand balances for foreign currency, this could only be done by selling such balances to another non-resident. These transactions between two non-residents had no effect on the country's gold and foreign exchange reserves.

Emigrants from South Africa were allowed to transfer a portion of their capital when leaving the country by way of a settling-in allowance. Moreover, these amounts were only transferable via the financial rand mechanism and did not lead to a loss of foreign exchange for the country. Any balance exceeding the permissible amount had to be credited to a blocked account at a domestic bank authorised to deal in foreign exchange.

Individuals resident in South Africa were not allowed to acquire any assets abroad, while corporates could make direct investments abroad provided that they obtained exchange control approval. Such transactions were only allowed if these investments were financed by way of offshore borrowing without any recourse to South African capital markets. This borrowing had to be serviced from income generated abroad. Domestic institutional investors were generally not allowed to diversify their asset portfolios internationally.

After 1994, government opted for a gradual approach to the elimination of the exchange control regime, because the risk of applying a "big-bang" approach was just too great. A phased approach allowed the consequences of certain relaxations to be first absorbed before further steps were taken. Furthermore, such an approach allowed the economy to adjust slowly to the shocks created by the removal of capital controls which had been in place for a long time.

The sequencing of the removal of exchange controls was as follows:
1. The abolition of exchange control on non-residents, i.e. the abolition of the financial rand system.
2. The abolition of exchange controls on current account transactions.
3. Gradually becoming more lenient in the approval of applications for direct foreign investments by South African corporates.
4. Allowing institutional investors to diversify their asset portfolio internationally.
5. A progressive relaxation of all other controls on outward investments by residents, and the release of emigrant blocked funds.

The financial rand system was abolished in 1995 and considerable success has already been achieved in relaxing many other controls. Limits are still applicable on the amounts that residents and emigrants may repatriate from South Africa, but these limits have been increased progressively over the past ten years. Moreover, a foreign exchange control amnesty and accommodating tax dispensation were announced in February 2003 to allow individuals to bring funds back that were held illegally offshore or to pay a 10 per cent charge on funds remaining offshore. The amnesty offered individuals an opportunity to regularise their affairs. The period for filing for amnesty relief expired on 29 February 2004.

FISCAL POLICY

The liberalisation of South Africa's trade relations with the rest of the world was accompanied by considerable changes in the management of public finances. At the beginning of the 1990s an unsustainable fiscal situation had started to develop, and the deficit before borrowing and debt repayment of the government reached 7.3 per cent of gross domestic product in the fiscal year 1992/93. Government expenditure continued to rise relative to domestic production, the tax burden increased, the public sector made increasing demands on the domestic capital market, the ratio of government's interest payments to gross domestic product rose steeply and government dissaving increased to unacceptably high levels.

The post-apartheid South African government therefore placed considerable emphasis on restoring fiscal stability. The economic strategy at first was to create stable macroeconomic conditions as a necessary precondition for sustained growth and employment creation. It was believed that by improving fiscal sustainability, poverty reduction and income redistribution would become attainable objectives over the medium term. The expenditure restraint applied by the national and provincial governments reduced the fiscal deficit before borrowing and debt repayment, to 1.5 per cent of gross domestic product in fiscal 2001/02.

This successful fiscal consolidation allowed the government to adopt a more expansionary fiscal policy stance from fiscal 2001/02. More emphasis was placed on infrastructural development and social upliftment than in the previous years. The government, however, continued to apply fiscal discipline and despite a decline in the growth of tax revenue, was able to contain the main budget deficit to an estimated 2.6 per cent of gross domestic product in fiscal 2003/04. Economic growth was primarily promoted by microeconomic reforms to boost the supply side of the economy, rather than by stimulating demand through rapid increases in expenditure and the lowering of taxes.

Throughout the past ten years, the objective of the South African government was to achieve a more equal distribution of income and alleviate poverty in combination with the application of fiscal discipline. Although the income tax structure has remained progressive, the authorities did not rely much on increases in tax rates as an instrument of redistribution. The overall tax burden did increase steadily, but this was more a result of broadening the tax base and greater efficiency in collection rather than increases in income tax rates. The value-added tax rate was kept unchanged, and indirect tax increases consisted mainly of higher excise duties on tobacco products and alcoholic beverages. However, some redistribution of income was achieved by providing partial relief for the effects of bracket creep on the lower and middle income tax groups, i.e. for the effect of rising income into higher tax brackets often simply because of inflation.

A number of measures were introduced to enhance efficient tax administration, such as the improvement of operational efficiency and effectiveness, the easing of the compliance burden, the provision of services to clients in the form of tax guidance and the encouragement of tax morality. A new institution, the South African Revenue Services, was created outside the National Treasury. The success achieved with these measures was clearly reflected in the strong growth of tax revenues.

In accordance with the objective of restoring stability in government finances, the capital spending of both general government and public enterprises was reduced at first. From fiscal 2001/02 the fixed investment of general government and public enterprises started to rise sharply, when the emphasis shifted to infrastructural development. In contrast to these changes, government consumption expenditure was kept at a level of about 19 per cent of gross domestic product over the past ten years. This was the combined result of a decline in the ratio of the government's wage bill to gross domestic product since 1998 and an increase in the corresponding ratio of non-wage expenditure.

An important aspect of the budget reform was the adoption of the Medium-Term Expenditure Framework in the fiscal year 1998/99 and the Public Finance Management Act of 1999. The Medium-Term Expenditure Framework consists of three-year rolling expenditure and revenue projections for the national and the provincial governments. This creates greater certainty and brings transparency to the budgetary process. The Public Finance Management Act has enhanced the accountability of public sector managers by emphasising disciplines such as regular financial reporting, sound internal expenditure controls, improved accounting standards, performance monitoring and independent audit and supervision systems.

The asset and liability management of government has also changed considerably over the past ten years. After years of isolation, the South African government established itself again as a credible borrower in the international capital markets. This is reflected in the upgraded credit ratings received from international rating agencies since 1994 and the continued interest in investing in bond issues of the national government. However, the government has maintained its foreign debt well within appropriate levels. At the end of December 2003 the foreign debt of the national government amounted to only 6.0 per cent of gross domestic product.

In the domestic market, the government's strategy has been aimed at reducing borrowing costs and risk, managing maturity profiles, diversifying funding instruments, increasing transparency and building credibility. The marketing of government debt through primary dealers was introduced in 1998, followed by a debt consolidation programme in 2002. The funding instruments were also diversified – from fixed income bonds and treasury bills to inflation-linked bonds, variable rate bonds and retail bonds. Moreover, considerable progress has been made in improving cash management through investments in interest-bearing deposits.

As a result of all these measures the government has been able to reduce its net loan debt from a peak of 48.1 per cent of gross domestic product in fiscal 1996/97 to 36.8 per cent in 2003/04. This not only contributed to lower interest payments on total public debt, but also to generally lower long-term yields in the South African capital market. The prudent measures applied by government have also brought about a decline in government net dissaving from the high level of 7.3 per cent of gross domestic product in 1992 to 1.1 per cent in 2003.

MONETARY POLICY

More normalised relations with the rest of the world made it possible for the authorities to focus monetary policy on the creation of a financial environment conducive to the fulfilment of the growth potential of the country. The objectives of monetary policy at the beginning of the 1990s were to reduce the rate of inflation to the average rate in trading partner and competitor countries; to manage the money creation process in such a way that an adequate, but not an excessive, amount of new money would be supplied to the system; to maintain positive real interest rates; to increase the gold and other foreign reserves to a comfortable level and to develop a sound financial infrastructure consisting of healthy financial institutions and financial markets.

The monetary policy framework applied can be described as "informal inflation targeting" because of the emphasis it placed on the reduction of inflation without specifying the time period over which it would be attained. It also differed from formal inflation targeting at first because an intermediate target, the growth in money supply, anchored monetary policy decisions. Later, towards the end of the 1990s, the Reserve Bank moved to an "eclectic" monetary policy framework. Although growth in money supply and bank credit extension were still regarded as significant contributors to inflation, the Bank began to closely monitor other financial and real indicators when taking decisions on the appropriate level of short-term interest rates.

In the 1990s, the Reserve Bank intervened heavily on its own initiative in the spot and forward market to influence supply and demand in the foreign exchange market. These operations were undertaken to smooth out large short-term fluctuations in the exchange rate, but the Bank stated explicitly that it did not target the level of the exchange rate. The extent to which the Bank intervened in the foreign exchange market was clearly reflected in the changes in the net open position in foreign reserves (NOFP), i.e. the net gold and other foreign reserves of the Bank, less the balance on its net oversold forward book. For example, on 30 September 1998 the NOFP reached a peak of US$23.2 billion.

Despite this active intervention, large fluctuations occurred in the weighted average external value of the rand, particularly during the second half of the 1990s in an environment of more liberalised exchange controls. The monetary policy measures, however, achieved considerable success in bringing the rate of inflation down. After inflation in the consumer price index had generally fluctuated around a level of about 15 per cent in the late 1980s and the beginning of the 1990s, it moved below double digits in 1993 and declined to 5.2 per cent in 1999.

In February 2000, the government announced that South Africa had formally adopted an inflation-targeting monetary policy framework to make monetary policy more transparent and accountable and to co-ordinate with other policy measures. The inflation target was specified as a range of 3 to 6 per cent in the overall consumer price index, excluding mortgage interest cost in metropolitan and other urban areas (the CPIX), i.e. a variant of the headline inflation rate. The headline inflation rate was not used, as it is affected directly by changes in the Reserve Bank's repurchase rate. By including price changes in metropolitan as well as other urban areas, the most comprehensive price index available in South Africa was used in setting the target.

In the application of inflation targeting, it was decided to leave the external value of the rand to the market, and not to intervene in the foreign-exchange market to influence the exchange rate. It was realised that this could lead to volatility in the exchange rate of the rand. Although the Bank would prefer to operate in an environment characterised by exchange rate stability, it takes cognisance of the fact that fluctuations in the external value of the rand are unavoidable in the current international monetary system of generally floating exchange rates. In these circumstances the authorities can only aim at creating underlying economic conditions conducive to exchange rate stability.

The exchange rate of the rand has proved to be central to the inflation outcome. For example, in 2002 monetary policy was dominated by inflationary pressures arising from a substantial depreciation in the external value of the rand in late 2001, combined with a sharp rise in international oil prices as well as in domestic food prices. These external shocks were responsible for a surge in the twelve-month rate of increase in the CPIX from a low of 5.8 per cent in September 2001 to a peak of 11.3 per cent in October 2002. Restrictive monetary policy measures and the subsequent recovery in the exchange rate of the rand then brought the rate of increase over twelve months in the CPIX down to 4.0 per cent in December 2003.

With the adoption of the inflation targeting framework, it also became the stated objective of the Reserve Bank to reduce the NOFP because of the negative effect that this position had on foreign investments into South Africa, on the assessment of domestic economic conditions by international rating agencies and, crucially, on exchange rate developments. The NOFP was accordingly reduced from the peak oversold position of US$23.2 billion at the end of September 1998 to an overbought position of US$0.9 billion at the end of July 2003.

The Reserve Bank then shifted its focus to reducing its oversold forward book and to gradually strengthening the official foreign exchange reserve position. The oversold forward book of the Reserve Bank, amounting to US$4.1 billion at the end of July 2003, was quickly turned around to an overbought position of US$38 million at the end of February 2004. The official foreign exchange reserves of the country were also increased from US$7.6 billion at the end of December 2002 to US$8.2 billion at the end of February 2004.

THE FINANCIAL SECTOR

In the period of political and economic isolation during the 1980s, the domestic financial sector continued to develop rapidly. Many improvements were made to the regulatory framework, such as the creation of a uniform legal framework for all deposit-taking institutions, the establishment of appropriate structures for the markets in new financial instruments, and the revision of rules governing the marketing of equities, bonds and derivatives. Moreover, the authorities endeavoured to promote proper risk management procedures and internationally accepted principles with the objective of preserving the soundness of financial institutions.

The efforts made to maintain an effective and efficient financial sector were hampered by the lack of co-operation with international regulators because of the sanctions referred to earlier. As a consequence, some regulations and practices started to deviate from international best practice. With the re-establishment of normal relations with the rest of the world in the 1990s, significant efforts were made to bring the rules and regulations on the activities of financial institutions in line with international best practice.

From 1994, South African financial institutions started operating on an increasing scale in major international financial centres and began opening branches or subsidiaries in other African countries. As part of this process, five large domestic companies transferred the primary listing of their stock to international bourses. This change gave them greater access to capital resources at lower cost and provided them with opportunities to expand their core business into other countries and regions. All these companies maintained secondary listings on the JSE Securities Exchange South Africa, and their market capitalisation on the JSE actually increased from 126 billion in 1997 to R471 billion in 2003.

Over the same period, international financial institutions were encouraged to conduct business in South Africa. Continuous attempts were made to level the playing field between local and international service providers. The regulatory authorities also actively encouraged the development of appropriate clearing, settlement, ownership-transfer and market information systems and insisted on proper intra-market and cross-market risk management systems, including capital adequacy requirements for market participants.

Increased international participation, the development of new financial instruments and other innovations became important reasons for a paradigm shift in financial sector regulation, away from an interventionist approach to a more market-based approach. Flexibility was increasingly applied, and more reliance placed on corporate governance, disclosure, transparency and accountability.

The operations of the financial markets in South Africa were also improved considerably to bring them in line with international norms. In 1996 bond trading was shifted from the JSE to the Bond Exchange of South Africa. This led to a substantial rise in turnover in the secondary bond market from R2 trillion in 1995 to nearly R12 trillion in 2003. Improvements to the JSE included electronic clearing and rolling contractual settlement, the dematerialisation of equity scrip and the implementation of an electronic trading system. The value of shares traded on the JSE increased from R62 billion in 1994 to R752 billion in 2003.

An important further development since 1994 has been the impetus given to providing access to finance and banking activities to small, medium and micro enterprises and underbanked communities. This challenge has been accepted with due recognition of the regulatory objective of achieving a high degree of economic efficiency and consumer protection in the economy. It requires an approach that introduces changes to achieve greater participation in banking while maintaining financial stability at the same time.

Developments in the regulatory framework of South Africa's financial markets during the past years have also been aimed at addressing empowerment issues. For this purpose, the financial sector has developed a Financial Sector Black Economic Empowerment Charter to promote increased black ownership of and access to financial institutions. This Charter, made public on 17th October 2003, sets out targets that will be pursued to December 2014 regarding, among other things, investment in human resource development; a procurement policy that favours accredited black economic empowerment companies; improved delivery of and access to financial services to a greater segment of the low-income population; the mobilisation of resources for empowerment financing; increased direct black ownership at the holding company level; the encouragement of shareholder activism in promoting the objectives of the charter; and directing a percentage of after-tax operating profits to corporate social investment aimed at education, training and job creation.

CONCLUSION

The normalisation of relations with the rest of the world has made it unnecessary to follow unduly restrictive fiscal and monetary policies in order to maintain a surplus on the current account of South Africa's balance of payments and created leeway for the promotion of economic growth. In the past ten years, a deficit has been recorded on the current account, but this deficit as a ratio of gross domestic product remained low and averaged only 1 per cent per year. Over the same period, net financial inflows from the rest of the world amounted to nearly R204 billion, compared with net financial outflows of about R45 billion from 1985 to 1993. As a result, the level of foreign investment in South Africa amounted to R736 billion at the end of 2002.

These developments have allowed the authorities to pursue more globalised policies while maintaining financial stability, which has contributed materially to a better growth performance of the domestic economy and improvements in the living standards of the population. South Africa's real economic growth doubled from an average annual rate of 1.5 per cent during the 1980s to about 3 per cent between 1994 and 2003. In addition, the average growth in real gross national income per capita, an indicator of living standards, improved from a negative figure of 1.1 per cent per year during the 1980s to a positive figure of 0.8 per cent between 1994 and 2003. Moreover, between 2000 and 2003 the average growth in real gross national income per capita amounted to about 1.5 per cent.

So, the future looks promising indeed.

T T Mboweni
Governor of the South African Reserve Bank

References

Calitz, Estian and Krige, Siebrits, "Changes in the role of government in the South African economy", *Economic Perspective*, Absa Group Limited, Second Quarter 2002.

Cassim, Rashad, et al., *The state of Trade Policy in South Africa*, Trade and Industrial Policy Strategies, Department of Trade and Industry, December 2002.

Cross, James, *Global Integration and Capital Liberalisation in South Africa*, Bank for International Settlements, Paper No 15, 2001.

De Kock, G P C, "The Monetary System and Monetary Policy in South Africa", *Final Report to the Commission of Enquiry into the Monetary System and Monetary Policy in South Africa*, Government Printers, Pretoria, 1985.

Falkena, H B et al., *Financial Regulation in South Africa*, SA Financial Sector Forum, Johannesburg 2001.

Republic of South Africa, National Treasury, *Budget Review* 2004, RP18/2004, Pretoria, 18 February 2004.

Republic of South Africa, National Treasury, *Medium-Term Budget Policy Statement, October 2003*, RP201/2003, Pretoria, 2003.

South African Reserve Bank, *Governor's Address*, 1994 to 2003.

South African Reserve Bank, Bank Supervision Department, *Annual Reports*, 1994 to 2003.

FROM LOCAL TO GLOBAL IN ONE DECADE

INTRODUCTION

Graham Mackay's essay on South African Breweries' transformation in the past decade from a South African company dominating its domestic market to a global brewer in over forty countries on four continents, is, while extraordinary, also an archetype of the experience of several other large South African companies. While the details of SAB Miller's global emergence are unique, the outline of the story reflects many aspects of the motivation and the experience of Anglo American, Gencor – now BHP Billiton, Rembrandt/Richemont and Old Mutual.

Previously trapped behind tariff walls and exchange controls, some of South Africa's greatest companies had become pot-bound, being forced to invest in South Africa outside their areas of core business, to produce a growing return for shareholders. Gencor, among others, saw the need to break out, and developed sophisticated financing instruments enabling it to list in London as Billiton plc. Others such as Anglo, De Beers and Rembrandt had earlier leveraged their European ties to build separate, comparatively robust businesses offshore. But South Africa's questionable international status before 1994, economic sanctions in the latter half of the 1980s and the high domestic cost of capital constrained opportunity and made such businesses vulnerable.

The transition to democracy, the opening of South Africa to the wider world and the decision by the Reserve Bank and Treasury to allow dual listings transformed the environment and brought about a new era in South African business. Graham Mackay's account of SAB's path is both a corporate history and a deeper parable.

SABMILLER

It has been a fascinating journey. Springing from its South African roots, SABMiller's rapid advance in the last decade has been a voyage of discovery – of overcoming many obstacles, learning new cultures, coping with many new languages and dialects and adjusting to dramatically different market requirements. All this has been done relatively quickly. There have been problems – and there have been the sceptics.

But today, barely a decade after South Africa became truly democratic and re-entered the world as a full and accepted member, I believe that SABMiller – and other South African companies – can look back on their achievements with more than a little pride.

A decade ago, we were a successful but almost entirely South African business – our only real prospect of major growth lay outside the country's borders. We entered new territories early, first in Africa and then in Eastern Europe and Asia. We acquired businesses at reasonable entry prices and in doing so, exploited the first phase of the global brewing industry's consolidation. Our move into the Americas marked phase two of this process.

Now, SABMiller is a truly international business in every sense of the word. We have a brewing presence in over forty countries across four continents, operate 121 breweries, and are ranked the third largest brewer in the world by volume. We sell 100 000 pints of beer every minute, every day of the year. That quenches a lot of thirsts. We hold strong positions in several markets and a unique portfolio of international premium brands, including Miller Genuine Draft, Pilsner Urquell, Peroni and Castle Lager.

At the same time, in the carbonated soft drinks market we remain one of the largest bottlers and distributors of Coca-Cola products outside the United States, with interests in Africa and Central America.

But we do not measure ourselves by size alone. Our growth, geographic reach, the quality and breadth of our brand portfolio, and our widespread distribution network are means towards the ultimate objective of delivering value to our shareholders.

We are proud of our achievements, but we are on a never-ending journey, acknowledging that many challenges lie ahead.

THE HERITAGE

Where did it all start? How have we come this far on our global quest? Our foundations are firmly entrenched in the heritage and success of a South African company, whose roots reach back more than a century.

The South African Breweries was founded in 1895, soon after the establishment of Johannesburg as a mining town. It was the first industrial share listed on the Johannesburg Stock Exchange in 1897 and its flagship brand, Castle Lager, was an immediate success.

The company grew over the years but because of taxes on beer in the 1950s, the demand for beer fell. To address this problem, the three largest brewers in South Africa at the time – Ohlsson's, United Breweries and SAB – consolidated. Although SAB was the smallest of the three, the new company retained the SAB name. In August 1962, South African Breweries was presented with a phenomenal market opportunity when an apartheid-era restriction on black people buying alcohol was lifted. This enabled the company to grow the beer market significantly, taking market share from sorghum beer.

From the mid-1960s to the early 1990s, SAB followed a strategy of growth through diversification. This was a consequence of the political isolation of South Africa at the time, and the fact that SAB already held 98 per cent of the South African lager beer market. Our strategy included launching a hotel division in 1966, acquiring a 49 per cent share in Appletiser in 1979, the purchase of Scotts Stores Group and Edgars in 1981 and 1982, and investments in the Lion Match Company, Da Gama Textiles and Plate Glass in 1987, 1989 and 1992 respectively. When, after the first democratic elections in 1994, SAB decided to focus on and develop its core business of producing beverages, we sold off virtually all these non-core businesses.

In the 1970s, we started expanding our operations beyond South Africa, beginning with sub-Saharan Africa, establishing breweries in each of our neighbouring countries, including Swaziland, Botswana and Lesotho. But the sanctions imposed on South Africa in the mid-1980s because of apartheid restricted SAB's expansion opportunities to the domestic market.

When sanctions were lifted in the early 1990s, it was obvious that to grow we had to move far beyond our borders – and quickly. Thus, by the end of the 1990s SAB was the largest brewer in Africa, and held interests in Zimbabwe, Tanzania, Mozambique, Angola, Ghana, Uganda, Kenya and Zambia. Over half the beer consumed on the African continent is now produced by SAB and its associates.

The new "free market" economy in South Africa saw the return of companies that had left the country in the apartheid years, and new giants entering the market. Many South African companies were quick to see the threats and opportunities this situation posed, and sought expansion abroad.

Political changes on a global scale in the early nineties also played an important role in SAB's expansion. The fall of the Berlin wall and the demise of communism opened up significant investment opportunities in central and Eastern Europe. SAB, with its experience in the developing world, was able to exploit the privatisation of state-held assets and purchase breweries in a number of countries.

Another factor affecting the global brewing industry was the trend towards the consolidation of brewers to form giant international operations, a trend that continues unabated.

Our philosophy is that you've got to link global aspirations to a value growth proposition. We operate with the underlying assumption that those who dominate the industry will thereby have access to economies of scale and will be able to create a superior, sustainable and long-term growth profile. That's the point of being one of the dominant players in the global industry. It's not about being cock of the roost and being able to crow about your size. If there is an economic logic to global consolidation, it is to access global economies of scale. If these are present, then we want to access them, otherwise our long-term value growth will be inferior.

Our strategy towards this objective is based on four goals: to drive volume and productivity in all our major markets; to optimise and expand existing market positions through acquisition; to continue to be alert to the typically smaller number of larger value-added opportunities, to enhance our position as a global brewer, and to grow our brands such as Pilsner Urquell, Miller Genuine Draft, Peroni and Castle Lager in the international premium beer segment.

GLOBAL EXPANSION

Our global expansion began with the acquisition of breweries in Hungary in 1993, China in 1994 and Poland and Romania in 1996.

SAB became the largest brewer in Eastern Europe in 1999 following its acquisition of Czech brewers Radegast and Plzensky Prazdroj, and became active in Russia and India. Our strategy was to focus on operating improvements and efficiencies.

The pan-African strategic alliance entered into between SAB and the Castel group, with effect from April 2001, capitalised on the complementary geographic profile of the two groups in Africa. While SAB's operations were concentrated in the south and east of the continent, the Castel group's interests were in sixteen mainly Francophone countries of west, central and north Africa. In addition, SAB had made carbonated soft drinks (CSD) acquisitions in Angola and Zambia, and had increased lager beer investments in Uganda and Mozambique.

The group entered a new region, Central America, in November 2001, with brewing and soft drinks acquisitions in Honduras and El Salvador. Management believed that this market offered potential for growth in both volume and profit, as per capita beer consumption was relatively low in these countries compared with other Latin American markets.

SAB had expanded rapidly in China, where our joint venture operation, China Resources Breweries (CRB), was well positioned as the country's second largest brewer. We purchased five new brewing companies in the 2001/2002 financial year in the northeast and southwest of the country, where CRB was the market leader. By entering into a majority-owned joint venture with the Blue Sword group, CRB also became the leading brewer in the highly populated Sichuan province. In total, SABMiller was involved in thirty breweries in China at the beginning of 2004.

SAB initially also acquired two new breweries in India, giving us a presence in four of the five largest beer-consuming states in the country. We also successfully launched Castle Lager, our South African flagship brand, as a premium product in the cities of Delhi and Mumbai. Subsequently the company formed a joint venture with Shaw Wallace Breweries Ltd, which was considered the largest international collaboration in India's alcohol beverage industry. The joint venture combined the brewing interests of both partners to form an entity with 35 per cent market share, the second largest in the domestic market.

By early 2002, SAB had total lager sales of 70.4 million hectolitres annually, and brewing operations in 24 countries. Some of the highlights included the turnaround of the Polish and Czech Republic operations, while Tyske Gronie had become one of the top brands in Europe, and Pilsner Urquell had grown 3.2 per cent in a declining market.

We had also moved our primary listing from the Johannesburg Securities Exchange to the London Stock Exchange.

THE LONDON LISTING

I have been asked many times why we changed our primary listing and chose London as our new headquarters.

The London listing, in March 1999, in which we were ranked immediately in the FTSE 100, was crucial to moving our global strategy forward because it gave us new opportunities for expansion, which we did not have in Johannesburg. It provided us with a listing in a deeper capital market.

The South African government was supportive of our decision and has done a fine job in ensuring that the economic fundamentals for a prosperous future for the country are in place. The leadership has also been courageous in pursuing an economic path that will have long-term benefits.

GLOBAL CONSOLIDATION

Before addressing the acquisition of the Miller Brewing Company, it is worth exploring what was happening to the global beer markets generally. The trend of consolidation, mergers and acquisitions intensified from 2000 to 2002. Yet no company had built a dominant position at global level, and much of the mergers and acquisitions activity had been driven by other factors. Some companies had withdrawn from non-core businesses, or acquired smaller local competitors; others had entered "new opportunity" markets such as China and Eastern Europe.

The global beer market, however, remained more fragmented. In 2000, the ten largest brewers accounted for less than 43 per cent of worldwide production. The largest of all, Anheuser-Busch, held less than 9 per cent of the total, and its leading brand, Budweiser, less than 4 per cent. By contrast, just three companies in the soft drinks sector accounted for some 80 per cent of the world volume, with Coca-Cola commanding almost half.

Consolidation of the brewing market is slow and inexorable, a sticky process advancing in fits and starts, more like an ultramarathon than a sprint. Beer is high in bulk but low in value, and it is difficult to centralise production because of high transport costs. At the same time, merging across borders between various countries is tricky because of local brand preferences and different regulatory requirements. In emerging markets there is more freedom to restructure, but markets are sometimes slow to appreciate the benefits of consolidation. This process is probably less than halfway through, and could last for another ten to fifteen years.

In 2002, eleven markets accounted for nearly 70 per cent of the beer consumed worldwide. In 2004 China surpassed the US as the world's largest beer market in volume.

Largest Beer Markets

2002 Rank	Market	1997 Hectolitres in millions	2002 Hectolitres in millions	1997 – 2002 Compound annual growth rate
1	United States	226.5	241.0	1.3%
2	China	187.1	238.0	4.9%
3	Germany	109.7	102.7	-1.3%
4	Brazil	81.4	86.7	1.3%
5	Japan	71.2	69.5	-0.5%
6	Russia	26.4	66.2	20.1%
7	United Kingdom	61.1	59.4	-0.6%
8	Mexico	45.8	51.4	2.3%
9	Spain	26.3	29.5	2.4%
10	Poland	18.8	26.7	7.2%
11	South Africa	25.2	24.6	-0.5%
	Top 11 Markets	879.5	995.8	2.5%
	All Other	410.0	440.7	1.5%
	Total Worldwide	1,289.6	1,436.5	2.2%
	Top 11% of Total	68.2%	69.3%	1.1ppts

Source: Plato Logic, April 2003

World's Top 10 Brewers

Rank	Brewer	Rank	Brewer
1	Anheuser-Busch	6	AmBev
2	SABMiller	7	Scottish & Newcastle
3	Interbrew	8	Modelo
4	Heineken	9	Coors
5	Carlsberg	10	Kirin

Source: Plato Logic, October 2003

NOTE: China became the largest market in 2004 and SABMiller moved to third position following the announced merger of Interbrew and AmBev in March 2004.

THE MILLER ACQUISITION

After the London listing, we continued to consolidate SABMiller as a global brewer. The markets, however, had been criticising us for a perceived risk of overexposure to emerging markets. The truth is that SAB had not been idle in this regard, and had been talking to a number of groups around the world. The decline of the exchange rate of the South African rand against the US dollar in 2001 obviously had an impact on the strong underlying performance of our South African operations. This, together with the weakening of other African currencies and political instability in some countries, contributed to a general feeling of "Afro-pessimism".

This was one of the contributing factors to our low PE ratio of around 14.5 at the time – well below those of other brewers such as Anheuser-Busch (24.4), Heineken (22.5) Diageo (18.8), and AmBev (18.7).

Although SAB was then the world's fourth largest brewer by volume, there was always the risk of a hostile takeover. We felt that the markets were underrating the company, and decided we needed to transform ourselves from a large brewer operating in emerging markets to a truly global player involved across a range of markets. Specifically, we sought a presence in a developed market.

The US beer market was very attractive to us. Firstly, it was the largest in the world, with a profit pool more than three times the size of the next market, which was China, followed by Germany, Brazil, Japan, Russia, UK, Mexico, Spain and Poland.

Three players dominated the US market – Anheuser-Busch with 49 per cent, Miller with 20 per cent and Coors with 11 per cent. The balance of the market was made up of niche players, who operated largely through imports, or as microbrewers. A key question facing the industry was whether this market would end up with one large-scale player and multiple niche players. SAB concluded that there must be room for a successful number two and felt that Miller could fulfil this role.

Miller was owned by Philip Morris but accounted for only 4 per cent of that company's business. Although Miller was profitable, its market share had steadily eroded over the years. We felt that, given time, we could turn this around.

Miller had been the second largest brewer in the US since 1977, and in 1991 had volumes of 50 million hectolitres and a market share of 20 per cent. The Miller brand portfolio had leading positions in all key market segments. The major brands were Miller Lite (premium light), Miller Genuine Draft (premium regular), Miller High Life (near premium), Milwaukee Best (budget), Fosters (imports) and a new portfolio of premium Flavoured Malt Beverage brands.

The company, one of the lowest cost brewers in the country, operated nine breweries across the US and had a strong national distribution network.

The deal was finally concluded in July 2002. SAB assumed US$2 billion of Miller's debt, and Philip Morris received equity of about US$3 billion in the combined group, which was renamed SABMiller plc.

SABMiller was now the second largest brewer in the world by volume, and had moved into the top tier of brewers. It represented a new chapter in our development and positioned us as a major participant in the ongoing consolidation of the beer industry.

In short, the deal provided us with:
- greater geographical balance between a cash-generative mature market and the cash-consuming developing markets;
- better access to capital markets through a lower weighted average cost of capital;

- the scale and critical mass to move into the first tier of brewers;
- an opportunity to put together a portfolio of international brands, which would in turn be underpinned by a global network of distributors;
- access to hard currency earnings and the large American profit pool; and
- an opportunity to "de-risk" the business.

Philip Morris openly acknowledged that brewing was not its area of expertise, and was not threatened by SAB's emerging market portfolio because of its own dealings in this sector. By contrast, SAB's business was beer. And the emotional attachment of the beer consumer to his or her product was different to that of the tobacco consumer, and the dynamics of branding were very different.

The deal also opened up a host of opportunities for cross-selling of our considerable range of products. SAB had, for instance, been building the famous Pilsner Urquell brand in the US – before the Miller acquisition – and access to Miller's sales force and distribution network has not only boosted this process, but also reduced costs. Pilsner Urquell, from the Czech Republic, was the world's first pilsner-type beer with a heritage going back hundreds of years.

We acknowledge that there are some important challenges in respect of the Miller acquisition and it will be critical for SAB to demonstrate to the sceptics that the company can in fact operate successfully in a first-world market.

OUR PEOPLE

I am often asked what I see as our key competitive advantage. Without doubt, it is our people. Brewing is a very competitive process; everyone has access to the same equipment, the same technology and the same suppliers. What differentiates companies is the quality of their people. A very strong people culture has always existed in our South African business, although I'm not sure if it is a characteristic of South African business as a whole. The long experience with South African emerging consumers certainly stood us in very good stead when we were moving into emerging markets. I would not have said it was necessarily the best training ground for moving into more highly contested markets against international competitors, which we did gradually in Europe and then in the US, because the market power we enjoy in South Africa is not easily found elsewhere.

However, our people have learned rapidly how to operate successfully in contested markets. Where South African managers are strong, I believe, is in their willingness to lead by example, to roll up their sleeves and get involved in the detail of business, and to show a strong commitment to making it a success. This is not a unique trait, but one that SABMiller has been able to harness quite effectively.

In our international development, we have deliberately sought to repeat the style of operation which has been successful in South Africa. While other companies' international expansion has been based on exporting brands, ours has been on exporting people. It is thus no coincidence that, at the beginning of 2004, more than 130 people from our South African business were installed in senior positions in our operations around the world.

I went through a phase of thinking that South African business was rather self-congratulatory about its prowess overseas. Now I believe there may be more justification to that than I thought. I don't know whether one can generalise about South African managers, but I do think they have adapted remarkably well to expatriate lives and expatriate roles.

THE BRANDS

Brand power is what the beer markets are all about. There are very few genuine international brands, and top sellers tend to be confined within any country's boundaries. But that is changing slowly. While it is true to say that there is a general decline in mainstream brands, the premium category, as I have mentioned, is in a growth phase in both the emerging and the developed markets. It is the imported brands that are showing the strongest growth. Heineken is clearly the leader in the international stakes. We are focusing on using SABMiller's geographic spread to promote our leading brands globally.

We have positioned Pilsner Urquell as SABMiller's premium international brand. It is now available in more than forty markets across five continents and is showing a strong growth rate. Two of our other brands, Miller Genuine Draft from the United States and Nastro

Azzurro from Italy, have also been included in our international portfolio. In Africa, Castle Lager is the continent's biggest beer brand.

Altogether, the company markets nearly 200 brands worldwide in hundreds of pack choices.

THE FUTURE

Some years ago we wanted to be on the list of top five brewers. Now we *aim* to consolidate our position as a top-tier global brewery. We are in a strong position to achieve this – and to meet our strategic vision of delivering superior long-term value growth to our shareholders. In this regard:

- We are confident that we will stabilise Miller, which will emerge as a strong, sustainable and attractive business. New marketing campaigns have been launched to re-energise the brands, and much work has been done to further segment the US market.
- In Europe, our businesses continue to benefit from macro-economic growth, with a further stimulus expected from accession of countries into the EU, and evolving consumer preferences for beer over spirits.
- Asia offers exciting prospects. We hold a leading position in China. Although China is now the world's largest beer market, it is still at an embryonic stage of its development. But consolidation will help improve the pricing environment and a growing beer culture will enable us to build a strong national brand and introduce at least one of our international premium brands. In India, we have a third of the market and a national footprint. We are working on improving product quality and introducing modern manufacturing disciplines and marketing.
- Central America remains an attractive market with a young population profile, and the potential to move consumers from spirits to beer. Our portfolio of African businesses, combined with our Castel alliance, diversifies country risk and gives us a unique footprint across the continent.
- And returning to our roots – in South Africa, where it all started – we continue to see opportunities to grow volumes and drive margin improvement. In an expanding economy, our aim is to grow our share of the drinks market in the short term through the introduction of new products and a shift from high alcohol drinks into beer.

However, the model and the approach we have used to get us where we are now may need revision to retain its effectiveness.

We will need to get better at three things:
- ◆ Managing and developing higher value brands in countries and across borders instead of concentrating mainly on local brand portfolios selling primarily in the mainstream;
- ◆ Systematic recruitment, employment and development of management talent worldwide rather than essentially relying on South Africa to provide us with a pool for our international operations, and
- ◆ Managing our corporate brand and our profile as a global company, rather than relying on the spillover from decades of effort in South Africa.

We are at some kind of crucial point – and so is the industry. We've arrived here together and we must leverage our existing platform through having the strongest brands, having the finest global talent and by managing our reputation successfully. Like South Africa, we have made considerable progress over the last ten years, some of it unnoticed and perhaps even unrecognised. But again, like South Africa, we have built the foundations from which we can continue to develop and deliver value to all our stakeholders.

It has been a long journey from the dusty mining town that gave birth to the enterprise now known as SABMiller, and we move confidently into the future.

Graham Mackay
Chief Executive, SABMiller plc

BLACK EMPOWERMENT: MYTHS AND REALITIES

HOW WE GOT HERE

Any meaningful review of black economic empowerment (BEE) in the first decade of democracy in South Africa needs to consider, first and foremost, how the country arrived, on 27th April 1994, at a point where it was able to confront its numerous social and economic challenges. More precisely, such a review needs to appreciate the extent of economic disempowerment and dispossession that prevailed for over 300 years in South Africa, and which constituted the awful legacy that the new democratic nation inherited.

Some, albeit a small minority, hold to the myth that, come the democratic change of 1994, the country's slate was wiped clean. This minority believes that South Africa was given a fresh start, unencumbered by the limitations of its troubled past. The reality, of course, is somewhat different. In assessing the progress of BEE over the last ten years, it is important to understand the full impact of three centuries of deliberate and systematic disempowerment. Not only does it help to comprehend the extent of the challenge we face today, it also helps identify those elements which must necessarily form part of any successful black empowerment programme.

One of the most devastating acts of economic disempowerment in South Africa's history was the removal of its indigenous people from the land they had occupied for centuries, initially through force of arms and later through discriminatory laws and a system of taxation designed to force Africans into the industrial labour market. For these communities, loss of land amounted to a loss of economic independence and for many a loss of a viable livelihood. Formalised in the 1913 Land Act and apartheid-era forced removals, this dispossession and its after-effects persist to this day – where access to productive agricultural land remains largely the preserve of a racially defined minority. While the industrialisation process of the last century has resulted in large-scale urbanisation, there remain significant numbers of South Africans living in rural areas. Land reform and rural development must therefore necessarily form part of any comprehensive BEE strategy.

Dispossessed of their land, black South Africans were confined to a particular role in the economic development of the country – serving as a cheap and bountiful supply of labour. Through a range of legal and social mechanisms, blacks were barred from any occupations above those of unskilled or semi-skilled workers. They were prevented from owning property, or owning or operating businesses and thus effectively prevented from building up any significant capital and resource base. This lack of capital, as we shall see, served – and continues to serve – as one of the biggest impediments to the large-scale entry of black South Africans into the mainstream of the economy at all levels. Ensuring access to finance therefore necessarily forms part of a comprehensive empowerment strategy.

The logic of the apartheid policy was that black people were destined only ever to provide cheap labour, a process which resulted in the deliberate denial of opportunities for decent education and skills development. The infamous system of Bantu Education sought not only to strip black people of their dignity, but also to cripple any efforts at self-development. It created a society in which the vast majority of citizens simply did not have the skills to advance beyond a certain economic level. The development of the country's human resource potential therefore forms an integral part of a comprehensive empowerment strategy. This is particularly important given the relative growth of the secondary and tertiary sectors of the economy, and the relative decline of the primary sector. Skills are in greater demand, and more important to the growth of the economy, than ever before in South Africa's history.

To compound the economic disempowerment of the country's majority, successive apartheid governments directed practically all available public resources towards meeting the needs of the small white minority. The social infrastructure of black communities was ignored for decades, resulting in miserable living conditions for millions. Without even the most basic social services – like adequate transport, health care, shelter, energy, water – black South Africans have been additionally disempowered. BEE therefore requires that public resources are redirected to meet the basic needs of the majority.

Precisely because the economic disempowerment of black South Africans was so far-reaching in its effect, and so broad in the areas in which it was effected, it was necessary, as we entered the era of democracy, that our efforts at black economic empowerment be similarly broad and far-reaching.

One of the myths about BEE is that it is essentially about the entry of blacks into the heights of the South African economy. That is certainly what is given the most media coverage and appears to draw the most attention. But BEE, if it is to be meaningful and sustainable, must achieve redress in all those areas where blacks have been disempowered. It must ensure the active participation and benefit of blacks in all sectors and at all levels within the economy. BEE is as much about black participation on the boards and in the senior management of the largest companies in the country as it is about the number of black engineers, accountants and IT professionals coming out of universities. It is as much about the percentage of black ownership on the JSE, as it is about the number of households in the country that are electrified.

EARLY EFFORTS, EARLY LESSONS

From the outset, in 1994, the newly elected democratic government set about the daunting challenge of reversing the effects of centuries of economic disempowerment. In doing so, it had to tackle a number of immediate problems. The economy was in a state of decline, the public debt had soared to unsustainable levels, many economic sectors were ill-prepared for global competition, and the government bureaucracy was fragmented, poorly equipped and badly managed.

The government introduced a range of mechanisms to halt the economic decline that had characterised the 1980s and early 1990s, largely through macroeconomic interventions such as the GEAR strategy and via tariff reductions and the removal of wasteful export incentives, the latter requiring structural change in a number of industries to achieve international competitiveness. Public finances were prudently managed, to bring the deficit down and steadily reduce the country's public debt.

These mechanisms were implemented alongside other elements of the Reconstruction and Development Programme (RDP), which sought to expand the provision of basic services to all South Africans, through greater investment in housing, health care, education, water, energy, transport and social infrastructure. All of these measures have been part of government's efforts to meet the basic needs of all South Africans – a stage in the process of empowering, socially and economically, South Africa's poor black majority.

Over the same period, the private sector has embarked on a number of BEE initiatives, including changes in ownership and proposals to stimulate economic growth. From the moment in 1993 when Sanlam sold 10 per cent of its stake in Metropolitan Life to a black consortium, the private sector began a period of sustained deal-making, selling stakes in companies, many of them listed on the JSE.

With the advent of democracy, the number of joint ventures between established white-owned businesses and black companies increased, as did the number of black companies and consortia taking equity in existing companies or unbundled entities. This process peaked in the period from 1996 to 1998. From just one empowerment transaction on the JSE in 1993, there were 111 in 1998. These transactions increased in value from R140 million in 1993 to R7 billion in 1996 and R21.2 billion in 1998. However, during these years, a handful of major deals accounted for most of this value.

Because of the lack of capital in black hands, efforts to source black capital through stokvels, trade union pension funds and retail schemes were unsuccessful. This led to the development of special purpose vehicles (SPVs) to fund these transactions. As the Black Economic Empowerment Commission (BEECom) noted in its landmark review of the empowerment process, between 1996 and 1998 SPVs were by far the most favoured financing structure, accounting for 52 per cent of black economic ownership. (An SPV is essentially a company established for the sole purpose of facilitating the purchase of an equity stake in a target company by a BEE grouping.)

However, the SPVs were premised on a continuing bull market. When the market hit turbulence, many empowerment groups were not able to meet their financial obligations as defined in SPV agreements, and some were forced to give up recently acquired shares in investee companies. The global financial crisis of 1998 exposed further BEE funding weaknesses and resulted in a situation where a significant number of SPVs were "out of the money", causing substantial losses for financiers, who withdrew from the market. From its peak of R21.2 billion in 1998, the value of empowerment deals on the JSE dropped to just R3.4 billion in 1999.

There were indeed a number of other flaws in the SPV funding mechanism which became apparent. Some of these are outlined in the BEECom report, published in 2001: "In structuring the transactions, advisors seldom critically assessed the potential of the instruments to transfer sustainable ownership. In the race to do the deal, advisors were often not rigorous in their appraisal of investment opportunities, resulting in many BEE consortia entering into deals they should never have considered. However, BEE consortia must also share the blame for not interrogating the contracts presented to them."

The report continues: "There are now few deals that involve the acquisition of minority stakes in JSE-listed companies. This is because BEE groups are under pressure from funders and the markets to demonstrate focus, move away from portfolio investments, and to become operationally involved. More recently, some BEE companies have been able to fund their acquisitions on the strength of their balance sheets. There have been very few new entrants and almost no new sources of funding."

The research conducted on behalf of the BEECom showed that the SPV approach had not translated into a meaningful transfer of ownership into black hands. Even under a best-case scenario, the funding structures implied a significant dilution of black ownership on the winding up of SPVs, with most of the financial benefits accruing to funders. The funding mechanisms were not designed to effect real ownership.

These shortcomings highlighted the perennial problem of the lack of capital in black hands. They also drew attention to the challenge of finding sustainable ways of leveraging finance, the lack of support to black companies, and the absence of a comprehensive view of black economic empowerment either in the private sector or in government. The weakness of the BEE exercise was not simply a concern for would-be participants – it was a challenge to the whole process of economic growth and sustainability.

The simple reality is that South Africa cannot have a strong economy unless the majority of its people are active participants in it – whether as owners or managers, workers or broad beneficiaries. BEE, in its broadest form, is central to narrowing the vast – and unsustainable – income gap in South Africa, stimulating economic growth, and harnessing the country's human resource potential.

As part of the effort to address some of these perceived shortcomings, the Black Business Council established the Black Economic Empowerment Commission (BEECom) to review what had taken place in the arena of empowerment, analyse the challenges and formulate recommendations that could be presented to government and other stakeholders.

GROWING UP, GROWING WISER

The BEECom report was one of a number of policy initiatives that provided improved focus and renewed vigour to the process of empowerment. It proceeded from the premise that conditions existed for government, the private sector and other stakeholders to agree on a common strategy for pursuing broad-based empowerment. These conditions had been created as much by the lessons of the early empowerment deals, as they had by the progress made by government in working to redress apartheid's economic inheritance.

This led the BEECom report to note in 2001: "South Africa's democratic government inherited a mismanaged economy, designed to serve the needs of a minority of the population and condemn the black majority to a vicious cycle of extreme poverty, unemployment and underdevelopment. Over the past seven years, [the government] has fundamentally transformed the country's political, economic and social landscape. It has entrenched the values of equality and freedom and laid the foundations for the country to chart a new path to economic development."

Central among the recommendations of the report was an "Investment for Growth" accord, whereby stakeholders were called upon to commit themselves to a targeted development investment strategy which, among other things, would increase the levels of fixed investment and promote economic growth. This targeted investment would be directed at developing black business, but would consist mainly of investments in social and economic infrastructure and human capital.

For its part, government was urged, subject to consultations with labour, to invest around 10 per cent of the assets of the Government Employees Pension Fund in areas of national priority over an adjustment period of five to seven years. Around 3 per cent of the fund's assets had already been allocated for investment in black economic empowerment.

A portion of proceeds from the privatisation of state assets should be invested in an agency dedicated towards rural development. Already government had earmarked some of these proceeds for a National Empowerment Fund, which would invest in black business.

This targeted investment strategy would include a commitment by the financial sector, particularly life and retirement companies, to divert a specified percentage of its total assets towards productive investments in areas of national priority over a similar adjustment period.

The private sector was challenged to make a concrete commitment to rural development and other infrastructural and economic initiatives in rural areas and anchor projects aimed at attracting investments into Industrial Development Zones. Such an accord would increase black participation in the economy because new investments in areas of national priority would create formal sector jobs, stimulate rural economies and promote the development of small and medium business.

The commission noted that a key condition for any successful programme of black economic empowerment must be the development of the capacity of the country's people. Education, training and targeted skills development is a necessity if black South Africans are to be empowered. It therefore argued for an integrated national human resource development strategy which covers the full spectrum of learning – including primary schools, higher education, adult basic education and training, life-long learning, youth learnerships, SMME skills development, and on-the-job training in the public and private sector.

It recommended that government use incentives and penalties to ensure that the higher education and training system would substantially increase its output of black graduates, particularly in the fields of science, information technology, business and engineering. Incentive schemes should be used to encourage institutions in this system to forge partnerships with secondary schools, to improve the quality of teaching and the standard of skills at this crucial level of education development.

The restructuring of state enterprises – which includes, but is not limited to, privatisation – could be effectively used by government as a tool for BEE. In addition to directing proceeds from the sale of state assets to rural development and black entrepreneurship, government should endeavour to involve black companies at all levels of the process, including large divestitures, strategic equity partnerships, concessions and strategic management partnerships. Any restructuring processes would be used to help develop black corporate advisory companies across a wide spectrum of disciplines, with the potential to compete against established firms.

Other key recommendations of the BEECom report included the implementation of the Integrated Sustainable Rural Development Strategy and the creation of an agency to streamline and co-ordinate funding and other initiatives in rural areas, including land reform; a national procurement agency located within the Department of Trade and Industry aimed at transforming the public and private sector procurement environment; and a National Black Economic Empowerment Act to create uniformity in policy and establishing the necessary institutional support and instruments with which to drive the BEE strategy.

It also called for an empowerment framework for public sector restructuring; an enabling framework aimed at improving access to finance for households and businesses through disclosure and reporting requirements in the banking sector; and the streamlining of public sector funding initiatives through a National Empowerment Funding Agency.

The commission said the success of these efforts could be measured, among other things, by targets that could be achieved in an incremental manner, which were measurable and annually reviewable. It said that within ten years:

- at least 30% of productive land should be in black hands;
- black equity participation in each sector of the economy should be increased to at least 25%;
- at least 40% of non-executive and executive directors of companies listed on the JSE should be black;
- at least 50% of procurement by government and state-owned enterprises (SOEs) should go to black companies;
- at least 30% of private sector procurement should be to black-owned companies, including SMEs and collective enterprises;
- black people should comprise at least 40% of the number of people in the professions and in professional training;
- in the event of restructuring, at least 30% of the equity of restructured SOEs should be owned by black companies and collective enterprises.

Given the relatively slow pace of change, particularly in the composition of the workplace, these are ambitious targets.

A TOOL FOR ECONOMIC GROWTH

The recommendations of the BEECom were widely discussed and formed the basis of extensive discussions between black business and government. These were followed by the publication of government's strategy for broad-based BEE.

This strategy aims not only to redress past racial imbalances, but to be a powerful tool for building the economy, accelerating growth and stimulating job creation. While it draws on the work of BEECom and contributions from the President's Black Business and Big Business working groups, it is founded on the basic policy positions outlined in the RDP – and thereby reflects an important continuity in policy.

One of the mechanisms outlined in the strategy is the Broad-Based Black Economic Empowerment Act, which provides the legislative framework through which government can provide direction to the empowerment process. BEE will clearly not be achieved by decree. Rather, the role of government is to encourage the process through, among other things, the publication of guidelines and codes of good practice on BEE. The strategy also includes the formalisation of partnerships with the private sector, including the use of industry charters and even enterprise charters.

The use of a "balanced scorecard" approach for measuring empowerment progress confirms the view of the BEE Commission that empowerment needs to be broad-based, covering a range of features within any company or industry. The scorecard represents a common approach to what economic empowerment is, and how it should be pursued. The tendency towards consensus on these matters cannot, however, change the reality that efforts towards empowerment will necessarily differ from one instance to another. One size will not fit all. But at least we know what the sizes are, and are developing an understanding of which situations are best suited to which size.

The scorecard is not merely intended as a guide to the private sector. Government has indicated it will use the scorecard when it grants licences or concessions, sells any state assets or enterprises, enters into a public-private partnership, or engages in any economic activity.

Government will also use the sale of stakes in state-owned enterprises to encourage BEE, by, among other things, offering discounted shares in any initial public offerings (as happened with Telkom) or ensuring worker or community ownership and management of state-owned enterprises. And both government and state-owned enterprises will promote empowerment through preferential procurement to increase the proportion of black-owned and black-empowered companies which provide products and services to the state.

PARTNERSHIPS AND CHARTERS

The strategy recognises that BEE will not be effective unless government and the private sector work together to achieve it. Its intention actively to seek innovative structured partnerships with the private sector is therefore most welcome.

Sector- and enterprise-based charters are one possible form of such a partnership, although government has indicated that it does not expect that every sector or enterprise will develop empowerment charters. These charters would include the vision of the sector or enterprise for achieving BEE targets and timetables; the specific mechanisms to be used to achieve these targets; an assessment of the financing needed to fund black economic empowerment transactions; and the institutional and management mechanisms that will co-ordinate, facilitate, monitor and evaluate the implementation of the charter.

Government has said it will "strongly encourage" sectors and companies which regularly engage with government, or are regulated by government, to develop charters. It will also seek to conclude enterprise charters with key companies in priority sectors to inject momentum into the empowerment process.

Already a couple of significant and far-reaching charters have been concluded. The petroleum, mining and financial services sectors have each developed empowerment charters. These agreements are not simply pragmatic responses to political and social pressure. Rather, they are necessary responses to economic imperatives, which dictate that growth cannot be achieved without a more equitable distribution of resources and more meaningful participation of greater numbers of South Africans in economic activity at all levels and in all sectors.

While each of the charters so far concluded have their own specific features according to the nature and requirements of their industry, there are a couple of common areas of focus. A central imperative of each charter is to develop human resources within the sector, and, in particular, ensure that the composition of the sector is progressively changed towards reflecting the demographics of the country.

The financial services charter, for example, commits each participating financial institution to invest in human resource development "across the full spectrum of skills, with special emphasis on increasing the participation of black people in skilled, strategic and operational leadership in the sector". Minimum targets have been set for each institution to achieve by 2008. Before 2008, the sector will determine the respective targets for 2014.

The charters also take a similar approach to the implementation of targeted procurement strategies to enhance black economic empowerment, which set incremental targets for increasing the value of procurement supplied by BEE-accredited companies. Some commit themselves to provide support to small- and medium-sized black businesses to help them benefit from targeted procurement programmes.

The charters also address themselves to the important issue of ownership, setting targets for companies in the sector not only for black ownership, but also women's ownership. They also deal with the issue of control, generally setting targets for black and women's representation on company boards.

A critical element of the charters is the issue of setting benchmarks and evaluating progress. In the case of the financial services sector, an independent "Charter Council" will conduct reviews of progress and assess changes to the environment in which the charter is to be implemented.

The development of sector-based charters has added a welcome dimension to the empowerment process. The early empowerment deals were by their nature sporadic, informed in many instances by short-term considerations, rather than an over-arching vision of the development of a particular industry. The process of developing and implementing these charters lends empowerment a far more strategic and comprehensive character.

THE WAY FORWARD

While there has certainly been progress with respect to empowerment, most significantly with respect to efforts to develop relationships between government and business, and to broaden national consensus on the need for, and form of, empowerment, the bulk of economic empowerment work still lies ahead of us.

Among the issues which each industry needs to address – whether through charters or other mechanisms – is a targeted, comprehensive and co-ordinated strategy to develop and transfer skills. A procurement strategy to promote black economic empowerment is also critical to the development and enhancement of black economic empowerment. This strategy should set out a percentage of the value of all goods and services procured over a period that will be sourced from qualifying BEE companies.

Mechanisms should also be developed to ensure the provision of basic savings and payment services to a greater segment of the population. This requires, of necessity, giving proper attention to the accessibility and affordability of banking services to the rural and poor. The latter should take place alongside the development of programmes to promote a greater savings culture in the country. This point is critical, and not merely for the financial services sector. Unless South Africans can achieve far higher levels of savings, their capacity to boost economic growth through domestic investment will always be limited.

Consumer spending is important. But sustained growth requires that South Africans substantially increase the proportion of their resources which go into savings. At the same time, the financial sector needs to increase access to credit for businesses and households, particularly black-owned businesses, co-operatives and collective enterprises. The industry needs to develop models for borrowing to such sectors in which risk can be effectively managed and value can be unlocked in a sustainable manner.

It is important, also, when looking at this issue, to acknowledge the substantial role already played by the public sector in the provision of credit and financial assistance to particularly the poorer section of society. The private sector would do well to draw on the experience of these public institutions, seeing what has worked and – importantly – what hasn't. It would also be useful for the private sector to engage with these public institutions to provide whatever insights, experiences and skills it may have to offer.

There can be no doubt that we are moving forward with BEE. As we do so, we are making progress in the pressing challenge of building our economy, developing our human resources and addressing the substantial gaps of income and opportunity which exist in our society. What will speed up this process and make it more thorough-going – and ultimately define its success – is the extent to which we can proceed along the path of BEE with a shared vision and a common framework for what needs to be done. Given what has taken place over the last ten years, the lessons that have been learnt and the extent of common ground achieved, the future for economic empowerment looks promising indeed.

Cyril Ramaphosa
Chairman, Shanduka Group (Pty) Ltd, South Africa

THE ROLE OF WOMEN IN A DEMOCRATIC SOUTH AFRICA

South Africa has undergone fundamental political and socioeconomic transformation since 1994. Despite having inherited a distorted economy, the new government has been successful in laying a sound and robust macroeconomic foundation. Our economy continues to perform well, relative to other emerging markets, and has demonstrated considerable resilience over the last ten years. There is a need, however, for economic advancement to be expanded to include a far greater number of South Africans.

The major sectors of the South African economy continue to discriminate against women. There are very few women in either executive or non-executive roles. While the country has been transformed significantly since the first democratic elections, women have been left behind in the race for economic empowerment and in appointments to corporate or board positions. Although an elite group of women is making its presence felt, most women find it difficult to succeed in what appears to be a man's world.

This is despite the fact that women were an integral part of the national liberation struggle, both within South Africa and in exile, and they were instrumental in shaping the policies of the ANC. Their protest against the pass laws was a clear indication that they considered themselves an essential part of the liberation struggle. The formation of the Women's League in the 1950s illustrated their determination to play a definitive role in the struggle, and paved the way for the rights that women enjoy today.

South Africa's democracy is firmly anchored on the principles laid down by the African National Congress, the Freedom Charter and in our much-admired constitution.

The ANC undertook to ensure that there is a minimum of 30 per cent of women in leadership positions at national and provincial levels. The gender balance in parliament ranks favourably with that of democratic countries like Sweden and Canada.

ADVANCES MADE BY SOUTH AFRICAN WOMEN OVER THE PAST TEN YEARS

In Government

South Africa's Bill of Rights proudly declares that "everyone is equal before the law and has the right to equal protection and benefit of the law. Equality includes the full and equal enjoyment of all rights and freedom".

South Africa's women have probably advanced further in politics, the public sector and in business over the last ten years than women in the most advanced countries have done over the past century. A culture established during the struggle years required women to partner their male counterparts in leading South Africa through the first ten years of democracy in every sector of society, though women are perhaps more prominent in government than in the private sector. This is partly why our first ten years of democratic rule has been so admirable and so remarkable, disproving the old notion that women are unequal to the task of governance and leadership. South African women have assumed leadership positions in the diplomatic service, foreign affairs, telecommunications, health, the public service, housing, minerals and energy, with varying degrees of success. They have held down onerous jobs while retaining their primary roles as mothers and wives.

In the Boardroom

Ten years ago there was a handful of women in South Africa's boardrooms. This too has changed; some companies in South Africa currently have at least two women on their board, with state-owned enterprises having made the greatest strides. Most chairwomen are generally to be found in state-owned enterprises, where transformation is clearly not an option but part of the democratic mandate. There has not been the same level of commitment in the private sector. The shortage of women among South Africa's top management and leadership ranks is not unique to South Africa, however.

In 2003 one of South Africa's mobile companies, Cell C, pioneered a "take a girl child to work day" project to broaden the knowledge base and aspirations of South Africa's girl children. This became one of the most public and widely supported campaigns ever undertaken. Programmes like these are essential to enable young girls to picture themselves as chief executive officers or in leadership positions.

The various industry charters which aim to broaden and transform participation in the economy will change the imbalance between men and women and in another ten years we will see a completely different picture in the private sector.

ECONOMIC EMPOWERMENT

Over the past ten years, some women have organised themselves into investment groups to take advantage of economic empowerment opportunities in diverse industries. This development was pioneered by the formation of Women Investment Portfolio Holdings (Wiphold) by Gloria Serobe, Louisa Mojela, Nomhle Canca and Wendy Luhabe in 1993. Wiphold began as an unlisted company following a national road show over six months to educate women in the provinces about the economy. The road show's theme was "Beyond labour and consumption". Women supported the initiative in large numbers, subscribing for shares to the tune of R24 million and making themselves investors in their own right for the first time in the history of South Africa. After a rights offer within the following twelve months, women raised an additional R76 million, making their total contribution R100 million. Wiphold had to obtain permission to register a company that would allow only women to be shareholders as this objective was a violation of the spirit of the constitution. Eighteen thousand women responded to the call for action. Wiphold subsequently listed on the Johannesburg Stock Exchange in order to raise substantial capital to expand its business. Women who originally bought their shares for R2 received an equivalent share in a Wiphold Trust, established to protect women's interests and to encourage women to become financially independent. The Trust currently has a strong balance sheet and has made a number of distributions. Over the past ten years, investors have received dividends of more than 300 per cent of their original investment, making Wiphold easily South Africa's most successful venture on behalf of women. Currently, more than 300 000 women hold shares in Wiphold.

The work done by the Women's Development Bank, pioneered by

Mrs Zanele Mbeki, in providing micro-loans has changed the lives of women in rural areas, where more than 40 per cent are breadwinners. Women have made inroads into various other sectors of the economy over the past ten years, but not to the extent that they might have.

HURDLES STILL TO BE OVERCOME

Because South African society is still extremely conservative and sexist, the assumption of leadership roles by women has created an adjustment dilemma for many men who feel they are losing power and authority. As women advance, some men find it difficult to relate to those who are successful. It may be one thing to support a non-sexist society in principle, but quite another to live with the consequences. At the same time, there has been a sharp rise in domestic violence, although this could be the result of more incidents being reported, as women find their voices at last.

When traditional roles change in society, unintended consequences tend to arise. Where both parents work, children are adversely affected. Over the last ten years we have experienced an increasing prevalence of drug-taking, suicides and other dysfunctional patterns of behaviour, which were exceptional in the past. More and more women are opting for a career, single parenthood or living with a partner instead of marriage. This is having consequences for the quality of family life, the nature of relationships and the overall well-being of society.

From an educational perspective, whereas in the eighties there were more men than women enrolled at universities, this pattern has changed in the last ten years. In most universities black women now outnumber black men, although the areas of study by women are still primarily in the "soft" disciplines. This change has implications for the quality of leadership in the future. We must guide women towards the study of finance, engineering, technology and other disciplines critical for the new economy. Women must come to regard themselves as potential chief executives or company directors.

With regard to resources and capital, women do not have the same access as men. Even having a woman as the CEO of a bank has not changed the way in which that particular bank provides services to women, although it has made an effort to educate women about financial planning and management in some instances. This goes to show that having a woman at the helm is not enough; the real focus should be on cultivating women in the middle and lower levels of industry in order to change systematically how organisations perceive and integrate women in business over time. In this regard, succession planning should be obligatory for all organisations.

We have not seen many women ascend to leadership roles in the trade union movement; the few women who were part of the leadership structure prior to 1994 have been absorbed into formal politics, despite the fact that women make up a significant number in the employment sector. This is not a model to be followed by other key stakeholders in our society.

The ordination of women in the church is another huge challenge. Some male priests have left the church because they could not accept women as equals. Needless to say, this sector of society remains sexist and patriarchal. Yet, on a more positive note, women across racial lines continue to provide remarkable and admirable leadership in non-governmental and community-based organisations.

Various awards recognising ordinary women doing extraordinary things in their communities have multiplied over the last ten years. This is an area that has received the most sponsorship support from the private sector. Most business women's associations which existed prior to 1994 have consolidated into one organisation which has significantly raised the profile of women over the past ten years. Compared to other countries, South Africa has done much better than most in advancing women. Yet, the greatest single obstacle is the growth and impact of HIV/AIDS on our young democracy. Women, often single parents with many mouths to feed, are bearing the brunt of the HIV/AIDS scourge. Young women in their twenties have been particularly affected by the virus.

Efforts to give effect to the sentiments in the constitution have varied greatly among government departments. An audit carried out three years ago found that there was a piecemeal approach to dealing with gender issues.

In parallel with developments in the public sector, women in various professions, industries and corporations have broken through the glass ceiling, taking up positions as CEOs and senior executives. The fact that women have remained under-represented in the private sector is a function of prejudice and the shortage of experience. Yet the success of women in the public sector suggests that experience is perhaps overrated in certain instances.

In 1985, the book *Vukani Makhosikazi: South African Women Speak* concluded that the South African struggle will never be won until all women are involved. Yet the South African government is to be commended for introducing groundbreaking and far-reaching laws, policies and programmes aimed at improving the status of women – even if the full emancipation of women has a long way to go. In Gauteng province for example, there is a Gender Policy framework to guide the executive council in complying with constitutional provisions that promote gender equality and equity.

Some of the guiding principles to achieve gender equality are:
- Recognition of the importance of affirmative action as a tool to implement employment equity;
- Recognition of the role of the State as an agent of transformation;
- Recognition of differences and inequalities among women;
- Recognition that economic growth is central to the empowerment of women, but not sufficient to achieve it;
- Recognition of the importance of focusing attention on black women and women in rural areas;
- Recognition of women's rights as human rights;
- Recognition that cultural, customary and religious practices are subject to equality;
- Recognition of women's contribution to the economy and society through unpaid labour.

These principles are intended to improve the circumstances of women, remove the obstacles that have been institutionalised, ensure equality and help create a single society. While democracy offers women opportunities and choices to make what they wish of their lives, the reality is that most women remain constrained by the weight of social and cultural prejudice, and by discrimination in society. However, as the prospects for women have improved, so too has the abuse of women and children increased, calling into question the vision of creating a culture of equal rights for men and women.

The current generation of women will have to plant seeds by example, by successfully assuming roles traditionally preserved for men, by bringing up children in an equitable manner, giving children of both sexes the opportunity to pursue their dreams and to realise their full potential. The generation that will really enjoy the fruits of democracy is probably our grandchildren's, because changing society's entrenched beliefs requires time, effort, courage, commitment and resilience.

Every generation has its own responsibility and our generation of women has the responsibility for ensuring that our society continues to advance the role and contribution of women, thereby helping to consolidate the gains of our young democracy. We can rightfully claim to have ensured that the voices of women will never be silent again. That in itself is a major achievement.

WOMEN IN THE ECONOMY

Where women have the greatest contribution to make is in the area of economic development. However, their contribution remains constrained as they continue to be regarded as minors and as high risk by the establishment. Women still have very limited or no access to capital beyond micro-loans.

There is still much prejudice against women. Democracy has helped to a significant degree, but it cannot overcome the prejudice and discrimination which is generally deeply embedded in people's attitudes. As a result, women are still worst affected by unemployment, and by unequal income levels which remain below those of men for the same work and (probably superior) performance.

Yet until we tap women's enormous economic potential and encourage women to take responsibility for their financial and economic independence, they will remain second-class citizens and the full potential of our nation will never be realised.

THE ROLE OF WOMEN IN THE DECADE AHEAD

Over the next ten years, women with experience will be required to mentor the less experienced and grow their confidence, so that individual voices can join together to become a powerful collective and a conscience for South Africa's democracy. Fortunately, many men in leadership positions in South Africa, particularly in politics, recognise this and are working hard to increase the number of women participating in the creation of a new society. Our task, as women, is simply to rise to the occasion. While it might be too optimistic to expect our generation of women to enjoy the full fruits of democracy, we have to ensure that future generations are left with a firm foundation and a legacy to harvest.

In the coming decade, therefore, I expect that women will write more, make a significant contribution to the robust policy-making process of the country, participate in public debate about matters that continue to constrain women, and even use their purchasing power in the economy to change the behaviour of those institutions that continue to marginalise women. We need to encourage more women to consider church leadership, to help with the challenge of rebuilding a value system that strengthens our people's moral obligations to one another. We also have to take advantage of the huge developments in information and technology.

South Africa has pioneered several initiatives to advance the cause of women, something that would not have been possible prior to democracy. As a second stage in the process of enabling women to become more independent financially, I was part of establishing South Africa's first Private Equity Fund for Women, which raised R125 million by the time it closed in 2003, ten years after the founding of Wiphold. This fund will help women grow their enterprises beyond start-ups, which is where most women entrepreneurs tend to be trapped because of a lack of capital and the prejudice of financial institutions. For women to raise loans from a bank, they are virtually expected to mortgage their children, pets and themselves, notwithstanding research findings which confirm that women are not a credit risk, and seldom default. This scarcity of capital has led to the emergence of "loan sharks", who take advantage of women and give them credit at exorbitant interest rates. Part of our focus over the next ten years has to be to teach women to live within their means, or to find alternative ways to access extra money that do not compromise them.

For many decades women in South Africa have been part of well-established social networks called "stokvels", comprising a group of ten or more women who usually convene once a month on weekends to put an agreed contribution into a common kitty that gets shared either annually or monthly by members. I believe that South Africa needs a development fund to which all working women can contribute amounts proportionate to their monthly earnings, ranging from R20 to R200 per month. This fund could be used to provide loans to women in need and to educate and train women in life skills, particularly in financial management, parenting and entrepreneurship. A fund of this nature could be used to attract additional monies from the private sector and government to support the systematic development of less fortunate women in South Africa.

Over the next decade South Africa will need to accelerate efforts and increase resources in order to address gender issues and promote the empowerment of women. The core to women's inequality is their lack of economic empowerment and the main reason for this is their lack of education and skills. Any strategy therefore needs to give disproportionate attention to these two areas. We also have to explore how information and communications technology can be used to improve the daily lives of women. The mobile industry has been instrumental in bridging the digital divide in telecommunications. Access to information, however, is still a problem for many women.

CONCLUSION

South Africa is a country alive with possibility and is constantly looking for collaborative solutions to its many challenges. We must bring issues out into the open and encourage dialogue and debate. Our challenge, over the next ten years, is to ensure that we broaden sufficiently the number of people who can take advantage of the opportunities that democracy offers.

For our freedom to be sustainable and for our society to alleviate poverty meaningfully, we will have to entrust women with resources, such as government grants, that will help them to look after and educate their families and prepare their children properly for the world. True empowerment in our society will only be achieved when women become equal partners in every sense of the term.

Ultimately, advancement is relative depending on one's status in life. For rural women who previously did not have access to housing, electricity, water or micro-loans, a few steps forward mean a lot. We should resist being complacent however and encourage greater mobility between sectors to broaden the skills base and leadership pool among women. Women have the great gift of compassion; we must use it to advance those who are less fortunate. While a decade is too short to undo more than three centuries of oppression, exploitation, and denial of human rights, programmes like "take a girl child to work day" will eventually reverse centuries of gender stereotyping that keep most women from living fulfilling and economically productive lives. The world remains largely patriarchal, and South Africa is no exception.

I am confident that in another ten years we will begin to see a critical mass of women who have the competence and the confidence to take control of their future through informed and not imposed career choices, and who have the skills required to enable them to assert their financial independence. We have begun to plant the seeds that will grow into the next generation of South African businesswomen.

The 2000 World Development Report, compiled by the World Bank, pointed out that while the number of girls enrolling in schools has caught up with the number of boys in many parts of the world, girls who attend school tend to be directed away from science, mathematics and other technical subjects in high demand in the labour market towards vocations considered more suitable for women. This will have to change. Africa must deliberately strive to maximise its intellectual capital and economic potential by investing in the resilience of its women.

It is quite possible, I believe, for South Africa to have a female president within the next twenty years, to give expression to the saying "the hand that rocks the cradle rules the world". Yet most women still remain on the sidelines of our economy: South Africa is still very much a man's world.

While our gender balance in parliament ranks fifth highest in the world, it is still male rather than female MPs who dictate government's priorities. Over the next ten years, therefore, the country will have to put gender interests above party political interests. And we women will have to keep gender on the agenda to ensure that real progress and meaningful empowerment is achieved.

All these advances, however, will come at some cost to the quality of family life and the value system of our society. Women will need, in the future, to balance family and professional life to ensure that they do not strengthen our democracy while creating yet more dysfunction in society. As the custodians of our value system, women will have to find a more meaningful way to contribute without neglecting their primary responsibilities. The "battle" between men and women needs to be managed in a way that allows each to contribute towards a partnership of greater value. The reality is that our contributions complement each other; so we need to become more competent at harnessing each other's gifts and potential. The participation of both men and women together strengthens the social, emotional and spiritual capital of a nation.

Most women in South Africa will agree that democracy has helped their cause, but it has also created new challenges which most do not have the experience to deal with. Yet these are the challenges of progress and of creating a society that could result in a breakthrough or a crisis, depending on how it is managed.

Wendy Luhabe
Chairperson, Industrial Development Corporation

Addendum: Statistics on women in South Africa over ten years
Most of these statistics are derived from the Black Management Forum (BMF), the South African Chamber of Business (SACOB), the National African Federated Chamber of Commerce (NAFCOC), the Commission on Employment Equity (CEE) and the Black Business Council (BBC) were issued in 2003, and most have since changed.

General
- 30% of seats in national parliament are occupied by women.
- Women occupy 20% of seats in the nine provincial legislatures.
- Women occupy 18% of seats in local municipalities.
- There are nine female ministers and eight female deputy ministers.
- Women account for 6,6% of directors on boards of SA companies.
- There were a large number of female nominees in the information technology sector for the African Achiever Awards 2002. (*Source: Business Day, 08/08/2002*)

Trends in 2000/01
- Women (all colours) held 38% of the management (top and senior) and professional category in the labour market.
- In the top management level, women held 13% of jobs.
- Women held 40% of all skilled jobs compared to 60% by men.

Trends in 2000/02
- Men held 88% of all top management positions in South Africa, compared to 12% for women.
- The percentage of women of all races remained unchanged at 38% of the management (top and senior) and professional category in the labour market.
- In the top management level, women held 12% of jobs.
- Women held 38% of all skilled jobs compared to 62% by men

On the other hand, this is how the Commission on Employment Equity (CEE) report reflected the progress in different sectors and positions:

CEE Report–2001 (2002)

Occupational level	(Female)
Top management	12 (12)
Senior management	21 (18)
Professional and middle management	43 (38)
Junior and supervisors	40 (46)

HIV/AIDS
The following information comes from the South African Medical Research Council's (MRC) report, "The Impact of HIV/AIDS on Adult Mortality in South Africa", released in 2003.
- Life expectancy is expected to fall from the current 54 years to 41 by 2010. Two groups particularly hit will be young women in their 20s and young men in their 30s.
- Astonishingly, the death rate amongst women in their 20s is higher than that of women in their 60s – the report describes this as "a unique phenomenon in biology". Dr Malegaparu Makgoba, the MRC president, introducing the report said: "There is no precedent for this in history. You have a situation where younger females who are supposed to be healthy and productive are dying in greater numbers than their mothers."
- Ten years ago the number of pregnant women tested for the HIV virus at antenatal clinics was one in a 100 – today the figure is one in four. Of all deaths at the Chris Hani Baragwanath hospital in Soweto, 43 per cent are attributable to AIDS.

Overall percentage of women in senior positions in corporate South Africa
Women represented on boards: 6,6%
Female non-executive directors: 13%
Female executive directors: 12%
Senior executive management: 17%
Senior management: 25%
Middle senior management: 24%
Junior senior management: 28%

Women and management:
White females: 16%
Black females: 7%

Women and the workforce:
Paid workforce: 39%
Service-sector employees: 68,4%
Legislative, senior management: 28%

A final fact
- South African women constitute 33% of the total workforce and receive 42% of the training.

CONFRONTING THE HIV/AIDS PANDEMIC IN SOUTH AFRICA: THE CHALLENGE FOR BUSINESS

In the mid-1980s, the South African Chamber of Mines carried out anonymous HIV/AIDS-prevalence tests at mine sites. The results showed a prevalence of less than 1 per cent. Twenty years on, similar company surveys suggest an infection rate of between 20 and 30 per cent. In parallel with the extraordinary political achievement represented by the relatively peaceful transition to democracy in 1994, a human catastrophe has been unfolding. While the first decade of full democracy in South Africa gives much cause for celebration, the major failure of all responsible parties has been to tackle the HIV crisis effectively. A huge challenge for the next ten years will be to stabilise and reverse the epidemic.

It is a particularly vicious twist of fate that just as South Africa's first multiracial government, after many years of struggle, was starting to redress the evils of apartheid, the HIV pandemic was reaching critical mass. Nelson Mandela readily concedes that his government should have devoted greater attention to the issue. But they were not alone in their neglect, and their distraction was not surprising. For all the criticism directed at his successor, Thabo Mbeki, on this topic, I would only venture that he has been right to emphasise poverty as a key factor in the rapid spread of the disease. In looking at preventive interventions this societal dimension cannot be ignored.

In a world where many people are enjoying standards of living undreamt of by previous generations, across much of sub-Saharan Africa perhaps the greatest health crisis in human history challenges our humanity and solidarity. Around the world over 8000 people are dying every day from AIDS. Approximately 600 of these deaths are in South Africa. What is more, the estimated number of new infections exceeds those dying by two-thirds, which means that the epidemic will worsen in the coming years. A recent publication by the US-based Population Reference Bureau has sought to predict the impact of the disease and estimates that over the next forty years South Africa's population may actually decline by over one-fifth. The potential consequences of this scale of mortality are profound in terms of social stability, loss of skills, economic dislocation and increased poverty. It is not surprising in this context that rolling back the epidemic was identified in 2000 as one of the Millennium Development Goals.

On the economic front, estimates suggest that the direct impact of HIV on growth might be an annual reduction of as little as a 0.3 per cent or as much as a 1.5 per cent. But the compounding effect of such a drag on development is likely to be serious as South Africa seeks to accelerate development and job creation.

Where do companies come into this equation? And what is the extent of "corporate responsibility"? These are the questions that Anglo American, along with other corporations, has had to address during the late 1990s and early 21st century. HIV is a social, rather than an occupational, disease. But it cannot be kept outside the perimeter fence. It is intimately linked with poverty, and with such African issues as high levels of migrancy, social taboos about sex and the lack of empowerment of, and sexual violence against, women. As a responsible employer and corporate citizen Anglo American has adopted an activist role over the past decade. We believe that business has a crucial role to play in combating the disease.

EVOLVING A STRATEGIC RESPONSE

Throughout the 1990s, Anglo American – along with many other leading corporates – was involved in education and prevention programmes designed to raise awareness of HIV and to minimise the spread of the virus. This involved a variety of approaches, including workplace talks; working with trade unions; condom distribution; treatment of other sexually transmitted diseases; anonymous site-level prevalence testing and the use of industrial theatre. Although the continuing, and seemingly inexorable, rise in the rate of infection casts doubt upon the effectiveness of these approaches, there is some evidence to suggest that the level of infection is often higher in surrounding communities than at major industrial operations. This may indicate that without such employer prevention programmes, things would have been even worse.

Key challenges in implementing education and prevention programmes include achieving consistency of message; trust; ensuring cultural appropriateness and reducing denial and stigma. They remain highly relevant today. There can be no question, under law, of anything other than voluntary testing (which should be accompanied by competent counselling) and there must be no discrimination against those who are HIV positive. People will only confront their own HIV status if they feel confident they will be handled fairly. The inconsistency of messages in the past, between companies and parts of civil society on one hand and some parts of the government on the other, has been a significant impediment to effective education efforts.

Anglo American has always been keen to pursue partnership opportunities. Thus, for example, from the late 1990s onwards Anglo Coal was instrumental in the development of the PowerBelt project in Mpumalanga province – which has amongst the highest HIV-prevalence levels, at around 30 per cent of adults. The project was designed to complement internal initiatives taken by the coal companies in the areas of education, prevention and STD treatment, by establishing a partnership across the industry with government, community groups and external funders. Its activities have included a baseline community survey, with a focus on demographics, condom usage, TB and STD management, school and youth issues and social upliftment priorities. The project has resulted in a co-ordinated and much more effective local approach to the prevention and management of HIV in the community.

Amongst the outputs of the project has been a peer-education approach to delivering prevention messages to sex workers – getting them to work together to insist, for example, on condom use. This approach was originally developed in Zimbabwe and has enjoyed some success. In 1999, Anglo Coal received an award from the Global Business Council on HIV/AIDS for its work in the Kriel district of Mpumalanga. The Kriel project now involves the active participation of the owners and managers of sex establishments and shebeens – which are used, *inter alia,* as condom distribution points.

We have been mindful, too, of the poverty dimension to the spread of infection, including the lack of empowerment of women. Thus, for example, one Anglo colliery made over its bakery to a local women's co-operative, so as to give the women concerned incomes to divert them from having to resort to sex work. Mondi Forests has also launched several income-creation programmes, including woodlot growing schemes.

Similar multi-agency approaches have been pursued in other parts of South Africa – showing the vibrancy and commitment of both business and many parts of civil society to tackling the AIDS crisis. AngloGold's work at Carletonville and in some rural labour-exporting areas, and initiatives by Anglo's Namakwa Sands operation in the Western Cape, also deserve particular mention.

Leadership and full management engagement have also shown themselves to be crucial to the success of workplace and community HIV programmes. At Greenside Colliery, for example, Anglo's manager John Standish-White has taken a close personal interest in challenging taboos. He made sure that discussion of sex was made open and personally went to meet local prostitutes to understand the nature of local challenges. There is a passionate promotion of safe-sex messages at Greenside where Standish-White has shown real and active concern for the welfare and safety of his workforce.

TAKING STOCK

By 2001 drug costs were falling. This began to stimulate a debate about facilitating wider access to antiretroviral therapy (ART) in developing countries. My colleagues in Anglo American were also taking stock. As the epidemic was becoming more mature, evidence was growing of increased absenteeism, people becoming ill and increased mortality. It had become abundantly clear that however good and creative our prevention and education programmes were – and they continue to make a real difference – they were not cutting the mustard in preventing the spread of infection. High HIV prevalence also contributes to the spread of TB and is inimical to embedding a safety culture if a view that "life is cheap" becomes entrenched.

Our head of medical services, Dr Brian Brink, had gradually come to the view that a key ingredient was missing from our strategy – an incentive for employees to confront their status through voluntary counselling and testing. At that point a number of operations were providing wellness programmes for HIV-positive employees. These included nutritional and healthier lifestyle support and timely antibiotic treatment of opportunistic infections. These programmes have proved effective in postponing the onset of AIDS, in reducing hospitalisations and in keeping individuals healthy for longer, but they are not, in themselves, likely to produce a large increase in life expectancy. Brian Brink had identified, however, that the provision of antiretroviral therapies has the potential to change attitudes to the disease. ART might, after all, extend life expectancy by, say, eight to ten years. This might, he reasoned, cause many more people to reject the stigma and denial that help to perpetuate the spread of the disease, and motivate them to be tested.

Anglo American had already, through awareness programmes and anonymous prevalence testing, sought to ensure that all our operations were developing plans to manage the impact of the epidemic in relation to, for example, loss of skills, training programmes and recruitment. The company has to ensure the continued viability of our businesses for the benefit of the three-quarters of employees who are not infected as well as, of course, our shareholders. Thus, around this time increasing thought was being given to the costs of not providing treatment – with the prospect of a quarter of our workforce being dead within five to ten years. In addition, Clem Sunter, a leading guru of scenario planning and chairman of the Anglo American Chairman's Fund, co-wrote with Alan Whiteside a powerful book challenging South African business to adopt a more proactive approach to treatment. In the book, they argued that the costs of inaction might well exceed those of treatment over the longer term.

A number of other multinationals, including Heineken in East, Central and West Africa, BMW and Daimler-Chrysler in South Africa and Debswana in Botswana were also embarking upon treatment programmes by early 2002. But none of these had the spread of operations or the number of staff (about 120 000 in South Africa) employed by Anglo American.

Anglo looked at a number of models for introducing ART, including through pilot programmes and in association with the Chamber of Mines. Moving straight to a full roll-out was daunting. There were fears about how closely the complicated drug regimen would be followed in an African context – with the risk of causing increased resistance to the drugs involved. In the politically charged atmosphere surrounding ART, there was apprehension about how the government might respond. There were concerns also about whether it would be sustainable to limit the employer's funding of treatment to employees – as we eventually decided we would have to do – and also about how to handle both the logistics of a complex roll-out and difficult issues such as how to continue treatment for retrenched workers. All of these complexities argued for a feasibility study approach – which might also enable better projections for group-wide costs to be made. However, militating against these arguments were the urgency of the situation and the knowledge that a feasibility study could not generate meaningful feedback for some three years. Such a period of relative inactivity was profoundly unattractive.

Discussions were held, too, with the Chamber of Mines, but these progressed slowly and seemed destined to result in pilot projects, predominantly at Anglo American, AngloGold and De Beers operations.

Thus in August 2002, my colleagues on the Anglo Executive Committee had to confront some fundamental questions about the nature of corporate responsibility. It was undoubtedly defensible, and in line with most other company policies, to abdicate a leadership role on HIV/AIDS to government. However, the committee also judged that the company had the capacity to contribute to changing the terms of debate as well as directly prolonging the lives of many of its employees. They decided that all Anglo group companies would be encouraged to make antiretrovirals available to those who had reached the stage of infection where such an intervention was clinically recommended.

Anglo's announcement was dismissed by a rival CEO as "throwing drugs at the problem" and by the Minister of Health for lack of consultation. But the overall response was very positive from staff, civil society and many others in the corporate sector. Indeed a number of other corporates have subsequently announced their intention to make ART available to employees, and in some cases to dependants, including Goldfields, Rio Tinto and Old Mutual.

I must acknowledge the response of our shareholders. They have been strongly supportive of the move, despite the fact that we cannot, at this stage, be confident of either the gross or net costs of the initiative. We know that there will be savings in training, absenteeism, recruitment and productivity. Nevertheless, we expect there to be a significant net cost, but it will be containable. Moreover, in some situations raw figures cannot be the sole determinant of actions and a company may need to make a judgement about the wider context of its actions.

SUCCESSES AND DISAPPOINTMENTS

Following our ART announcement, we went into an intensive period of preparation. By the end of 2002 we had generated clinical protocols (available on www.angloamerican.co.uk), prepared with the advice of South African clinicians and the London School of Hygiene and Tropical Medicine. Over sixty sites have had training and are now licensed to dispense ART, and we have recruited two health economists to monitor the impact of the intervention. A not-for-profit drug supply agreement has been finalised with GSK, while several other research-based pharmaceutical manufacturers supply their antiretroviral drugs on a similar basis through the "Accelerating Access Initiative". Anglo's drug cocktail is explicitly designed to minimise side effects so that those on the medication will be able to continue to work and to support their families.

The encouraging news from Anglo's experience to date is that adherence to the treatment regimen is reported to be good. Moreover, and most encouragingly, over 90 per cent of employees on ART are back to normal work. In some cases the drugs have had a remarkable, transformatory impact.

Last year I visited Goedehoep colliery and saw not only some of the industrial theatre and small business projects for women, but also heard of the first five or six people there who were on antiretrovirals. The eyes of the nursing sister in charge were absolutely sparkling with the delight of seeing these very sick people returning to work. These dramatic, visible effects have an enormous impact on colleagues and lead to the hope that others will be encouraged to come forward for testing and wellness programmes.

Financially, too, developments have been in the right direction with the cost of our first line regimen drugs having already dropped from $1,250 per head per annum to about $750. Of course, on top of this there are significant laboratory, clinical and management costs. In total, ART costs were around $3,000 per capita in 2003. But with falling drug costs and the ability to spread the fixed costs across a wider number of patients, we expect this to fall to some $1,700 per head in 2004 and to $1,300 in 2005.

The disappointment is that after about a year of full roll-out, we only have some 1350 employees on treatment. This is the biggest, directly administered, corporate ART programme in the world and hundreds of people who are now on it would probably be dead without the treatment. Nonetheless, there are some 6000 employees whom we estimate are at a stage of infection where ART should be administered. We also have some 3500 employees on wellness programmes, which means that they know their HIV-positive status and are having their immune system regularly monitored to judge when ART should most effectively be given. This accords with our estimate that nearly 30 000 Anglo employees in southern Africa are HIV positive.

The response indicates – as has been the experience of longer standing programmes such as those at Debswana or Heineken – that denial and stigma cannot be tackled overnight. But, as Nelson Mandela has observed, we need to "break the silence". We will be looking at those operations which have had the greatest success in Voluntary Counselling and Testing – to see what cultural and climate issues may be involved. We will also build upon some outstanding examples of leadership by some of our managers.

Along with other major corporates, we are looking at how we can increase access to ART for dependants, and the communities associated with our operations. The biggest project in this category is a partnership which Anglo American has formed with the South African NGO loveLife, the Mandela Foundation, the Henry J Kaiser Foundation and the Global Fund to fight AIDS, TB and Malaria. The partnership is aimed at transforming 38 government primary healthcare clinics in communities associated with our operations into a network of adolescent-friendly clinics, geared to offer comprehensive HIV/AIDS prevention services. (Youth from 12 to 21 years form a key target group for prevention and treatment initiatives.) The aim will be initially to make these clinics accessible and attractive places for young people to visit initially for help with prevention, education and STD treatment, but then for them to become part of the distribution infrastructure for ART. We hope, too, to mobilise international donor funding for other community-based projects, to which Anglo American will contribute organisational capabilities.

A PARTNERSHIP ROUTE?

During 2003, there were significant and optimistic shifts in government policy towards HIV. Much of the previous ambivalence has disappeared and ART will be made available in stages from April 2004 through the public health system. This does not let the corporate sector off the hook, however, since it will take some years before ART is available across the health system. Moreover, now is the time for all the key players in South Africa to join together in partnerships to push back the advance of the epidemic.

No business should be operating in a highly affected country without a clear AIDS policy and a strategy for dealing with the epidemic. Every company should understand the potential impact of HIV on its operations and take action to minimise that impact in a compassionate manner. Management, unions and employees should be committed to working together to prevent infection and to provide care and support for those who are infected. I would underline the potentially crucial role that organised labour can play in making programmes successful.

Access to treatment has opened up a more hopeful landscape in the fight against AIDS. Along with the trade unions, government, the corporate sector, the churches and community groups, we need to give priority to keeping people safe from disease and to forging a common strategy. The scale of the challenge is enormous. It is not for the faint-hearted. It is a challenge, however, to which business is well equipped to make a substantial contribution. We must bring about a scaling-up of education prevention and treatment programmes at a community level.

It is a matter of concern that a gulf exists between the performance of some of the leading companies and some other corporates. HIV poses a significant risk to most companies and yet a large proportion do not appear to be attempting to manage it. Recent studies by the Bureau for Economic Research (BER) for the South African Business Coalition on HIV and AIDS indicate that 9 per cent of companies feel that HIV has already had a significant adverse impact on their business – whilst 43 per cent anticipate it doing so in five years' time. In a survey conducted in Autumn 2003, more than a third of companies reported an adverse impact on productivity or increased absenteeism; 30 per cent reported higher than normal labour turnover rates and 27 per cent had lost experience and skills. However, against this backdrop, only 41 per cent, even then, had an HIV/AIDS workplace awareness programme; only 26 per cent had a policy; only 18 per cent have a Voluntary Counselling and Testing (VCT) programme in place and only 6 per cent are offering ART. Companies like Metropolitan

Life, in the financial services sector, have been admirable in urging other companies to address the impact of HIV/AIDS as a core element of their risk-management strategies.

A great deal remains to be achieved across all the major and public and private sectors in South Africa. At Anglo, we have come to learn that partnership models – set up with shared objectives and an understanding of differing working methods – are crucial in reinforcing prevention messages and mobilising a wide coalition of interests in the community. The scale of the HIV epidemic and its implications for many African societies demands the full involvement of the corporate sector. But while companies are very effective in delivering programmes and handling logistics we are not always the most listened to or credible source of advice on issues like "safe sex". Nor are we necessarily best configured for handling many aspects of social care. We in the private sector undoubtedly bring skills to the table, but we also have to recognise what we are not so good at. The great advance represented by the Mbeki government's announcement of its ART programme means, I hope, that the divisions of the past are behind us, and that all elements of South African society can now work together in tackling the scourge of AIDS.

Sir Mark Moody-Stuart
Chairman, Anglo American plc

ICT IN SOUTH AFRICA: RECOLLECTIONS OF AN EXTRAORDINARY DECADE

Extraordinary change. These two words best describe the evolution in information and communications technology (ICT) in South Africa in the decade from 1994 to 2004. ICT is an industry in which continual change is the norm. However, the changes in ICT in South Africa after 1994 have embraced much more than technology – politics and regulation, community and globalisation, e-government, citizenship and aid, and transformation have all helped to modernise and change the face of ICT in South Africa.

Dimension Data is honoured to be recognised by the World Economic Forum as a leading African ICT company and to share some of our thoughts and experiences of ICT in Africa, and in particular South Africa, over the past decade. It is important to remember that ICT in Africa did not start in the 1990s. The continent possesses a long and rich history of achievement in ICT since the first long-distance telephone line was installed between Addis Ababa and Harar in Ethiopia[1] in 1894, only eighteen years after Alexander Graham Bell spoke the famous words: "Watson, come here; I want you."

TECHNOLOGY ALWAYS IN FLUX

Although technology is in a constant state of flux, it is rare that changes in technology have a profound effect on the entire industry. During the 1990s, however, two technologies – the internet and GSM mobile telephony – did just that, and altered the landscape of the ICT industry. In both instances South Africa was among the first countries in the world to adopt these technologies and remains a world leader today.

---

[1] *Internet from the Horn of Africa: Ethiopia Case Study*, White paper published by the International Telecommunications Union, July 2002.

The first commercial internet links in South Africa were established in 1993, only two years after the National Science Foundation in the USA opened the internet for commercial use. One of the companies involved in bringing the internet to South Africa as a commercial tool was Internet Solutions,[2] now part of Dimension Data. By 2001, according to researcher Mike Jensen,[3] there were over 750 000 dial-up internet users in South Africa. In 2004 we estimate that there are more than 5000 organisations with fixed-line internet access, providing mostly web connection, but at the very least e-mail, for an additional 1 500 000 users. This gives a total of 2 250 000 South Africans with access to the internet, approximately 5 per cent of the population. Given the world average for internet access of 6.7 per cent in 2000 (ibid.), this represents a remarkable achievement for a country so geographically isolated from the main concentration points of the global internet. The 5 per cent penetration in South Africa compares with 3.2 per cent in Latin America, 2.3 per cent in East Asia, and 0.4 per cent in both sub-Saharan Africa and South Asia (ibid.).

Through constant innovation, the South African commercial sector has exploited the high levels of internet access with great success. In early 1997, First National Bank and Nedbank simultaneously launched the first online banking initiatives in South Africa, with Dimension Data providing the enabling security technology in both instances. Remarkably, this development took place only four years after the first web browser had been released. By the end of 2003, according to technology research organisation World Wide Worx, the number of South African internet banking users topped the one million mark.[4] This represented a growth of 28 per cent year-on-year during 2003, with a growth of over 30 per cent expected for 2004.

The first GSM mobile telephony services in South Africa were launched in 1994, only two years after the first GSM networks were launched in Europe.[5] The first network providers were Vodacom and MTN, joined in 2001 by Cell C.

Initial market projections were for only 500 000 GSM users in South Africa. Today the country has 18.5 million and Africa 34.6

---

[2] http://www.is.co.za
[3] Writing in *Information and Communications Technologies for African Development*, United Nations ICT Task Force Series II.
[4] Source: http://www.the worx.biz
[5] Source: http://www.gsmworld.com

million GSM users, the latter being approximately 2.6 per cent of the world total of 1.32 billion users.[6] South African GSM penetration is more than triple the fixed-line penetration of 5 million lines. What is more, African growth rates for GSM users are expected to top 100 per cent in 2004, compared to little over 50 per cent growth worldwide (ibid.).

The foresight of the South African government and private sector in becoming one of the first countries in the world to adopt and implement the GSM cellular standard afforded ICT service providers such as Dimension Data[7] an entirely new customer base. Two examples are the next generation network built for MTN and the network performance management system built for Vodacom. Moreover, the strong South African cellular industry created the necessary skills pool for us to undertake work in the cellular industry elsewhere in Africa and globally. Today Dimension Data has rolled out more than one-third of all cellular masts in sub-Saharan Africa and has used South African service-provider skills to develop systems for customers such as Telstra in Australia and BT Cellnet in the United Kingdom.

CELLULAR TECHNOLOGY SPURS GROWTH

Cellular growth in turn has spurred the growth in many sectors of ICT outside the cellular industry itself. One example is call centres. The Department of Trade and Industry (DTI) estimates there are now 100 000 call centre seats in South Africa, with the majority of calls coming into these centres from mobile rather than fixed-line phones.

The call centre industry is undoubtedly one of South Africa's best examples of mass job creation through the effective use of technology. The result is that the DTI has identified the call centre industry as a key component of its SAVANT (South African Technology Vanguard) public-private sector partnership programme to market South African ICT skills on a global basis.[8] Dimension Data has attracted to South Africa a 570-seat call centre serving North American consumers, through the support both of this programme and the Minister

[6] http://www.cellular.co.za/stats-main.htm/
[7] See http://www.didata.com/about/abt_casestudies.asp for more information and case studies.
[8] http://www.savant.co.za

of Trade and Industry, Alec Erwin. Public-private sector partnerships of this kind are critical to attracting services-based export business to South Africa and, in our view, are essential to local ICT growth in the future.

The GSM short message service (SMS) is by far the most rapidly growing GSM application in South Africa. Over Christmas/New Year 2003, more than 133 million SMS messages were sent via South Africa's three cellular networks. This type of application has created an entirely new ancillary industry. Many participants are innovative small and medium enterprises providing services such as news, weather and sports updates, integration into corporate messaging systems,[9] and most recently even applications to check registrations for the South African general elections in April 2004.

The internet and GSM cellular services have not only transformed technology and business in South Africa, they have also created platforms for future applications that are only now beginning to be exploited. Both technologies require strong co-operation between government and the private sector if they are to reach their full potential. The creation of this enabling environment, allowing the large-scale emergence and adoption of new technologies, represents possibly the greatest single structural change in South African ICT before and after 1994.

POLITICS AND REGULATION

When South Africa was reborn in April 1994, the new government inherited outdated legislation governing the ICT sector. Before long, a number of new laws were passed by parliament that directly or indirectly affect the ICT industry. These included the:
- Broadcasting Act, No. 4 of 1999
- Interception and Monitoring Prohibition Amendment Act, No. 77 of 1995
- Sentech Act, No. 63 of 1996
- Telecommunications Act, No. 103 of 1996
- Telecommunications Amendment Act, No. 12 of 1997
- Telecommunications Amendment Bill, No. 65 of 2001
- Electronic Communications Security (Pty) Ltd Act, No. 68 of 2002

---

[9] See http://www.vine.co.za/ and http://www.itouch.co.za/ for examples.

- State Information Technology Agency Amendment Act, No. 38 of 2002
- Electronic Communications and Transactions Bill, No. 8 of 2002.

The initial thrust of the new legislation was to modernise the sector in line with international best practice, address the participation of blacks and women in the sector and extend services to previously under-serviced rural areas. As an example, some of the objectives of the Telecommunications Act of 1996[10] were to:
- promote the universal and affordable provision of telecommunication services;
- promote the provision of a wide range of telecommunication services in the interests of the economic growth and development of the Republic;
- ensure that, in relation to the provision of telecommunication services, the needs of the local communities and areas are duly taken into account;
- encourage ownership and control of telecommunication services by persons from historically disadvantaged groups;
- promote the empowerment and advancement of women in the telecommunications industry.

The impact of this legislation on the ICT industry has been marked and in many instances has stimulated business opportunities that could not have been envisaged prior to 1994. The Telecommunications Act of 1996, for instance, provides for the establishment of value-added network services and allows licensed private enterprise to offer organisations managed network services on a shared platform. Today, value-added network licensees such as Dimension Data, authorised under the Telecommunications Act, provide outsourcing services on a shared platform to more than 150 large South African organisations. The positive impact of world-class, value-added network services on electronic business and the wider South African economy cannot be overstated.

An additional and critical piece of legislation is the Electronic Communications and Transactions (ECT) Bill of 2002. This bill allows

---

[10] The Act is available online at http://www.doc.gov.za/ The section covering objectives is section 2.

for the recognition of electronic communications as legal tender and is widely recognised as being among the most advanced of its kind in the world today. It creates the enabling environment for the streamlining of many paper-based and unnecessarily bureaucratic areas of public and private enterprise in South Africa, once again advancing the overall efficiency of the economy.

More recently, the South African Minister of Communications, Dr Ivy Matsepe-Casaburri, published the draft Convergence Bill for comment. This bill is the enabling legislation that recognises and advances convergence in the information technology, broadcasting, and telecommunications industries. Without this legislation, South Africa could not take advantage of convergence to create efficiencies or enable converged applications such as Voice over Internet Protocol (VoIP). This bill is key to sustaining the global competitiveness of South African industry.

COMMUNITY AND GLOBALISATION

In 1994 South Africa was able to rejoin the world community and the African community of nations, after decades of isolation during the apartheid era. This allowed the country to participate fully in ICT initiatives on the African continent. The result is that Africa today represents one of the greatest opportunities for bilateral trade and growth for South African ICT companies. In addition, local ICT skills, such as call centre technology and software development, can be used to offer services to developed countries.

In July 2002, the African Union formally adopted the New Partnership for Africa's Development (NEPAD) programme, previously endorsed by the heads of state of the G8 countries. One of the founders and drivers of NEPAD is the South African president, Thabo Mbeki. Supported by the G8 Africa Plan of Action, the NEPAD programme places strong emphasis on both ICT development and ICT for development.

The G8 Africa Plan of Action undertakes to assist Africa to create digital opportunities. The latter are broadly defined as access to modern digital telecommunications, broadcasting, and technology infrastructure, and services such as electronic education and telemedicine. The G8 member states undertake to do this by:

- encouraging the G8 Digital Opportunities Task Force (DOT Force) to focus on Africa;
- working toward the goal of universal access to ICT;
- encouraging and supporting public-private partnerships for ICT; and
- supporting entrepreneurship and human resource development with ICT.

The NEPAD initiative has created an environment in which African countries can work together to pursue ICT initiatives. Early success stories include:
- constructing and launching, in 2002, the 28 000-km Sat-3/WASC/SAFE fibre-optic cable network to link African countries to each other and to Europe and Asia;
- the establishment of the African Connection and Ministerial Oversight Committee in 1998 to serve as an institutional framework for telecommunications initiatives with regional scope; and
- the creation by South African Minister of Communications, Dr Ivy Matsepe-Casaburri, of the African Advisory Group on ICT, consisting of twelve eminent African ICT experts who meet twice a year to advise African ministers of information and communications.

NEPAD has also established a task team focused on the ICT sector, the NEPAD e-Africa Commission. The e-Africa commission will:
- develop a broad NEPAD ICT strategy and action plan;
- serve as the primary advisory body to the NEPAD Heads of State and Government Implementation Committee on the development of an effective ICT programme in Africa; and
- undertake a number of tasks and projects related to ICT in Africa.

NEPAD has created the environment for ICT growth in Africa through intra-African collaboration. The first large-scale evidence of this is in the cellular industry, where MTN and Vodacom have become two of the largest GSM cellular players on the continent. As an example of the scale of this investment, by January 2004 MTN Nigeria had built more than 700 GSM base stations, providing coverage to 83 cities and more than 1000 villages and communities throughout Nigeria.[11] A further example

---

[11] http://www.cellular.co.za/news_2004/Jan/011704-mtn_nigeria_opens_64_el_circuits.htm

is Vodacom's establishment of Vodacom International in 2001, with the objective of generating more than 30 per cent of Vodacom's revenue outside South Africa by 2004.[12]

NEPAD and the general spirit of African co-operation has enabled many related industries to expand beyond South African borders, of which MultiChoice with its DSTV platform is the best-known example. This platform now provides digital satellite television services to fifty countries and 936 000 subscribers, most of them on the African continent and the Indian Ocean islands. The DSTV platform also provides the basis for rudimentary internet access and interactive television. No doubt convergence between broadcasting and ICT will enable this platform and its successors to provide the necessary infrastructure for many more ICT applications in Africa.

According to the 2004 IDC[13] Black Book, pure information technology (IT) initiatives, excluding telecommunications and broadcasting, in Africa and the Middle East were worth US$19.4 billion in 2004, of which South Africa comprised US$5.274 billion. The other key markets in the region are Egypt, Israel, Saudi Arabia, Turkey, and the United Arab Emirates. These five total US$9.366 billion while the rest of the region put together totals US$4.787 billion – less than the South African market on its own.

However, looking forward from 2004 to 2007, the rest of the region will grow from a regional share of 24.6 to 26.9 per cent whereas South Africa will decline from 27.1 to 25.1 per cent. The growth of the South African market is estimated at 8.7 per cent for 2004 compared with 14.8 per cent for the "Rest of Region" (excluding the countries named previously). These statistics reflect the fact that African countries previously under-serviced by information technology are now investing in technology at an unprecedented rate. This in no small part reflects the success of NEPAD and its partners in creating digital opportunities in Africa.

Prior to South Africa's emancipation from apartheid as well as Africa's new spirit of co-operation and the NEPAD initiative, it would have been inconceivable for any South African ICT services firm to access the wider African market. Today, as indicated by the aforemen-

---

[12] http://www.vodacom.co.za/about/corporate_profile/subsidiaries.asp
[13] A global market intelligence and advisory firm in the information technology and telecommunications industries.

tioned statistics, Africa represents one of the best growth opportunities for ICT in the world, and certainly the most attractive growth market for South African ICT service organisations such as Dimension Data.

E-GOVERNMENT

In 1994, the South African government inherited fragmented systems that did not provide a single view of the citizen across all government functions, or allow citizens to view government as a single service provider rather than as a group of unrelated departments. Prior to 1994, all government systems were proprietary in nature and government expenditure on ICT was fragmented, with a strong lock-in of incumbent suppliers. As a result it was very difficult for new suppliers, particularly those such as Dimension Data who provided open systems based on then fledgling open internet-based standards, to gain a foothold.

Today this situation has changed comprehensively and government has become one of the largest procurers of ICT goods and services in South Africa. Estimates for government expenditure on ICT in 2004 vary between R12 billion and R17 billion or between 21 and 33 per cent of total ICT expenditure in the South African economy. Let us reflect on how the new government created such large growth so quickly.

One of government's first steps was to consult widely with international peers and experts to develop an e-government vision and an execution plan. A body established for this purpose was the Presidential National Commission on Information Society and Development,[14] of which I am privileged to be a member. The result is that today a key tenet of e-government is the provision of a "single window" into government. This approach is fully endorsed and supported by the Working Group on e-Government in the Developing World, in which South Africa is an active participant. In 2002, this working group published a roadmap which emphasises that e-government is about transforming government to become more citizen-centric.[15]

In order to plan and execute its e-government vision, South Africa established the Office of the Government Chief Information Officer (OGCIO) within the department of Public Service and Administration. In addition, each government department has appointed a

---

[14] http://www.pnc.gov.za/
[15] http://www.dpsa.gov.za

chief information officer (CIO), and all CIOs become members of the Government Information Technology Officers (GITO) Council. The GITO council's objectives are to:[16]
- develop and prioritise government objectives and policies and integrate them with the other national macro socioeconomic development strategies;
- deploy and use IT for improved service delivery;
- co-ordinate and consolidate IT initiatives in government;
- leverage economies of scale;
- enhance security and inter-operability; and
- make e-government a success.

In January 2003, in order to lend legislative support to the work of the GITO council, the government amended the 2001 regulations governing the public service to include a number of clauses related to ICT. Amongst other things, these regulations oblige the head of any government department in South Africa to:
- publish an information plan;
- publish an information infrastructure plan in support of the information plan; and
- publish an operational plan that enables the implementation of the information infrastructure plan and information management.

Government also established the State Information Technology Agency (SITA), through the SITA Act of 1998, in order to create a central agency to execute interdepartmental projects related to e-government. These include the official procurement of ICT products and the creation of services such as a shared network and shared back-office systems.

A key aspect of government's ICT vision is the use of open standards. These include the following (ibid.):
- the use of XML (extensible mark-up language) standards for data integration;
- the use of web browser interfaces;
- the alignment with internet standards; and
- the effective and appropriate use of open-source software.

[16] http://www.dpsa.gov.za/e-gov/2001docs/e-govt%20a%20common%20understanding/e-govtCommonUnderstanding.pdf

In Dimension Data's view, this enlightened approach is essential to the success of the e-government vision of creating one window into government. To realise this vision, it is critical that government enforces these standards rigidly for all new systems – not an easy task in such a large organisation.

The highest-profile initiative aimed at realising the e-government vision is the Government Gateway project, which aims to create a portal through which citizens can access all the services they receive from government, from cradle to grave. The Minister of Public Service and Administration, Geraldine Fraser-Moleketi, announced in February 2004 that the initial implementation of the Government Gateway was up and running. (The web site is located at http://www.services.gov.za.) The portal provides information about 4600 government services and is available through the internet, through kiosks and service points located at government offices and the South African Post Office, and via telephone through the government call centre on the 1020 national telephone number.

A further departmental initiative is the "single view of the customer" project within the South African Revenue Services (SARS). This project is now live, and will save SARS "hundreds of millions of rands each year". It allows SARS to consolidate the registry of 9.5 million tax-payers nightly, matching all tax-paying entities with individual tax payers The project is of such a world-class standard that the US-based software company whose technology has been used has embarked on a global road show to demonstrate its implementation to governments around the world.

Today the South African government sector offers the greatest growth opportunity for South African ICT services companies, outside that of the continent of Africa itself.

CITIZENSHIP AND AID

In 2000 the member states of the United Nations adopted the Millenium Declaration in order to create a global partnership for human development. The Declaration has eight Millenium Development Goals, a key objective of which is bridging the digital divide.[17] The eighth goal is to "Build a Global Partnership for Development",

---

[17] http://www.developmentgoals.org/Partnership.htm

which involves co-operating with the private sector to make available the benefits of new technologies, especially information and communications. The December 2003 World Summit on Information Society (WSIS) in Geneva[18] reiterated that ICT is only an effective tool for development and poverty reduction if it forms part of a broader, more comprehensive national development strategy.

Prior to 1994, few non-governmental organisations (NGOs) active in South Africa focused beyond the end of apartheid. Today this has changed, and many NGOs are active in pursuing the various objectives of the Millenium Declaration, the WSIS, NEPAD, and the South African government with respect to overcoming the digital divide. Some of the more worthwhile initiatives of this kind are:

- The Africa Global Information Infrastructure Project (AGIIP), launched by the USAID Leland Initiative, in 21 African countries.[19] This is a five-year, US$15 million project to extend internet connectivity, increase their capacity to use information in decision-making, broaden the African user-base of information systems and provide training.
- The Digital Partnership, an initiative of the International Business Leaders Forum (IBLF) established in May 2001 to facilitate innovation, training, and access to the internet through a sustainable public-private partnership model.[20] The Digital Partnership uses reconditioned technology to provide access to the internet for learning, personal development, and citizenship to students, teachers, and communities. It embarked upon a full-scale roll-out in South Africa in July 2002 in partnership with the Department of Communications and with the then director-general, Dr Andile Ngcaba, as its chairman. The Digital Partnership has received a commitment of more than 150 000 refurbished personal computers from its corporate partners for use in South Africa. It is also active in a number of other African countries and in developing nations around the world.
- SchoolNet SA, founded in November 1997 as a non-profit educational organisation, creates communities of educators and learners who use ICT to enhance education in South Africa.[21] It was formed with the assistance of the Centre for Educational Technology and

---

[18] http://www.itu.int/wsis/
[19] http://www.usaid.gov/leland/
[20] http://www.digitalpartnership.org/
[21] http://www.schoolnet.org.za/

Distance Education, part of the South African Department of Education.

From the point of view of ICT services organisations such as Dimension Data, these initiatives are critical, as the people reached by these programmes represent future growth markets, both directly and as technology-enabled customers of private and public sector organisations. Without these initiatives the long-term health of the ICT sector in South Africa and Africa would be seriously jeopardised.

TRANSFORMATION

There is no doubt that the legislative, social, and economic environment prior to 1994 gave white South Africans preferential access to education, capital, and employment. In a skills-based industry such as ICT, the net result of these policies was the limited participation of blacks in the industry. The change in government in 1994 removed the legislative barriers, but the resulting social and economic inequalities will have to be addressed over a much longer period through a concerted and ongoing public-private sector partnership. If the economic needs of all South Africans are not met, we cannot create a sustainable economy, and the impact of such a failure will be catastrophic for all industries in South Africa, including ICT.

In order to redress the situation, the post-1994 South African government included transformation in its policies right from the outset, starting with the Reconstruction and Development Programme (RDP). Transformation was subsequently formalised through a number of acts of parliament and its progress was reviewed by several commissions. The result of this process was the publication in March 2003 of a strategy for broad-based black economic empowerment by the Department of Trade and Industry (DTI).[22]

This broad-based strategy is best illustrated by reference to the scorecard for black economic empowerment published by the DTI as an appendix to the overall strategy. This scorecard suggests that companies should be measured on their achievement in four areas:
1. Direct empowerment – consisting of equity ownership and managerial control, with a proposed weighting of 30%.

[22] http://www.thedti.gov.za/bee/bee.htm

2. Human resource development – consisting of employment equity and skills development, with a proposed weighting of 30%.
3. Indirect empowerment – consisting of preferential procurement and enterprise development, with a proposed weighting of 30%.
4. Initiatives such as corporate social investment, with a proposed weighting of 10%.

Government indicated that industries should use this broad-based strategy as a framework to develop sector charters or face the imposition of legislation governing transformation in each sector. The mining and financial services industries have already published sector charters. The ICT Charter working group has recently released the first draft of the ICT Charter for comment.[23] Dimension Data is optimistic that this charter will be finalised shortly, thereby creating the necessary certainty regarding transformation imperatives in the ICT industry and ensuring its long-term sustainability.

Dimension Data itself has not waited for finalisation of the charter; for the past eighteen months it has implemented a broad-based transformation programme in line with the DTI's strategy document. Most recently we announced the first phase of a transformation of equity ownership in our South African business. Dr Andile Ngcaba, formerly director-general of Communications, will lead a consortium that will ultimately own 25 per cent of the equity in Dimension Data South Africa. Many other ICT companies have already initiated transformation programmes, which bodes well for the future of the industry in South Africa.

In Dimension Data's view, effective transformation is possibly the most important development affecting the long-term health of our industry in South Africa. While the progress made by both government and the industry over the ten years of post-apartheid South Africa is remarkable, the industry nonetheless still has much work to do to become truly representative of the South African population at all levels.

SUMMARY AND CHALLENGES

Extraordinary change. By now it should be apparent why these words characterise ICT in post-apartheid South Africa.

In technology, the twin revolutions of the internet and GSM mobile

[23] http://www.ictcharter.org.za/

telephony stand out among many other advances. These technologies have created a platform for improved communications and the better use of information in South Africa, and increasingly throughout Africa. Both demonstrate the positive impact of free-market forces on a modern digital infrastructure. The challenges that remain are the full exploitation of these platforms through the development of appropriate applications, and putting an end to the continuing tug-of-war with monopolistic, state-owned, fixed-line telecommunications interests.

In the areas of politics and regulation, South Africa is unrecognisable. The post-1994 government has passed legislation to modernise and align the South African ICT industry with respect to telecommunications, electronic communications and transactions, broadcasting, and most recently convergence. This legislation provides the enabling framework to allow South Africa to take advantage of the latest technologies and remain competitive in global terms. The challenges in this arena are primarily in regulation, in arbitrating between vested interests with respect to the interpretation of legislation, and in devising legislation to keep up with an ever-changing technological landscape.

In international terms South Africa is now part of the African and global community and a key driver of ICT in Africa and the developing world. Ten years ago this would have been unimaginable. NEPAD and specifically its e-Africa commission have opened up the African continent to ICT services, both in spirit and in deed. As a result Africa today represents one of the fastest-growing ICT markets in the world. The challenges in this arena are twofold: to acquire sufficient skills and sufficient capital to implement the recommendations of the e-Africa commission effectively.

In e-government, South Africa now has a comprehensive strategy to implement ICT and create a window for the citizen into government. To implement the strategy, the South African government has global and local advisors, including the Presidential National Commission on Information Society and Development, as well as the necessary managerial skills through the Government Information Technology Officers council and state structures such as the State Information Technology Agency. The challenges in this area are to deepen and broaden the skills base both within government and the broader community, and to co-ordinate ICT initiatives and enforce adherence to standards in such a large and disparate organisation.

Citizens, aid agencies, the private sector, donors and non-government organisations are now key participants in ICT within South Africa. The USAID Leland Initiative, the Digital Partnership and SchoolNet are but three among hundreds of examples of initiatives aimed at bridging the digital divide. The key challenge here is not to become dependent on aid and to ensure that South African and African ICT objectives are developed in the interests of Africa and not of foreign organisations and governments.

In transformation, a comprehensive strategy is in place to address the systematic exclusion of blacks from the economy under the apartheid government. The ICT Charter will shortly be finalised, providing a roadmap for transformation in the sector. The main challenge is to ensure that empowerment creates and does not merely redistribute value.

ICT in South Africa is irrevocably and unrecognisably different today from 1994. Whilst many challenges remain, South Africans can justifiably be proud of their first ten years of ICT freedom under a post-apartheid government.

Jeremy Ord
Executive Chairman, Dimension Data plc

THE ROLE OF TECHNOLOGY IN MEETING DEVELOPMENT CHALLENGES

SETTING THE CONTEXT

The world today is divided by technology – into those who have access to it and those who do not. This demands bold new thinking on the part of those concerned with development.[1] Technology creates opportunities for developing countries to take a quantum leap forward, to develop their productive and creative capacities and to become integrated into the global virtual economy. The internet has opened exciting new opportunities for human capital development, which should result in more informed, empowered and creative citizens – a precondition for economic development. With wireless technology advancing and consumers becoming more adventurous, mobile phones are poised to take the great leap beyond the voice market. The new marketplace offers options such as polyphonic ring tones and downloadable games. Innovation is now commonplace.

The linkage between technology and development, if it is to be sustainable, must integrate economic, environmental, social, gender, governance and leadership aspects. This is a prerequisite for the successful implementation of policies aimed at enhancing the social capital and productive capacity of society. As a result of the impact of technology, development as a concept is rapidly evolving.

Development is intrinsically about social ownership and is political in nature. Today, there is virtually no technological constraint preventing access: even a remote village, lacking both telephones and electricity, can be connected to the internet through using a satellite dish and solar power. A disaster in a remote village comes quickly to public attention, thanks to information and communications technology (ICT). In over-

---

[1] Jeffrey Sachs, 2000. "Sachs on Globalisation: A new map of the world", *The Economist*, June, 24–30.

coming the challenges of the "digital divide",[2] the role of technology is crucial. And bridging the divide is a precondition if a revolution in creativity[3] is to flower worldwide.

At the turn of the millennium, technology began to dominate the agenda, prevailing over issues such as health, water and sanitation, education and food security that had always been part of the dialogue on development. Yet if advances in health, trade, education and economic development are to be implemented and sustained, an understanding of the culture of a society is critical.[4] Increased sponsorship of culture, heritage and the arts, via a partnership between the corporate sector and private foundations, is necessary for new technological inventions to take root and flourish.

Technology's impacts and linkages pervade a number of industrial services and new economic sectors. Software applications are transforming entire business models and stimulating the discovery of new products and markets. A key issue for stakeholders is how to interpret information in order to gain insights about how innovation will unfold, and to identify new market opportunities. The gaps between what worked in the traditional market and the new cyber-market will have to be filled by innovative and timely actions, such as "Bluetooth" which enables one to reach other computers effectively while mobile. Technology is a powerful tool[5] in the hands of people – in government, development agencies, academe, policy- and decision-making positions – who lead the drive for sustainable development and rely on technology to make it happen.

TECHNOLOGY AND DEVELOPMENT FRAMEWORK

Because of its cross-cutting nature and its ability to add value to initiatives that help to lift people out of poverty, technology plays a pivotal role in social and economic development. While this is technology's strength, a concern is the depth of the digital divide – both domestic

[2] The G8 meeting in Okinawa, with the formation of the Digital Opportunity Task Force (DOTForce).
[3] Ashfaq Isahaq, 2001. "On the Global Digital Divide", *Finance and Development*, Vol. 38 No 3.
[4] Report to the G8 "On Culture in a Worldwide Information Society"; http://www.medicif.org
[5] "Information and Communications Technologies for Sustainable Development" 2002. A Discussion Paper prepared for the DBSA by the Wits LINK Centre.

and international – and the risk of reinforcing existing inequalities in the global economy. In the field of social justice, however, technology can be deployed to empower marginalised communities, especially in times of great economic and social change.

In developing strategies to achieve a networked economy, the fundamental elements of good governance and leadership are often relegated to the periphery. The quality of leaders is a critical element in sustaining development. Competent leaders provide the insight and energy required to meet development challenges. Good business models and strategy matter. A guiding vision, policy certainty and transparent regulation are also necessary if technology is effectively to address economic growth and poverty reduction, as well as other issues such as competitiveness, employment opportunities and the digital divide.

Sustainable development provides a framework for thinking about how to tackle the development challenges and to bring about a better quality of life for all. A sustainable development framework requires policies that ensure more economic opportunities; decision-making processes that are inclusive, participatory and transparent; and options that are innovative.

A comprehensive approach to sustainable development demands a combination of development policies that build productive capacities and work in tandem to create a dynamic investment/export nexus for sustained growth and development. Additional policies must aim to create sustainable livelihoods, through ICT and other applications, in the fields of health, education, labour market policy, small and medium enterprises and rural development. The key constraints remain resources and capacity which places leadership and good governance at the core of effective policy implementation and regulation.

The daunting task for policy makers is to measure the likely effect of ICT on development, make recommendations for its diffusion, and guard against exaggerated claims about the internet's potential to resolve a host of development problems that have so far proved intractable.[6] Ultimately, the intention must be to arrive at policy decisions that are most likely to expand the frontiers of opportunity. The

---

[6] Goldstein, Andrea and David O'Conner, 2001. "Navigating between Scylla and Charybdis", *OECD Observer*, February 8, 2001.

key issue is deciding where the quality of ICT assets, including internet access, will make the greatest difference to development and competitiveness. Policy makers need such analyses[7] when designing policy and making investments to upgrade ICT infrastructure roll-out and promote ICT diffusion.

ICT DIFFUSION IN THE ECONOMY

Local research has explored the diffusion[8] of ICT in eight growth[9] sectors in the South African economy. The survey broke new ground that will help us to capitalise on the efficiencies of technology. It provided information, among other things, on how net-based applications are changing business practice, modifying the pool of corporate resources and interacting with business strategies.

An analysis of the ICT diffusion indicates high levels of e-mail and internet usage. In emerging industries and community initiatives, small business owners, artists, crafters and tour operators in the townships are becoming empowered through their use of technology, but much still needs to be done to make ICT more accessible in rural and peripheral areas.

ICT plays a crucial role in stimulating development by modernising delivery systems. As the ICT survey results confirm, the challenge in South Africa is to catalyse the rural economy to leapfrog development. The lack of connectivity and the relative high costs of ICT and internet access are serious barriers and require investment in infrastructure, systems and know-how. For South Africa to become connected in the e-commerce pyramid, and integrated into the regional and world economy, a technological intervention and new partnerships are needed.

To ensure that development strategies in relation to ICTs are premised on democratic values and good governance, the focus has to be placed far more on the human aspects of affordable access, such

---

[7] Goldstein, Andrea and David O'Conner, 2002. "An Introduction to the Debate on Electronic Commerce and Development", OECD, Paris.

[8] This section draws on research by Miller, Esselaar and Associates, 2002: "The diffusion of ICT in eight sectors in the economy needed for growth of South Africa", Commissioned by DTI, sponsored by the EU.

[9] The eight sectors included: the Automotive industry; Biotechnology; Clothing industry; Cultural tourism; Deciduous fruit; Health care; Multimedia technologies and Platinum mining.

as ensuring that citizens have the skills to use enhanced services, in order to be more effective in the networked economy and to access development opportunities.

Another critical factor if technology is to fulfil its potential is that of human capital development. Far more important than financial capital is the right quality and mix of human ingenuity. Development intellectuals contend that the lack of social capital[10] and political instability were limiting factors in Africa's development. In sub-Saharan Africa, the incidence of extreme poverty has actually increased in recent years.[11] The continuing rise in extreme poverty is a tragedy, even if the Millennium Development Goals (MDGs) for poverty reduction at the global level are achieved. If these goals are to be met, we must re-ignite the development process.

Multiple layers of skills are required, starting with the need for more maths and science scholars as well as increased numbers of engineers and scientists. The arts and humanities are as important for creativity as the more nuanced requirements of the sector such as regulatory and policy formulation capacity. Research and innovation are also critical if ICT is to fulfil its rightful development potential.

The internet can provide a dynamic platform for individuals and organisations to fulfil their creative potential. There is a growing awareness that creativity should be a central focus of public policy. Venturelli[12] warns that "a culture persists in time only to ... [the] degree it is inventing, creating, and dynamically evolving in a way that promotes the production of ideas across all social classes and groups". Indeed, without creative dynamism, once productive societies fade away. Developing creative capacities is the defining challenge for individuals, organisations, societies, and governments.

As in any developing economy, it is up to government to provide the essential catalysts of institutional and infrastructure delivery support. New technologies open up access to capacity building and training opportunities. Together with these technologies, a concerted drive to catalyse human capital development can set the country on the path of development and renewed growth.

---

[10] Letters to the editor, *Finance and Development*, Vol. 40 No 4, 2003, p. 3.
[11] Loungani, Prakash, 2003. "The Global War on Poverty: Who's Winning?", *Finance and Development*, Vol. 40 No 4, pp. 38–9.
[12] Shalini Venturelli, 2001, *"From the Information Economy to the Creative Economy"*, Center for Arts and Culture, Washington D.C.

The success stories in ICT today appear to be found in the private sector, although the industry is currently experiencing many difficult challenges. There is a consensus that the following broad steps are needed to maximise the positive impact of ICTs:
- Make the provision of ICT services in low-income areas, which represent the majority of households, sustainable;
- Introduce regulated competition in order to speed up infrastructure roll-out, increase services and bandwidth, and reduce costs; and
- Pursue development applications in a holistic manner within a policy framework.

The identification of challenges is often a powerful spur to action. A realistic assessment of the prospects for improving access and affordability to community operators can become the catalyst for setting the roll-out process in motion. The challenges we face and what can be done to tackle them will be addressed in the sections that follow.

CHALLENGES

The developmental focus in the ICT sector has been on access, and therefore on the provision of infrastructure. Access requires a personal computer (PC), electricity, a telephone service and an internet service provider (ISP). At the local level, the costs of building the necessary infrastructure and procuring equipment and services have to be financed. Access to infrastructure is a necessary, but not a sufficient, condition for sustainable development.

While projects aimed at using technology to address South Africa's development challenges abound they tend to be small, and there is insufficient collaboration among groups and agencies. Collaboration and integration are key factors driving the successful application of ICTs to development challenges because they help to aggregate demand, lower costs, increase the number of services offered and expand education and training opportunities.

Another challenge is to lower the hurdle of ICT access. Location is relevant for ICT diffusion to outlying areas, where it is not possible, for example, to operate a 56K modem. Location supposedly does not matter in a virtual world, but it does in remote areas of South Africa, where affordable technology options are still quite limited. High access costs are a serious deterrent and here telecommunication monopolies are partly to blame. But low telecommunications network density[13] in rural areas can also inhibit connection to the internet via a local phone call and require more expensive alternatives.

ACCESS

One option to overcome the leased-line charge hurdle is to provide access to communities via internet cafés, or to make ICT more accessible by replicating the Grameen Phone experience (see below). The cost factor explains why the internet remains simply a medium for providing e-mail services in peripheral areas. E-mail is cheap because it requires minimum time online, but while it may save costs and bring other benefits, it represents an under-utilisation of the web's potential, as demonstrated by the ability of portals[14] to spread knowledge across the dynamic network of development.

Increasingly, the realisation is dawning on government that it has to construct internet portals, similar to those that provide a one-stop shop for consumers, to improve public service delivery. The development landscape is rapidly changing: taxpayers can file their tax returns online; and farmers can access the web to learn how to improve crop yields.

Yet the internet threatens to magnify the existing socioeconomic disparities, between those with access and those without, to untenable levels, because internet density is still much higher in wealthy and educated communities. Action is needed at the local, national, and regional levels to bridge the digital divide.

Students, for example, are able to connect to the internet at their schools or at libraries or homes, at community centres, or in shopping malls. People in poor areas cannot afford such an array of choices. In most villages and towns, a single central access point can make a difference in the lives of hundreds of people, as the Grameen Phone experiment in Bangladesh has demonstrated. Village pay phones (VPP), based on cellular radio technology, provide access in the rural areas of Bangladesh. As is the case with Grameen micro-credit borrowers, the operators are mainly women. The VPPs have provided significant benefits, yet a still underexplored aspect of the Grameen

---

[13] Users as a percentage of population.
[14] Such as the World Bank's Development Gateway: www.developmentgateway.org

Phone exercise is the degree to which access to mobile telephones by poor rural women can leverage investments made with micro-credits or open new investment opportunities.[15]

E-COMMERCE

By applying web-based tools, technology can address and overcome some of the constraints experienced by entrepreneurs. Marketing opportunities on the internet abound for SMMEs especially. In the cyber-market, exposure adds significant value to any business. Websites attract consumers to electronic marketplaces and services; thereby harnessing the power of mobile technology.

E-commerce is evolving rapidly, with the corporate landscape being continuously transformed by start-ups, acquisitions and failures, and with new technologies emerging all the time. Digital trade in goods and services already makes it easier for artisans, musicians and other artists in developing countries to reach global business-to-consumer (B2C) markets, cutting out layers of middlemen and improving a seller's bargaining power. In some developing countries, B2C e-commerce offers important export as well as local marketing opportunities.

By international standards, local marketing budgets do not measure up to competitive norms. Consolidating various web initiatives in one domain would provide a more focused approach to marketing and e-business.

E-TRAINING

When it comes to training, computer-based instruction can leverage the efficiencies of digital networks by translating the principle of "learning by doing" into concrete actions. ICT professionals have even managed to train themselves on the internet, where e-learning works well for self-motivated staff. As strategic thinking is key to staying ahead of the competition, training also needs to be given in the area of strategic management.

In order to link entrepreneurs into the global business-to-business (B2B) system and to deliver service of international standard, the

---

[15] Goldstein, Andrea and David O'Conner, 2002. "An Introduction to the Debate on Electronic Commerce and Development", OECD, Paris.

government should partner with the private sector in replicating successful e-training programmes. Many local role players see themselves as highly innovative early adopters, and even world leaders in the areas of products and services as well as in market innovation. Increasingly the focus is shifting towards innovation and creativity in order to explore opportunities. Knowledge on how to create value from innovation, invent new markets and reinvent existing ones is supported by the ICT diffusion survey responses in South Africa.[16]

After starting out as a medium for communication and information, the internet has quickly become a place for learning and transacting. It offers unprecedented communications-, learning- and transactional opportunities for those connected to the web. The introduction of ATMs in the financial services sector has resulted in gains in labour productivity rather than in total factor productivity. Over time, as more suppliers and customers use the internet in their front- and back-office systems, and to connect with trading partners, the benefits of internet-enabled collaboration are likely to become more pronounced.

E-LEARNING

In the human resources domain, there are manifold opportunities to incorporate multimedia options into computer-based instruction. The internet could be a powerful tool for this purpose. Private business and technology activists in SA are working to ensure that the industry becomes globally competitive and services are of global standards. Becoming competitive requires being responsive to local customer needs and at the same time being focused on global opportunities.

Several major universities serving the African continent, especially the University of South Africa, are placing their course materials online. More significantly, the internet itself is bringing about a revolution in learning and education. New approaches, involving radical changes in attitudes as well as the incorporation of new research into how learning takes place and how to make education more effective, are taking root. With their students at the centre of the learning process, schools can become fundamental agents for change, helping to re-ignite the educational system and stimulate lifelong learning.

---

[16] Miller, Esselaar and Associates, 2002: "The diffusion of ICT in eight sectors in the economy needed for growth of South Africa", commissioned by the DTI.

The internet is a place not only to acquire knowledge but also to create, document, and store it. Users in Africa are coming together to create knowledge networks and to exchange ideas on education with those on other continents.

E-DEVELOPMENT

The growing recognition of the internet as a powerful factor in economic development has led to e-development – the pursuit of new opportunities available to those with access to the worldwide web. The hope is that e-development will ignite and inspire creative ideas and innovative solutions to development challenges – not merely to come up with old ideas dressed up in new clothes.

The founding director of the African Dream Project (ADP) tells of the role technology plays[17] in exploring niche markets. Nearly every week, a new community in the project gets connected to the web, publishes its own website, starts up e-commerce, or embraces e-learning. Internet-based websites market cultural tourism packages in remote, inaccessible and underdeveloped areas. The ADP website straddles more than 23 routes[18] in 56 towns from the Cape to Cairo. The diffusion of knowledge enables networking to take place between route members.

Technology is impacting also on the field of resource management. Innovation is discernible in applying Geographic Information Systems (GIS) to the management of nature conservation, particularly in the Peace Parks Foundation. Other conservation agencies also use GIS for identifying and prioritising heritage areas. Digital photography captures San rock art for preservation purposes. In similar vein, the Contemporary African Music and Arts (CAMA) developed a computer-based "context"[19] to focus on African music and art. By building a relationship network and by documenting and dissemi-

---

[17] The African Dream Website, www.africandream.org, won the 2002/3 Golden Web Award, the accolade of the International Association of Web Masters and Designers, presented to those sites whose web design, originality and content have achieved levels of excellence.

[18] The route concept was replicated from the very successful wine route in the Western Cape, South Africa.

[19] CAMA documents a wealth of materials within African institutions through a multimedia network archive for African arts and culture, by acknowledging cultural creativity on the continent.

nating audiovisual materials about their lives and work, artists and musicians are using information technology in an African context via the Culture Africa Network – CAN.

However, the existence of a technology infrastructure is not a sufficient condition for the emergence of a durable social or business network. That results from repeated interactions through which parties build reputations for trustworthiness and gain confidence in each other. This poses a challenge for prospective new entrants. Does disintermediation – i.e. the shift from face-to-face to virtual transactions – facilitate the entry of newcomers into global markets? The question lies at the core of the debate on e-commerce and development.[20] Closely related to this is the building of trust, which is crucial to becoming accepted as a global player in the market. Small entrepreneurs are particularly vulnerable, and face the challenge of building virtual trust to be able to trade effectively in the market.

Given access as well as a technology-literate workforce, the digital revolution can serve as the engine of economic growth and development. To this end, governance is necessary to regulate complex internet issues, ranging from privacy and security to taxation.

GOVERNANCE

Governance incorporates ethical dimensions into the areas of consumer protection, security of transactions, privacy of records, and the treatment of digital signatures. These issues are related to the recommendations on good corporate governance contained in the King II Report[21] and are receiving attention by all partners in the private sector, civil society and government officials. With respect to the governance aspects of e-commerce, government has strengthened patent law and given guidance on intellectual property rights. Strong copyright protection is especially appealing to music companies. Research

---

[20] Goldstein, Andrea and David O'Conner, 2002. "An Introduction to the Debate on Electronic Commerce and Development", OECD, Paris.

[21] These issues concur with the King II Report on Corporate Governance. The principles apply to all private and state-controlled companies and all public sector administrators. The code guides directors to keep their eyes on internal operations. A culture of corporate governance ensures adherence to the principles by all, including the media, to build investor confidence. Non-financial issues, such as ethics and ICT are incorporated, so that the transparency dimension is adhered to in the code of good corporate governance.

indicates that most music publishers will not provide their content to mobile operators unless they are explicitly offered digital rights protection.[22] Mobile operators' control over device software and hardware is essential if they are to provide this protection.

IGNITING A CREATIVITY REVOLUTION

Entrepreneurship triggers innovation and structural change, and spurs the creation of new enterprises, both large and small. It is critical to making markets dynamic, evolutionary and competitive.[23]

The introduction, by new growth theorists, of ideas and knowledge as factors in the production equation recognises that the new economy is a creative economy, characterised by potentially high output. High levels of innovation, epitomised perhaps by the first odyssey in space by an African,[24] suggest that Africa may be well placed to explore global business opportunities.

In making a case for a creativity revolution to flower, Ishaq[25] argues convincingly that "a creativity divide has existed in the world since long before there was a digital divide or a technology gap. The digital revolution can finally close the creativity divide by fostering and supporting human creativity worldwide. For this to occur, however, the global digital divide needs to be bridged and the internet's potential as a creativity playground for children needs to be harnessed. This would ensure that the next generation is more imaginative, innovative, creative, and artistic".

Exposure to the arts and humanities helps people understand other perspectives and fosters greater awareness of others' needs and aspirations, and is therefore critical to participating in our increasingly multicultural, global society. The arts and humanities promote forms of thinking that allow people to deal with ambiguity and complexity, to treat situations flexibly and form imaginative responses. Creativity, an important part of people's cultural identity, is expressed

---

[22] Helmut Meier, Roman Friedrich, and Hanno Blankenstein. "Business Models: A Master Model for Mobile Multimedia", *Strategy and Business*, HBS, Spring, 2004.
[23] Eldis poverty briefs: "Challenges to SIDA's Support to Private Sector Development: Making Markets Work for the Poor", Provisional edition, October 2003.
[24] Mark Shuttleworth was the first African in space.
[25] Ashfaq Isahaq, 2001. "On the Global Digital Divide", *Finance and Development*, Vol. 38 No 3.

in different ways. Creative skills are essential for an ever more knowledge-based and global economy. Our competitive strength depends on the imagination and innovation of our industries, institutions and people and are important requirements for success in both the local and the global economy.

FUTURE OPPORTUNITIES

Looking to the future, what challenges and opportunities lie ahead? Third-generation (3G) high-speed networks and portable multifunction phones will soon achieve data transmission power similar to that of personal computers.[26] Developing the market in mobile data communication – all signs indicate that multimedia[27] mobile data (i.e. sounds, pictures, video, and text transmitted through wireless networks) – constitutes the biggest ever business opportunity for the wireless telecom industry.

For many wireless telecom operators worldwide, mobile data service is more than a new market opportunity: The network connection is rapidly becoming a commodity, and revenue growth from traditional voice and text services is slowing. The transformation evident in the mobile industry and its impact on business is apparent from the following:[28]

"But the shift from voice to data services won't be an easy one. Indeed, mobile operators won't succeed without making substantial changes to their business models. Currently, their revenues come mostly from time- and volume-based fees charged to customers for connecting to their networks. This connectivity stratagem is not well suited to the world of data services, in which the network is a less valuable asset than the content that is transmitted through it. The

---

[26] For instance, France Télécom's Orange introduced the Motorola MPx200, which uses the Microsoft Windows operating system, marketing it with special services "exclusive to Orange".

[27] The world's first multimedia mobile data service, in Japan, caught on quickly with teens, who were captivated by playing games, e-mailing text messages, and downloading ring tones from the internet. Today, consumers of all ages around the world fancy possessing a mobile device for communication and entertainment.

[28] Helmut Meier, Roman Friedrich, and Hanno Blankenstein. "Business Models: A Master Model for Mobile Multimedia", *Strategy and business*, HBS, Spring, 2004, p. 2 of 7.

focus on connectivity has also isolated mobile operators within the wireless value chain. Because they were able to grow and profit in the past simply by owning the network, mobile operators had little reason to seek value from other sources.

"We believe a new 'integrated services' business model – one that encourages productive partnering and more varied approaches to value creation – is the most promising option for the wireless industry. Operators won't simply provide a connection to the network; rather, they will position themselves to directly influence and profit from every aspect of the wireless experience: reliable connections, clear reception, attractive and easy-to-use phones, useful and fun applications, good customer service, and more."

Mobile operators will need to create value from their networks, as well as the handset and content, as they face aggressive new competitors in the digital value chain that are intent on getting their piece of the wireless action.

In the past, the wireless industry has been hurt because many players were not winners in their relationships with others in the value chain. This is changing as demand for wireless products and services grows, and companies discover that collaboration is the best way to accelerate innovation, increase profits, and enrich the overall market. Plain old-fashioned voice service remains the mainstay of the wireless business, and will continue to be for the next several years. The use of a higher-cost, higher-risk, but higher-value-added integrated service model, which aims to capture more value from the different types of content carried over the network, is a critical element in the value chain. But partnerships are crucial to the mobile operator's ability to expand revenue streams, grow market share, and capture *more* value from the customer relationship. Collaboration with content partners is another critical element in the integrated model.

Growing "co-opetition" in the wireless industry, as well as changes in the power structure of the value chain, will determine how mobile operators respond and adapt to their new market dynamics. This has lessons not just for wireless players, but for companies in all industries facing today's familiar mix of "business uncertainty and compelling opportunity".[29] The worldwide growth of the mobile data

---

[29] Helmut Meier, Roman Friedrich, and Hanno Blankenstein. "Business Models: A Master Model for Mobile Multimedia" *Strategy +business*, HBS, Spring, 2004.

marketplace has been quite phenomenal. Leading mobile operators are bringing out ever more creative products, such as preloaded software applications. With added multimedia value from the network connection services, these applications will have a positive impact on revenues and profits.

In the wireless industry, or in any industry where the case for change is clear but the path less so, all partners need to understand the interests of other participants, anticipate their potential plays and devise their own responses.

CONCLUSION

The opportunities are vast and the challenges daunting. Government is under severe pressure to meet rising expectations and services. The potential and the prospects are enormous, but it will require committed leadership by government, a full understanding of e-business principles, and a clear strategy for overcoming the barriers to change. Government will also have to deal with the fear and hostility of the unions whose perception is that jobs will be lost. Here, technology – although crucial to making it all possible – is the least of worries.

Effectively breaking out of the vicious circle of poverty involves more than improving levels of nutrition, health, shelter, or education. The key question is whether technology will ultimately provide the opportunity for the poor to develop, and even leapfrog into prosperity, or whether the digital divide will deepen with time.

The diffusion of technology, lack of social capital and the environmental limits to growth all require a new paradigm in development where global forces of competitiveness, information technology and sociocultural dynamics have an impact. At the same time, if the industry is to create jobs it needs to improve information networks, incorporate more innovation and capitalise on its human resources. Global business is a strong stimulator of social change and transformation is a catalyst for innovation.

The challenge is to understand cultural diversity and draw on this knowledge to make social and economic development more effective. Farsighted support programmes now incorporate these ideas and these initiatives need to be supported, promoted, and replicated.

In order to demonstrate real commitment to technological development, all stakeholders and partners in the industry are supportive of the New Partnership for Africa's Development (NEPAD).[30] The organisation brings a focus to bear on business strategy and builds an awareness of intellectual property issues. More importantly, NEPAD aims to create the right climate to attract investment and create broader access and infrastructure roll-out.

We must guard against becoming mesmerised by technology systems, however; personal touch still builds stakeholder and customer relationships.

Last but not least, by improving the quality of relationships, our citizens can make a big difference to the attractiveness of our country, region, or city as a place to live, work and play. This goes beyond the delivery of services through the internet, and to the essence of digital democracy and is a vitally necessary step in the creation of a virtual community of political, corporate, and civil society leaders.

Jay Naidoo
Chairman of the Board, Development Bank of Southern Africa, South Africa

---

[30] This is already happening in the regional World Economic Forum meeting annually.

A DEMOCRATIC SOUTH AFRICA: THREE PERSPECTIVES ON THE ROLE OF CULTURE AND THE CONTRIBUTION OF ENTERTAINMENT AND THE MEDIA

1. THE CONTRIBUTION OF THE ENTERTAINMENT AND MEDIA INDUSTRIES

INTRODUCTION

Looking back ten years, it is apparent that South Africa's transition to a constitutional democracy owes as much to the pressure exerted by the arts and entertainment world as it does to the manoeuvrings of political and financial institutions. The light came in gradually through cracks in the apartheid structure. Glimmerings emerged in the 1950s, when the Union of Southern African Artists and the Arts Federation campaigned to have the members of the British entertainers' union, Equity, challenge discrimination policies.

Musicians such as the classical violinist Yehudi Menuhin defiantly gave performances in the townships. The white US jazz musician, Tony Scott, insisted on playing to integrated audiences and then inviting on stage our own Kippie Moeketsi. A black and white musician performing together! It seems ludicrous now – when our musicians are nominated for Grammies, our dancers illuminate international stages and our actors occasionally win Oscars.

As the late commentator Bloke Modisane observed, all this was made possible because some people held fast to an "unafraid sense of justice".[1] Such a fearless sense of justice remains integral to our sense of who we are – and want to be – as South Africans. Past achieve-

---

[1] *Blame Me On History* by Bloke Modisane, Simon & Schuster, New York, 1986.

ments will count for little if we do not confront the future with the same defiance.

Each year, we celebrate our diverse cultures and artistic achievements through increasingly popular festivals, such as the Awesome Africa Music Festival, the National Arts Festival, Aardklop, the Kora Music Awards, the Klein Karoo Nasionale Kunstefees, Oppikoppie, Suidooster, the Spier Festival, the Oude Libertas Festival and SA Music Week, as well as many local events that express the endeavours, aspirations and successes of our people.

The coverage of and reporting on these arts events, not surprisingly, is robust. In ten years consumer magazine titles grew from 278 to more than 530. More than 12 million readers turn to magazines for information and entertainment,[2] while nearly 10 million consult the daily and weekly newspapers. In the past two years alone, three new daily newspapers have been launched successfully.

The South African Broadcasting Corporation (SABC) performs its function as a public broadcaster, reaching out in all eleven official languages.[3] SABC's ten newsrooms employ over 300 journalists, producing more than 200 news bulletins, plus approximately 30 hours of current affair programming. The government also intends creating two regional broadcasters to give expression to marginalised African languages.

The country now tunes in to some 96 radio stations, some 13 of which are commercial and over 70 are communal.[4] It is estimated that more than 320 people out of every 1000 own or have access to a radio, compared to the 45 people out of 1000 who buy a newspaper. (However, 450 out of 1000 read a daily paper.[5])

A privately owned free-to-air television station, e-tv, has been launched. The pay channels, M-Net, SuperSport and the like, add value for their customers with increasingly diverse bouquets, while MultiChoice offers technology and service.

The South African film industry is small but growing. This year, construction of an international-standard film studio began in the

---

[2] Source: AMPS2003, ABC and The Media Buyer.
[3] The eleven languages are:
Sesotho sa Leboa (sometimes referred to as "Sepedi"); Sesotho; Setswana; SiSwati; Tshivenda; Xitsonga; Afrikaans; English; isiNdebele; isiXhosa; isiZulu.
[4] Source: ICASA.
[5] Source: Nielsen Media Research/AdEx 2003.

Western Cape and a similar project is planned for KwaZulu-Natal. At the Cannes Film Festival 2004, SA had eleven entries.

South Africa's vigorous entertainment and media business, backed by the Films and Publication Act, 1996, which dismantled the limitations imposed by previously censorious edicts, is increasingly competitive. But many feel that the regulatory environment needs to be further revised and liberalised. Regulatory bodies such as the Independent Communications Authority of South Africa (ICASA) and associations like the South African National Editors' Forum (SANEF) are trying to create a vibrant, professional environment.

CONTRIBUTION OF THE ENTERTAINMENT INDUSTRY

Over the last decade, the media and entertainment industry has been instrumental in breaking down social barriers and portraying the nation's kaleidoscope of cultures. The industry's landscape today reflects a mature democracy, marked by fierce competition and a variety of niche-market products. The industry is on its way to a highly digitised future and is being continuously reshaped by advances in delivery technologies.

TELEVISION

Television was introduced in South Africa only in 1975. But since then it has played an important role in the development of a broad South African culture. The growth of the economy, together with the development of democracy in the last decade, has widened television's scope, not only in the material available, but also in the challenge of delivering targeted commercial programmes to a diversified audience.

Television's challenge is to identify the shared aspirations of the audience without delivering homogenised programming. This requires an understanding of existing social structures and an appreciation of South Africa's new and unique culture. A nuanced view of the country's television audience has helped to strengthen the principles of the new democracy – and at the same time cultivate a healthy respect for differences.

Like other state institutions, the South African Broadcasting

Corporation (SABC) has undergone extensive restructuring to fulfil these requirements. It is called upon to serve all eleven official languages[6] and enjoys the highest aggregate audience ratings. It is funded from both compulsory licence fees and advertising. The SABC's stated aim is to provide coverage of national developments in a multi-channel milieu of competing television stations and local and international news organisations, while simultaneously protecting its independence as a reliable, non-partisan source of information for the South African public.

The independent television channel, e-tv, airs both international programming and strong local content. Movies, news and sport are its strengths. E-tv has taken on the SABC and pay-television, and made inroads into a highly contested market. Its ratings have increased spectacularly over the past few years.

The growth in the television industry has facilitated a range of new programming that is more reflective of our entire society. Soap operas and series form an important element in the programming mix and local stories often beat Hollywood productions in the ratings.

The range of local programming provides a barometer of the country's cultural mix. The fact that it competes with international shows for local audience ratings in this sophisticated and saturated market demonstrates that the South African audience, while hungry for the quality of international content, is also interested in itself. This propensity for self-examination has provided fertile ground for the rise of reality TV in South Africa, a phenomenon that reflects South Africa's complex social structure.

Pay-television offers the most hospitable environment for reality TV in South Africa, largely due to its transformation into a digital multi-channel platform that caters simultaneously for a general prime-time viewership and a multitude of smaller, niche audiences. This extended content capacity means that reality-TV formats are moulded into dedicated channels with a higher frequency of prime-time shows and interactive TV applications.

---

[6] The largest language groups in South Africa are:
   isiZulu 23.8% (10 662 400 speakers)
   isiXhosa 17.6% (7 884 800 speakers)
   Afrikaans 13.3% (5 958 400 speakers)
   Sepedi 9.4% (4 211 200 speakers)
   English 3 673 600 (speakers).

The pay-television industry mirrors the cultural kaleidoscope that is South Africa. From its early beginnings in 1986, it has grown from a single-channel analogue terrestrial offering into the current DSTV (digital satellite) bouquet, that offers a sophisticated cross-section of world-class channels.

South Africa pioneered the development of pay-television and conditional access systems in the developing world. Today, the Irdeto system is used by more pay-television operators worldwide than any other. MIH has grown its pay-TV business to countries elsewhere in Africa and also in the Mediterranean and in Asia.

In summary, the South African television industry is a mature, sophisticated and highly competitive environment that plays a pivotal role in the development of the country's new democracy.

COMMUNICATION AND DIGITAL ENTERTAINMENT FORMS

A decade of democracy, and the resulting freedom of information, has driven strong growth in other areas of digital entertainment. The internet started early in this country and in 2000 South Africa had 50 per cent of all internet connections in Africa. However, this figure has now declined to below 25 per cent as the growth of internet connections has stalled owing to high prices and a lack of innovation, born of a continuing telecoms monopoly. Today, a mere 6.5 per cent of the population (approximately three million people) enjoys internet access. Competition in fixed-line telephony in some form is expected soon.

On the internet content side, the South African *co.za* domain has become a ubiquitous element in above-the-line marketing. Most leading brands in South Africa have their own websites. In addition, secure transactions take place in online banking sites, auctions, and e-commerce ventures selling everything from books to groceries. E-mail, the killer application of the internet, is now the preferred mode of business communication.

News and sports sites are also particularly vigorous, catering mostly to users on corporate local area networks (LANs) at work. Yet broadband services in South Africa have been neglected, and connections number below 30 000. Until the broadband infrastructure rolls out, content services for broadband cannot develop.

Telkom, the fixed-line monopoly, runs a national telecom backbone, which in addition to carrying all basic voice and data traffic, has been used to package a residential asymmetric digital subscriber line (ADSL) broadband service.

State-owned broadcasting signal distributor, Sentech, is currently trying to get a wireless broadband service, MyWireless, off the ground. MyWireless is based on third-generation (3G) cellular technology and aims to construct more than 400 base stations.

The country's plan to licence a second network operator (SNO) to compete with Telkom, has been a shambles. Now that there is a largely new cast of executives in the Department of Communications, progress is eagerly awaited by an industry suffering from extremely high telecom charges, especially on international routes, and little broadband roll-out.

Wi-Fi hotspots have been installed, but sparsely, and have not yet gained widespread penetration.

The challenge is to make the internet as accessible to the population as cellular communication already is. A draft Convergence Bill aims to overhaul the IT, broadcasting and telecom sectors and to clarify the relationship between the regulatory body, ICASA, and the executive of the Department of Communications – which has seemed reluctant to grant ICASA the sort of independence enjoyed by the Federal Communications Commission (FCC) in the United States or the Office of Communications (Ofcom) in the United Kingdom.

Distance learning initiatives have been implemented in some rural schools, with corporations making generous donations of hardware and software to encourage computer literacy and use of the internet among schoolchildren. In attempting to bridge the digital divide, both the government and the private sector face a stern challenge: how to promote growth in this area, while taking a pragmatic view of what the majority of the population of the country actually needs in terms of the internet.

The mobile phone (cellular) industry has been a great success story. It has experienced unprecedented growth in South Africa and the existing three licence holders, Vodacom, MTN and Cell C, today have some 18 million customers. The industry adopted an innovative pay-as-you-go pricing strategy that required no credit checks, making connection possible for people from all walks of life. Cellular connections far surpass fixed-line connections: Today cellphone ownership beats fixed-line ownership by a ratio of three to one. Indeed, cellphones are now seen as the preferred means of communication for the young and the poor.

Currently, the government is considering whether to issue a fourth cellular licence. Sentech may also offer voice services. However, the monopolistic, fixed-line telecom has so far resisted any efforts to open up the market, and has proved effective over the past few years in winning regulatory battles with the government and regulator.

On the content side, a large number of wireless application service providers (WASPs) provide popular ring-tone and logo download services to cellphones. South Africans make extensive use of SMS technology for alerts, customer relationship marketing, as a payment gateway for charitable donations and for micro-payments for digital, rights-managed, online content. Banks use SMS alerts and WAP menus to give mobile users access and to provide added security.

Digital media delivery mechanisms have also made some advances in the market, but create difficult scenarios for the rights management of both local and licensed international content. Piracy of music on the internet is as much a problem in South Africa as elsewhere on the globe.

DVD has had a strong impact on the local market, making digital-quality home reception of movies popular and opening up new revenue streams for video rental businesses. The introduction of rewritable DVDs will make it difficult to protect intellectual content.

Paid-for internet content models are expected to develop in South Africa, using billing systems such as mobile phones. While this facility is still in its infancy, opportunities exist for the development of new content forms for exploitation across both internet and mobile platforms. To a large extent, this will be driven by improvements in DRM systems that allow for the protection of content.

The development of broadband is also urgently required. Currently, internet access in South Africa ranks among the most costly in the world and this is delaying the development of new generation content and services for the internet.

Radio

Ten years ago the segment comprised only the government-controlled SABC and two private companies: 702, and Capital Radio. As pointed out by the present Minister of Arts and Culture (then

Minister of Posts, Telecommunications and Broadcasting), Dr Pallo Jordan, the situation "was a scandalous denial of access to modern communications to millions of our people in the rural areas . . . and the urban townships". That scenario has radically altered.

Two years ago the SABC was split into public and commercial divisions. The SABC now reaches more than 24 million listeners. Today, thirteen commercial radio licences reach some 7 million listeners. In addition, more than 60 community radio stations, governed by non-profit principles, serve various communities.

It is estimated that some 32 per cent of the country own or have access to a radio, compared to only 4.5 per cent that buy a daily newspaper. Media buyers Radmark estimate that "80% of 15–24-year-olds listen to [radio] each week". Radio gets about 15 per cent of the country's total ad spend (about R2-billion).[7]

The outstanding growth of regional radio provides an indication of the country's changing media consumption. Stations such as the top regional commercial station, Jacaranda 94.2, have shown a sharp growth over the last four years, and now reach more than two million listeners each week. Similar growth was experienced at Kaya fm and the African language (Zulu) station Ukhozi,[8] the country's largest with just under seven million listeners.

Talk radio flourishes and has added a diversity of voices to the nation's ongoing conversation with itself, via broadcasters such as Yfm's DJ Fresh's giving air to local kwaito sounds to the debates of Tim Modise on 702 Talk Radio/Cape Talk and the probing investigations of John Perlman on SAfm.

The National Association of Broadcasters (NAB), which represents the country's major broadcasters,[9] wants to make the industry more competitive at a global level and recently drew up a ten-point plan that it says will facilitate media convergence.

Convergence is happening not just in terms of media platform innovation, such as radio stations adding value to their programming

---

[7] Source: Nielsen Media Research/AdEx. 2003.
[8] Source: Radmark. An analysis of four years of radio, taking into consideration the 15 per cent population growth in the country.
[9] The major radio players and their main stations are:
  Kagiso Media (East Coast, Jacaranda and OFM)
  Makana (P4 Cape Town, P4 Durban, Kaya FM)
  Nail (Jacaranda, Kaya FM, KFM)
  Primedia (Highveld, 702 Talk Radio, Cape Talk).

by online streaming, reward clubs on websites, print magazines and sponsored events, but also culturally. Despite our diverse languages and cultures, as our democracy grows up we find we have more in common than it seems. Much of this is driven by the demands of the new South African consumer.

Earlier this year, ICASA indicated it was willing to increase the number of commercial radio licences.

Satellite radio, delivered with digital signals and initially used in South Africa for distance-learning projects, may grow with Worldspace Southern Africa. Satellite radio can deliver crystal clear, commercial-free music and talk shows tailored to individual tastes. The technology, however, requires digital radios that process satellite transmissions. Worldspace's satellite beams down more than 40 channels across Africa and the Middle East.

Print Media

Newspapers

Change and reform are always risky, and these risks escalate when information is suppressed. South Africa is fortunate in having an independent newspaper industry that strives to achieve standards of journalism and management compatible with those in mature democracies.

Drawing inspiration from newspapers internationally and in spite of restrictive laws, South African newspapers played an important role in preparing the country for fundamental change during the 1980s and 1990s. It is difficult today to imagine how South Africa might have evolved without a vigorous and diverse newspaper industry.

Along with the rest of the country, the newspaper industry has transformed in many significant respects over the last ten years and has benefited from a stronger economy and a new dispensation in which press freedom is protected by the constitution. The tension between politicians, business, the broad civil society and the press is as healthy as in any democracy. Insufficient progress, however, has been made in scrapping some of the security legislation left over from the previous dispensation.

Important changes in media ownership patterns have also taken place. Black shareholders now own significant stakes in several newspaper groups. Today all major newspapers are owned by focused media groups, rather than conglomerates as previously.

Similarly, the composition of newsrooms has changed, and there has been a significant increase in the number of black journalists and editors. Serious debates about controversial issues of race and gender have sensitised newspapers as to viewing and reporting on these matters. Generally, newspapers have broadened their news coverage to reflect more groups and some have re-focused their content on new reader markets. Readership patterns reflect a healthy increase in black readership, while white readership of some papers has declined.

In line with general economic growth, advertising spend has risen slowly over the last ten years. Today, newspapers have a 29 per cent share of the total pool.

Circulation figures show that newspaper sales peaked during the hectic days of the fist democratic election in 1994, and slowly declined after that. Over the last ten years, daily papers have lost two per cent of their readers. However, the weekly papers show more than 18 per cent growth over the same period. Total sales for dailies and weeklies in 2003 amounted to 9 243 243, a two per cent growth over ten years. Advertising spend in the same period grew steadily.

Over the last few years a tabloid press has emerged, opening a new market of consumers that are literate, but have not been regular readers before. The four regional editions of the *Daily Sun* jointly constitute a circulation of more than 300 000, making it the biggest-selling cluster of daily newspapers in the country.

In the Sunday market, while the mighty *Sunday Times* still dominates, the *Sowetan Sunday World* and *Sunday Sun* have achieved significant growth. *Isolezwe*, a new Zulu-language daily, is expanding fast and attracting new readers. *Soccer Laduma*, the first focused sports tabloid, has also achieved spectacular readership.

In the aftermath of change in our political dispensation, a number of small but influential "struggle" newspapers failed to survive. Nonetheless, new titles emerged and today we have a very competitive, perhaps even over-traded newspaper industry. (A city like Pretoria is an example, with seven daily newspapers, more than many a bigger metropolis in the First World.)

The Newspaper Association of South Africa (NASA) listed 31 mainstream regional or national, and 123 community newspaper members in 1993. Today these numbers are 43 regional or national and 186 community papers respectively.

In 2003, the Audit Bureau of Circulation (ABC) stated that the number of national and regional members had increased from 42 to 49 between 1993 and 2003. Sold community papers went up from 31 to 48, and free papers from 73 to 106 in the same period.

In the process of opening new markets and seeking commercial opportunities, some newspapers are serving communities that were inadequately served in the past. The main growth achieved by the new sold and community papers has been among black readers, where the lower cover price of new titles makes them more affordable. In addition, distribution and availability of newspapers in rural and urban communities, while not yet ideal, is improving. Jobs and small business opportunities have been created for independent distribution and sales agents.

In support of true community media, the government has created the Media Development and Diversity Agency (MDDA), with funding contributions from media groups in South Africa. The MDDA is now operational and should stimulate development in community radio in particular (radio being the medium with by far the deepest penetration of society).

South Africa can be proud of its virile and competitive newspaper industry, reflective of a mature democracy.

Magazines

The fight for the magazine market is fierce: it's congested, volatile and unforgiving. Yet its evolution reminds us of how dynamic our own society is and how eager we are to embrace and explore the complexity of our globally connected world. We are hungry for information, and the power of the printed word remains strong.

An indication of this desire for useful information is the increase in business-to-business magazines, which have almost doubled in number of titles, from 361 in 1994 to 610 in 2003.

Readership figures reflect the sustained impact of increased education: in 1993 some 13 per cent of the population received no schooling at all. By 2004 this figure had halved. At the same time, the number of students passing the highest school level went from 22 per cent to 34 per cent. In time, this youth market will become the target ground for new publishing ventures.

In 1994, six magazine titles sold more than 200 000 copies each, yet in 2003 only two managed to do so. The significant growth over the last ten years has occurred in niche publishing: in 1994 some 29 titles sold fewer than 50 000 copies each. In 2003, 75 titles achieved these sales. In 1994 only six magazines sold between 50 000–99 000 copies; in 2003 this had trebled to 18.[10]

Magazine advertising spend over the same period shows a decline against other media.

Fierce competition in the women's magazine market has not discouraged new entrants. Inspired by the growth of such titles as *True Love* and the launch of the local version of *Shape* and *O*, *Glamour* joined the fray this year, and *Marie Claire* acquired a new publisher. With more than 18 titles vying for a place in the consumer's handbag, attrition is expected and some stalwart titles are already experiencing a decline in readership.

The launch of a South African edition of *Men's Health* in 1997 and *GQ* in 2000 paved the way for the lads' magazines, which market was soon dominated by the locally licensed edition of *FHM*. Traditional male domains such as car and sport publications have also experienced growth, the most successful example of which is *Kick Off*, a fortnightly local soccer magazine read by some 1.8 million fans.

But it's in the teen and tween markets that most launches have occurred over the past three years. A variety of titles have been launched, from *Seventeen* to the home-grown *Wicked* and *Saltwater Girl*. It is here that our most common social ground is stabilising, as global markets morph into global cultures and the divide between shopping and entertainment becomes more porous.

Tied in with globalisation is the enhanced appeal of celebrities. Titles such as *tvplus*, the magazine for soap aficionados, the celebrity features in *You* and *Huisgenoot* (the biggest-selling local title) and the recent entry into the field, *heat*, have all exploited this theme.

MOVIE INDUSTRY

The South African movie industry grosses more than R8.5 billion per year. It receives some funding and subsidies from government, mainly through the National Film & Video Foundation of the Ministry of

---

[10] Source: Media Manager and ABCs.

Arts and Culture. In addition, the Department of Trade and Industry offers an incentive package that encourages Hollywood studios to do business here.

The corporate player is the Industrial Development Corporation (IDC), which invested some R130 million in 16 films in 2003 alone. Most were joint ventures with international production companies.

The public sector has created parastatal organisations, such as the Gauteng Film Office and the Cape Film Commission. These organisations market and facilitate film productions and focus on stories about South Africa and its people. In recent years, SA has seen releases ranging from vernacular cultural preservation pieces to popular slapstick situation comedies.

Film schools have also made a contribution, and there has been impressive representation of South African film talent at places like the Cannes Film Festival. Local talent gained an extra spring in their step earlier this year when the 2004 Best Actress Oscar went to Charlize Theron.

South African cities, Cape Town in particular, have become a popular destination for location shoots by international filmmakers and offer world-class production crews and facilities to both feature film and commercial producers. And the business is growing. A consortium led by South Africa's most successful producer, Anant Singh, recently unveiled plans to build a R400 million film studio complex at Faure, outside Cape Town.

In common with the rest of the world, fewer South Africans are visiting local movie houses. Movie distributors have employed innovative customer relationship management programmes to bolster attendance figures. DVDs will continue to have a sizeable impact on local movie theatres, but will also stimulate production.

As is happening in the United States, video and DVD distribution channels are proving more lucrative for the producers and distributors than traditional movie theatres.

MUSIC INDUSTRY

Our music industry has also made some impression on the international scene, and has always been in the vanguard of social change. "South African jazz", a sustained fusion of rooted local musical traditions with much admired imports, has an appeal for international audiences. Coupled with the growing popularity of television shows such as *Project Fame, Idols* and *Popstars*, local music talent is moving into the spotlight on the national stage.

From the 1930s, when Dan Twala was booking local iscathimiya entertainers to perform in the Bantu Men's Social Centre, through the 1950s, when Miriam Makeba and Letta Mbuli played in now-vanished jive joints in Sophiatown, Jamestown and Dikatole, our music survived. In the 1960s, Makeba, Hugh Masekela and some other artists went into exile but their music endured. In the 1980s, Johnny Clegg joined with Sipho Mchunu, and Juluka rocked internationally; Paul Simon recorded with Ladysmith Black Mambazo. The country's musical transformation is reflected by our new national anthem, *Nkosi Sikilel'i Africa* (God Bless Africa).

The growth of local music has been hard fought for. From the 1930s, when Eric Gallo launched what became South Africa's largest recording label, to the restructuring of the industry in the 1990s, local artists struggled to acquire either public recognition or financial remuneration.

Today, the biggest problem facing the industry is pirated versions of local and international artists. It is estimated that piracy accounts for between 25–30 per cent of all sales locally (slightly below the world average). Organisations such as the South African Music Rights Organisation (SAMRO), the Record Industry of South Africa (RISA) and the South African Federation Against Copyright Theft (SAFACT) have been joined by the Ministry of Arts and Culture in the battle against piracy. The ministry recently appointed lawyers from the Legal Aid Board solely to handle infringements of artists' rights.

Our musicians continue to forge ties that bind our nation, but the industry needs to implement marketing strategies that will establish our local artists at home and on the international scene. In return, the government should actively seek to assist in the promotion of local talent and reward those who do. As the music pundits say: "Promotion is preferable to protection."

Sport

In 1995, at a stadium in Johannesburg, an elderly statesman pulled on a green and gold rugby jersey with the number "6" on the back and raised the hand of the Springbok rugby captain. Nelson Mandela's gesture became a symbol of something greater than Francois Pienaar's team winning the Rugby World Cup. We went from being underdogs to world champions. The following year, we hosted the African Nations Cup, in 1999 the All Africa Games and in 2003, the Cricket World Cup. Recently South Africa was chosen to host the FIFA's 2010 Soccer World Cup. We have gone from pariah state to popular host nation in one decade.

Professional sport, like other forms of entertainment, depends on corporate sponsorship and television coverage to pay the bills. Last year, the fourteen rugby unions received more than R100 million from the SuperSport TV channel alone.

Sport sponsorship also contributes. In 1993, its combined direct and leveraged spend amounted to R523 million: ten years later, it had reached almost R3 billion. A portion of this money goes towards player development, the benefits of which may be seen in the successes of our athletes, rugby, cricket and soccer stars, as well as of many in less publicised sports.

CONCLUSION

Foreign visitors to South Africa are often struck by the size and character of the local media and entertainment industry: competitive, loud, diverse, opinionated, respectful of the constitution, strangely tolerant – rather like the country itself.

Koos Bekker
Managing Director, Naspers

2.
FORGING A NEW CULTURAL IDENTITY

When one reflects on South Africa's transition from the brutality of apartheid to a peaceful democracy, one cannot help but wonder how this was achieved. While the apartheid regime was dividing people according to their race, a unique culture was taking root – a culture that saw people of all races coming together to fight a common enemy, each bringing their own attributes to what has become a new South African culture – of reconciliation, harmony and unity, a nation of free people.

This was clearly acknowledged in President Thabo Mbeki's remarks on the occasion of the adoption of the Republic of South Africa's new constitution in 1996, when he declared,

"I am an African"
"I owe my being to the Khoi and the San whose desolate souls haunt the great expanses of the beautiful Cape . . . I am formed of the migrants who left Europe to find a new home on our native land. Whatever their own actions, they remain still part of me . . .

In my veins courses the blood of the Malay slaves who came from the East . . .

I am the grandchild of the warrior men and women that Hintsa and Sekhukhune led, the patriots that Cetshwayo and Mphephu took to battle, the soldiers Moshoeshoe and Ngungunyane taught never to dishonour the cause of freedom.

I am the grandchild who lays fresh flowers on the Boer graves at St Helena and the Bahamas, who sees in the mind's eye and suffers the suffering of a simple peasant folk . . . I am the child of Nongqause. I am he who made it possible to trade in the world markets in diamonds, in gold, in the same food for which my stomach yearns . . .

I come of those who were transported from India and

China . . . who taught me that we could both be at home and be foreign . . .
Being part of all these people, and in the knowledge that none dare contest that assertion, I shall claim that – **I am an African**."

This important declaration by the President sent out a clear message to all South Africans that each one of us is a member of the new democracy. It emphasised that this is a country built on diversity; that it is important to find common ground among all people in order to create a new national identity and a new sense of patriotism. The binding force is the mix of different cultures that cements the nation together, resulting in what Archbishop Desmond Tutu has called the miracle of "the Rainbow Nation".

The arts and entertainment communities of South Africa have played a significant role in the building of the new nation. To redress the social and political injustices of apartheid, artists of all kinds committed themselves to a nonracial, non-sexist, united, free and democratic South Africa. This was no mere sloganeering. South Africa today sustains its democracy by adhering to these principles.

In exploring the role and contribution of the arts and entertainment sectors in South Africa, one must recognise that both internal and exiled South African artists, musicians and writers were at the forefront of popular campaigns to make the international community aware of the horrors of apartheid. They employed their talents and international profiles to expose the Nationalist Party regime and to drum up international support for the struggle against apartheid. It is no wonder then, that in a democratic South Africa, the arts, media and entertainment sectors provide the cohesion to bind the nation. Their contribution to democracy in South Africa is evident from their pioneering and innovative work in music, the performing arts, film and later television (regular broadcasts began in 1976).

MUSIC AS A WEAPON

One of the key elements in the days of struggle was protest music, the songs of liberation – the tunes and lyrics of Vuyisele Mini, Hugh Masekela, Vusi Mahlasela, Abdullah Ibrahim, Miriam Makeba, Mbongeni Ngema, Sophie Mgcina, Dolly Rathebe, Busi Mhlongo,

Letta Mbuli, Caiphus Semenya and a host of others. These artists used their music as a weapon in the struggle against apartheid. Many of them were exiled abroad and when they returned home triumphantly and began playing to local audiences, one could sense the emotions they aroused among people who had been sustained by their music in the dark days of apartheid. Theirs was a generation that found solace, comfort and strength in making music, while they fought for the freedom of their people.

The collaboration of South African and international artists, after the release of Nelson Mandela, has created a global audience that normally might not have listened to South African music. Shining examples are Ladysmith Black Mambazo's partnership with Paul Simon, and Lebo M's contribution to Disney's Lion King. Today, South African musicians such as Vusi Mahlasela, Yvonne Chaka Chaka, Brendan Jury, Danny K and Busi Mhlongo are in great demand internationally, on the strength and merit of their own music.

Today a new genre of music has emerged – kwaito, the true sound of the new South Africa. Kwaito is a pulsating blend of hip-hop, house, mbaqanga, jive, ragga and rap and boasts the biggest array of new stars, among whom are Arthur, the late Brenda Fassie, M'du, Aba Shante, Bongo Maffin, Boom Shaka, Spokes H and Jimmy B. Kwaito is difficult to ignore as its locally flavoured lyrics and irresistible beat pounds out of minibus taxis, radios, clubs and township taverns across the country. The lyrics – a medley of English, indigenous languages and street slang – truly reflect life in this country, creating a distinctly South African style of dancing, dressing and performing. Kwaito is now South Africa's pop music – a mixture of everything that 1990s youth grew up on.

Other forceful forms of music that served not only to conscientise but also as a strong healing force included the African music genre of iscathimiya and maskanda. Both of these music forms are considered to be too traditional for the commercial arena, and have been severely marginalised. During the apartheid years they spoke of the suffering and pain of the oppressed, and they enjoyed very limited support from the recording industry. Yet, they remain popular. Rooted in the migrant labour system, they are the soul music of thousands of Zulu workers who had to leave their idyllic rural worlds and migrate to the urban cities in search of work. Often illiterate, they eked out a living doing basic manual work in atrocious conditions – sending home money every month to their loved ones. The music enabled workers to give expression to and bring meaning and comfort to their lives in a harsh and bleak urban world. Exponents of iscathimiya include the world-famous Ladysmith Black Mambazo, and thousands of other groups found especially in KwaZulu-Natal and in the mining compounds and hostels of Gauteng. Maskandi artists include Mfiliseni Magubane, Phuzekhemisi and Pathekile Lukhosi.

African jazz was also in the forefront of the struggle, not only in making people aware of the harshness of life under apartheid, but as an expression of the people's indomitable spirit. It gave hope in a bleak, dark world. Jazz luminaries included Hugh Masakela, Abdullah Ibrahim, the late Basil Mannenberg Coetzee, Robbie Jansen, Sipho Gumede and Jonas Gwangwa. There was also the pennywhistle legend, Spokes Mashiyane. Sax jive, flute jive and vocal varieties of jazz, collectively known as mbaqanga, was popularised in the 1950s by groups such as the Manhattan Brothers, the Skylarks, Johnny Dyani, Dudu Pukwana and veteran sax man Ntemi Piliso. The African Jazz Pioneers and other popular groups such as Stimela and Bayete celebrated the rich legacy of South African jazz.

PROTEST THEATRE FLOURISHES

Like protest music, protest theatre was the mainstay of the theatrical community in the days of apartheid. In the mid-1980s, at the height of the struggle, there was an unprecedented degree of cultural activity. Talented people with few or no resources would go on stage and perform brilliantly. Outstanding playwrights and actors such as Mbongeni Ngema (*Sarafina!*), Percy Mtwa (*Woza Albert*) and others performed on makeshift stages in the townships, and then moved on to venues such as the Market Theatre in Johannesburg and the Stable Theatre in Durban. Their performances also encouraged people to speak out against the prevailing regime.

HIV/AIDS is a subject of great concern to the theatrical community as well. Pieter-Dirk Uys's extremely effective *For Fact's Sake* and Robyn Orlin's FNB Vita Dance Umbrella piece *"we must eat our suckers with the wrapper on"* are recent offerings. Phyllis Klotz and the Sibikwa Players' *The Stadium,* an examination of the live-fast, die-fast aspects of township sex culture told with humour, kwaito and dance, brings the fight against AIDS down to a level where everyone can be educated about the dreaded scourge. Theatrical veterans such as Zakes Mda, Gibson Kente and Mbongeni Ngema have also taken the battle against AIDS to the stage, creating shows that serve not only to entertain, but also to highlight the threat posed by the deadly virus.

Another area that has contributed greatly to South Africa's democracy is radio. The ANC's Radio Freedom played a vital role in the fight for freedom. As a result of the rationalisation of the airwaves in the mid-1990s, a new and vibrant medium has emerged that reflects the demography of the country . Ethnic and commercial radio stations attract listeners of all races and cultures. South Africans are now listening to the same radio stations and are exposed to the same range of views and opinions, as their sense of unity keeps developing.

HELPING THE YOUTH TO DANCE

In the 1990s, a new genre emerged – traditional theatrical entertainment fused with multiculturalism, of which *Umoja* and *African Footprint* are the outstanding examples.

Todd Twala and Thembi Nyandeni (two members of the original cast of the show *Ipi Tombi*) travelled around the country in the 1990s and became increasingly disturbed by the large number of teenagers from disadvantaged communities with huge potential but no access to work, education or training. They established a performing arts school, where they began teaching young people to sing and dance. A few years later, they had not only trained a large number of children, but also created a ten-man tribal music group, Baobab, which subsequently performed around the world. After teaming up with producer Maurice Fresco, 700 performers were auditioned and a cast of 36 chosen for a new production. Leading theatrical director Ian von Memerty was commissioned to do the scripting and assist with direction, and *Umoja – The Spirit of Togetherness* was born.

A similar motive inspired the success of *African Footprint*. It began as Richard Loring's vision of empowering South African youth, especially talented young black dancers, through theatre. He was determined to create a unique song and dance production as a showcase for emerging talent. His resolve, strengthened by the fiery words of passion and love of acclaimed poet, Don Mattera, and exposure to the dramatic fusion between traditional and Western, modern dance forms by award-winning choreographers, Debbie Rakusin and David

Matamela, materialised into the "explosive stampede of song and dance" that is now *African Footprint*.

The creation of these outstanding dance pieces has given a profile to traditional dance forms as well as fusions of dance that enable audiences to appreciate various ethnic cultures through the medium of song and dance. Pre-1994, racially mixed audiences would not have watched the same show in the same venue. Today, the situation is vastly different.

FILM COMES INTO ITS OWN

The South African film industry has also undergone major change since the achievement of democracy. During the apartheid era, the Nationalist government vigorously promoted film production and segregated cinemas. In collaboration with big business, the regime instituted a state subsidy scheme to support film-making that directly underpinned the apartheid ideology or at least sought to portray apartheid in a good light. Afrikaans films predominated, especially between 1956 and 1963. This was insular cinema at its best, providing a comfort zone for Afrikaners and a reassurance that apartheid would endure. Themes focused especially on issues of love, of the Mills and Boon variety, with buckets of melodrama thrown in. Social reality was ignored. Stereotypes of blacks as uncivilised, lazy, unintelligent and fit only for domestic chores were further entrenched in the narrative and visual language of these films. In the 1970s, there was some attempt to pre-empt criticism that there was no cinema for black people. A black film industry was born, but it was controlled by the apartheid regime. Badly made low-budget films, shown in township halls, shebeens, schools and churches, reinforced apartheid ideology, and promoted the "Bantustan" homeland policy.

By the early eighties, as grassroots, community and non-governmental organisations and a critical anti-apartheid press (the *Weekly Mail*, *Vrye Weekblad* and others) began to emerge, so too did a group of filmmakers, who used their medium to address the socioeconomic and political realities of South Africa. Many of their films and videos were banned, some of them were hounded and imprisoned by their regime, but the tide could not be stopped.

For the first time also, black and white filmmakers began working with each other, producing news, magazine inserts, documentaries and short and full feature films, primarily for international broadcasting and cinema release. These films included *Mapantsula*, *Place of Weeping* (which I produced while on the run from the security police), *The Stick*, etc. Short films and even animation work marked the beginning of a new, critical South African cinema, whose themes were associated with the nonracial, non-sexist democratic ideals of the liberation movements. From the 1980s to the present, these films and filmmakers have grown from strength to strength.

Since the advent of democracy, the South African government has played a significant role in promoting arts and culture and especially the film industry. Through the ministry of Arts and Culture, it initiated the National Film and Video Foundation (NFVF) – a statutory body to promote and enhance the equitable growth and development of the South African film and video industry, nationally and internationally. The foundation provides funding for training, development, production, exhibition, marketing and distribution. It also has a host of other projects and goals, which include policy and research. An important feature is that, unlike the apartheid regime, the new government provides arm's-length funding to the Foundation. It does not interfere in the selection of films and documentaries for funding and encourages the development of a critical South African cinema. Since the formation of the NFVF, several marginalised voices have emerged, heralding the dawn of a dynamic new phase in filmmaking. Many films supported by the NFVF have gone on to win awards at major international film festivals.

The NFVF, in collaboration with the departments of Arts and Culture and Foreign Affairs, is also spearheading the signing of co-production treaties. Currently, South Africa has a co-production treaty with Canada, and recently, a similar treaty was signed with Italy. A memorandum of understanding with regard to film also exists with India. More treaties can be expected in the future, thereby integrating South Africa into the international film production fraternity.

As a result of these and other initiatives by broadcasters such as the SABC and e-tv, new themes have emerged in both film and television, resulting in the industry becoming far more intercultural. Documentaries are commissioned to relate the history of the struggle and situation comedies now tackle intercultural and interracial prejudices (*Suburban Bliss*, *Going Up*, *Madam And Eve*). There are programmes offering health education through the medium of entertainment (*Soul City*); dramas around human rights issues made in part-documentary style (*Rhythm and Rights*); documentaries providing an African perspective on conflict resolution (*In Search of Common Ground*); a drama series that re-examined interracial relations during apartheid (*Homeland*); docu-dramas on key anti-apartheid figures, and a new breed of magazine programmes that represent the entire spectrum of the nation.

In cinema, the Afrikaans language film *Paljas*, made in 1996 and produced by myself (Anant Singh), a producer of Indian descent, and directed by a white Afrikaner, Katinka Heyns, marked a turning point in the South African film industry. The film was South Africa's first ever entry for Academy Award consideration, and was nominated as the country's official entry by a multiracial South African committee under the auspices of the Independent Producers' Organisation, chaired by Mfundi Vundla. This was an example of real change, where the film industry had transcended race and ethnicity.

Today, the themes of many local films are based on reconciliation and identity, as in *Paljas* and *Cry, The Beloved Country*. Comedies parodying South African life have been immensely popular, breaking box-office records while playing to integrated audiences. The most successful South African film of all time was *Mr Bones*, starring South Africa's king of comedy, Leon Schuster, who also conceived the idea and co-wrote the film, produced by Anant Singh. It became the highest earning South African film at the local box office, grossing more than R32 million.

Recent film productions have tackled social issues that affect the lives of all South Africans. They include *Yesterday*, directed by Darrell James Roodt, the touching story of a rural woman infected with HIV/AIDS by her mineworker husband, whose only motivation to live is to see her young daughter start school; *Red Dust*, starring Hilary Swank and Chiwetel Ejiofor and directed by Tom Hooper, a courtroom drama based on the Truth And Reconciliation Commission hearings, and *Forgiveness*, on the same theme, starring Arnold Vosloo.

IMPROVING INSTITUTIONAL CAPACITY

Government has also realised that the promotion of the film industry could also impact greatly on the South African economy. Unlike in the apartheid era, the new government instituted measures to improve the institutional capacity of the arts (especially film). For example, in May 2002, film was declared to be one of the rapid growth areas of the economy.

The remarkable growth in the South African film industry is evidenced by the formation of the Cape Film Commission in the Western Cape, and the Gauteng Film Office. In KwaZulu-Natal, a Durban Film Office has recently been opened and there is discussion about the formation of a KwaZulu-Natal Film Commission. The Western Cape provincial cabinet has recently chosen the Dreamworld consortium to establish a Film City near Somerset West. In KwaZulu-Natal, Videovision Entertainment has been selected by the eThekwini municipality to build a world-class studio in the city of Durban.

The establishment of film commissions, film offices and the building of studios will all help to improve the institutional capacity of the film industry in South Africa. Organisations in the industry, who worked against almost overwhelming odds during the apartheid era, have now emerged as leaders in their field. One such organisation is the Gauteng-based Film Resources Unit which screened films banned by the former regime. It has initiated an audience development programme in black townships, where there are hardly any cinemas, by bringing a mobile screening studio to these areas. Today, the Film Resource Unit distributes African films to the whole world, and aims to develop an audience for locally produced South African film. It has also set up a Video Resource Centre, where people can rent, watch and buy videos. Moreover, it trains young unemployed people all over the country in marketing and film distribution. The Unit also plays an invaluable role in strengthening marginalised film industry voices in South Africa and the continent.

One of the many legacies of apartheid education is the critical lack of black scriptwriters in South Africa. The South African Scriptwriters Association (SASWA), administered by members who contribute their time and expertise on a voluntary basis, has initiated programmes to provide training for scriptwriters, both currently working and aspiring. This is another organisation that has shown incredible commitment to fostering emerging talent in the film and video industry in South Africa. Other organisations such as the Independent Producers Organisation and the National Television and Video Association of South Africa play an important role in the promotion of film and video.

EXPLOITING THEIR FREEDOM

Just as in the past, when arts and culture played such a vital and vibrant role in the struggle for freedom, South African artists today are exploiting their freedom in our new democracy. The arts are infused with themes that deepen and defend democracy, and where necessary, artists speak with a bold and critical voice whenever such freedoms come under threat. Personal histories are now being brought to light and other social issues impacting on society are being addressed through music, dance, theatre, films and other art forms. These issues include the HIV/AIDS crisis, corruption, the high levels of crime, gender awareness, gay and lesbian issues, the search for roots, culture and identity and a host of other topics that form part of the daily debate in democratic South Africa.

A number of these themes are reflected in one of the most innovative projects ever initiated by the South African Broadcasting Corporation (SABC): "Project 10 – Real Stories from a Free South Africa". This was commissioned by SABC 1 and supported by the National Film and Video Foundation and the Binger Film Institute. Ten films were directed by young South African filmmakers, whose brief was to produce personal and intimate films about how they had experienced or understood the last ten years of freedom in South Africa. Many of these productions have received critical acclaim at major film festivals, including the Sundance and Berlin Film Festivals. Project Ten indicates that we have a new generation of young and exciting filmmakers who will uphold the tradition of making films that educate and entertain, and also continue to articulate socioeconomic, political and personal issues that affect our society. At the heart of this project is the industry's desire to forge social cohesion and thereby to contribute to the deepening of South African democracy.

These are exciting times for the South African film industry. The year 2004 has seen more than fifteen local film productions that tell South African stories, each contributing to the development of South Africa's identity, to the fabric of the country's evolving culture and the perception of the country and its peoples at an international level.

Anant Singh
Film Producer, Videovision Entertainment, South Africa

3.
THE MEDIA AFTER TEN YEARS OF DEMOCRACY

In 1990, when Nelson Mandela walked out of jail, South Africa's media landscape was as plain as the Free State veld. Radio and television blindly supported the National Party government (which effectively owned them). In one way or another Anglo American owned almost all 23 English language newspapers. Only the *Natal Witness, Daily Dispatch* and *Weekly Mail* were independent, and *The Citizen* had been started covertly with taxpayers' cash to support the apartheid regime. All English-language newspapers except *The Citizen* were implacably opposed to the National Party.

But while they opposed "the Nats", these papers were not in favour of the recently unbanned African National Congress, mostly because the ANC had resorted to urban violence in an attempt to bring about a revolution. Curiously, even the *Sowetan* – perceived as the major "black" newspaper – seemed to favour another liberation party, the Pan Africanist PAC.

All Afrikaans daily and Sunday newspapers supported the National Party, with their eyes wide shut. Their political journalists occasionally criticised "the party" but were slavish in supporting it against any threat. One dissenting Afrikaans weekly, *Vrye Weekblad*, was quickly closed when it lost a major defamation claim against a pro-apartheid general.

This pretty bland newspaper landscape changed quickly after November 1993 when Irish businessman Tony O'Reilly bought the best titles – including the *Sowetan* – from Anglo. Anglo wished to unbundle ahead of the election, realising that the concentration of media ownership would be a target for those wanting to label the forthcoming election unfair.

But, as the French have it, *plus ça change, plus c'est la même chose* and indeed things stayed the same, only the owners were now different. This prompted some of us to try to start alternate media which would put forward the views of the ANC, the SA Communist Party, the PAC and anyone else who needed a voice. So I went to New York to ask George Soros for some money to do this, but he said a firm "no". He felt that it was the newspaper groups' responsibility (but still gave me US$ 5 million "to help democracy" via his Open Society Foundation, an amount which has now topped US$300 million).

AN INFORMED ELECTORATE

On April 27th 1994 *The Star*'s headline read: "Vote, the beloved country". Alan Paton, that prune-faced, sour and somewhat bitter author of the classic tale of a rural hick robbed by city slickers, *Cry, the Beloved Country*, probably squirmed in his grave, but even he might have conceded that the headline captured the moment. Somehow, when the founding democratic election was held, amid much jubilation and with voters standing in long lines, all political parties had received sufficient coverage in the media for the electorate to make an informed choice. Some of Soros's money financed community radio stations, which helped. But all media went out of their way to try to ensure the electorate was as informed as possible.

Big differences emerged between editors, differences in personality rather than politics. Some predicted disaster and civil war, and others, such as my newspaper *The Star*, dared suggest to an incredulous world (and to withering criticism) that the election would be reasonably fair and would reflect the will of the people. As critics around the globe accused *The Star* of "sunshine journalism" (a semantically curious conjunction, considering most stars are suns) the optimists were proved correct, and the so-called "miracle" occurred.

The ANC swept into power with little bloodshed and no thoughts of revenge. President Mandela stunned the world with his policies of reconciliation and his sure-footed handling of global affairs. South Africa became flavour of the month, then of the year, and managed to stay there through the decade as well.

The media went into mild turmoil. Critical black reporters, previously significantly absent from the national broadcaster's radio and television newsroom, were thieved wholesale, first by television, then by radio. The unfortunate English-language newspapers which had bred and trained critical journalists were denuded.

Then a second wave of thieves raided the newsroom: a new and desperate batch of cabinet ministers, deputy ministers, provincial ministers and even mayors needed trained, independent, capable official spokespeople. Promising young reporters were offered a BMW and double their salaries to join the government and put out pompous statements by ministers or answer queries from their erstwhile colleagues.

TEN YEARS LATER

But the wheel has turned, and after ten years things have stabilised. *The Star* now has a shortage of white male reporters, the very creatures of whom government complained there were too many. South Africa's journalists are still underpaid, under-qualified and appallingly lacking in basic skills. However, even that is starting to change for the better as the job market becomes tighter and titles trim staffs, enabling news editors to be more picky.

And the SABC? It moved from being "His Master's Voice" for the apartheid government to displaying a degree of independence, but it still heavily favours boring speeches by ministers rather than the real news. It has already been through two boards and, under a highly independent chairman in Vincent Mphai, started to alter the old philosophy that radio and television do not rock the political boat.

Alas, the latest SABC board appointees are mostly people who are not shy to publicly proclaim their loyalty to the ANC. The party has such an enormous majority that it could have risked appointing independent thinkers to the board. But politicians everywhere like to be in control, to get even more votes than a two-thirds majority.

And what of newspapers, now that we are, in 2004, at the end of a decade of democracy? Most are still around, and there are five or six new titles on the scene.

A new tabloid *The Sun*, less than two years old, is now the biggest daily newspaper, and has no political reference point – thundering only that it supports "the readers" rather than a political party. Even older papers – such as *The Star* – show little political allegiance to anything except democracy. This may be because the ANC was so certain to win the elections that there is no credible alternative.

Most commentators find it difficult to say where Independent's fifteen titles stand politically. The same goes for other important titles, such as the major weekend newspaper, the *Sunday Times*. All are critical of government, but hasten to show support for both the ANC's policies and the government's regular calls for patriotism.

In television, South Africa has one truly independent free-to-air station, e-tv, Cape-based and Cape-biased, e-tv does strive to be independent and objective in its news coverage. Unfortunately, it lacks the skills and cash of the public broadcaster. It is also virulently anti-American (like many viewers), pro-Arab and pro-Iraq, and perceived as anti-Israeli. Opinion-formers and decision-takers often question e-tv's judgement.

There is also the wonderful world of DSTV – some sixty cable channels brought into wealthier homes and hotels by digital satellite. DSTV's bouquet offers some of the best channels from around the world, including 24-hour news services from Sky, CNN and BBC, plus the sophistication of Discovery, National Geographic and the History channels, together with the best sports coverage on the planet. Eight channels are devoted only to sports. Where else in the world could you watch a single golf game on six channels, each bringing you the same game but following different two-balls?

A COMPLEX LANDSCAPE

The media landscape in any sizeable country is complex. Extrapolated over a decade of transition, the complexity multiplies exponentially. Yet it really is quite simple – for those who live on the surface. Only when you start probing deeply does the stratification get difficult. So it is with the South African media.

Superficially, newspapers divide into those which are popular, and those which try to be serious. But in South Africa the popular papers have serious articles with business sections that are arguably better than the more up-market newspapers. And the latter also carry "pop" stories. So some observers try to divide newspapers into "black" and "white" – only to discover that those traditionally seen as white (like *The Star*) have a majority of black readers. Or try to divide the holding companies into English or Afrikaans, only to discover that an Afrikaans newspaper company publishes the biggest English newspaper.

So how have the media evolved and what has been their contribution to democracy in South Africa? Primarily, access to the media is now open to people of all political persuasions, even if most media now support the government. For in truth the overwhelming majority of people in the country (at the very least some 65 per cent) support the ANC government and it would be odd if the country's media did not reflect this.

South Africa has a multitude of media disciplines, in which there are the stars and the also-rans. Besides journalists, there are owners, promoters, marketers, advertisers and sponsors. There is – as in any healthy democracy – criticism aplenty, from politicians, business people, ideologues and ordinary readers, listeners and viewers. Yet, as in every free society, the media simply have to do their best every day, while absorbing and standing up to the pressure.

A BAD YEAR FOR THE MEDIA

In 2003 a succession of scandals rocked the South African media. Plagiarism by a brilliant columnist was uncovered, and he was eventually fired. Then the country's top editor (Mathatha Tsedu of the *Sunday Times*) was fired, with muddled reasons given for his dismissal. Another editor of a major weekly (Vusi Mona of *City Press*) admitted to a judicial commission that he had not taken due care (or any care at all, it seemed to the watching public) and was "reckless" in publishing a damaging story about the national director of public prosecutions. He also damaged himself and antagonised journalists everywhere when he disclosed the contents of an off-the-record briefing. He left his paper under a dark cloud.

There was more: a reporter sold a story to a rival publication when her editor refused to publish it (it later turned out to be false). The editor of *Elle* magazine resigned after allegations of plagiarism. A *Daily Sun* reporter was arrested for perjury after claiming to have been hijacked (the paper rather unfortunately ran the story as its main headline on page one).

In retrospect, 2003 was not a good year for the media, yet most of this was small beer compared to a reporter's making up of stories at the *New York Times*. For optimists, the very fact that these sins were uncovered indicated a maturing of the media in South Africa, a maturity perhaps absent when the newspapers' main mission was to dislodge the dreaded National Party and rid the country of the evil of apartheid.

A GROWTH IN OPPORTUNITIES

According to "SA Media Facts 2003", overall newspaper circulation – 1994 to 2004 – grew from roughly 3.5 million to 4 million copies. Circulation is not an accurate measure of readership, only of sales, and latest figures suggest that 45 per cent of the 30 million potential readers in the Republic read a newspaper on any one day. About 57 per cent access a magazine, 80 per cent television and 90 per cent radio. Only 4.6 per cent of the general population have "accessed the internet over the past seven days", according to research. Adspend on all media grew from R2.5 billion to R10 billion over the decade.

But it is the growth of media opportunities that had the greatest impact, a growth greater than exponential in the decade. In 1994 there were seven TV stations; now there are sixty plus (it changes almost monthly). There were 34 radio stations, and now 106. Consumer magazines have gone up from 250 to 515 and counting (this also changes monthly) and community newspapers from 0 to 272. Web pages have gone from 0 to 3 billion plus, although the number of people accessing them is small and elite.

Real change has taken place in newsrooms, where reporters had to unlearn a culture of constant criticism, which suited the apartheid era, and adapt to the role of a critical but constructive media. Naturally many reporters and commentators still shriek harshly at every perceived error by politicians, civil society or business. And that is right and good in a decent democracy, for society is the sum of many parts, and some parts need to be loud in pointing out the system's faults

But the pendulum of criticism has swung, and swung towards portraying South Africa in a good light. It has become fashionable to talk up the country's achievements rather than seek ways of belittling them.

A summit between the journalists and the Mbeki cabinet held at Sun City in the middle of the decade sent both sides – media and government – back to reconsider their positions, and an immense amount of good came from that soul-searching. Government realised that it was bad at communication: that it was foolish to believe that journalists and editors were unpatriotic at best and wanted a return to apartheid at worst. Editors returned to their publications having finally to face the fact that many journalists were under-skilled, arrogant, and abysmally ignorant of governance at local, provincial and national level.

Left unresolved was the hotly contested notion that there is a "national interest" which supersedes readers' interests, a position supported by all cabinet ministers and refuted by most editors. Many of us had suffered similar resentment at having "the national interest" thrust down our throats by successive apartheid regimes, which also, curiously, perceived us to be "unpatriotic". Comparing the two regimes is not productive, for the former was evil and the current one attempts to do good. This was another lesson editors had to learn: in the old days, newspapers represented the will of the people better than the white-elected government did. Now the government can rightfully claim to represent the will of the populace more legitimately than editors can. The difference is a profound one, as journalists have taken the better part of the decade to appreciate. As one apoplectic minister put it, simply but succinctly, "You were never elected to be editors, but we were chosen by the people!"

"Sun City" as it came to be called, had a profound effect. The South African National Editors' Forum (SANEF), under the leadership of Mathatha Tsedu, examined its reporters' skills and started to do something about them. Mbeki, who had brought his entire cabinet to Sun City for the two-day meeting, making some ministers fly back from Europe and central Africa, went away understanding that his frustrations were mirrored by editors who needed more communication, not less.

There are now repeated calls for a "Sun City Two", but the urgency has gone. Relationships between editors and government remain cordial but not too friendly, which is what they should be in a sound democracy.

STILL TOO MANY RESTRICTIONS

There are still many laws inhibiting the press. Idiotically, it is still not permissible to publish a picture of a bridge, for instance, because of an old apartheid law called the Key Points Act, which sought to keep secret vulnerable places which "the enemy" – the ANC – could attack. Perhaps in these times of world terror, such silly laws would find favour with the hawks of the Bush administration, but in South Africa they are mostly remnants of apartheid rather than a deliberate inroad into the freedom of the press.

Another change of note has been the shift from a narrow focus on South Africa's media interests only to those of Africa as a whole. A recent conference on Freedom of Speech drew participants from about forty African countries, and the South Africans who attended came to realise that they were not alone on the continent, had the fewest problems, and were indeed extraordinarily privileged.

And those words best describe the country's media. Extraordinarily privileged. To be part of the miracle, to be allowed to report it without fear or favour, to make money from doing so without any threat of being nationalised, to continue opening new newspapers, radio stations, television stations and, unlike in many other areas of the planet, to make good profits. We are privileged to be part of the excitement of this decade of celebration, to be able to look back on a job well done, to contribute to the forging of a new nation and to record its growing pains, its tribulations, its joys.

Parents know the delight of witnessing those first ten years of life. And parents also know – as do South Africa's journalists, editors, advertisers, educators and media executives – that they are extraordinarily privileged to be part of it.

Peter Sullivan
Group Editor-in-Chief, Independent Newspapers.

PHILANTHROPY IN SOUTH AFRICA: A FEEL-GOOD FACTOR OR A NET CONTRIBUTOR TO SOCIAL UPLIFTMENT?

How can I be happy when others are unhappy; how can I enjoy my wealth when others are poor?
— Eli Weisel, Holocaust survivor

BACKGROUND

Over the past twenty years, the story of South Africa has captivated the world. No nation has moved from pariah to admired status quite so dramatically; from economic isolation to economic integration quite so quickly; from global polecat to global favourite quite so emotionally. In many ways the story of philanthropy in South Africa is as dramatic. To understand this, we will review philanthropy in South Africa pre- and post-1994; examine new thinking and significant developments in the area of global philanthropy; and then discuss how philanthropy is currently contributing to transformation in South Africa.

Philanthropy can be described in a number of ways. In the purest sense, it is "giving without expectation of return". However, as elaborated upon later, there are limits to this approach which, in the context of corporate philanthropy, represents "old thinking". This chapter will review philanthropy in the strategic sense and, from here on, will use the modern term of corporate social investment (CSI), which is much more focused on determining where funding is going, how it is being used and what the expected returns are.

Historically, CSI in South Africa began in earnest during the 1980s. Even at that early stage the nature of giving had progressed beyond the fulfilment of basic welfare needs. The vibrant NGO and CBO[1]

---

[1] CBO stands for a Community-based Organisation – which along with NGOs (Non-Governmental Organisations) are sometimes referred to as NPOs (Not-for-Profit Organisations).

network that developed in those years addressed fundamental developmental needs within disadvantaged communities, such as schooling, job creation and the like. Organisations were frequently staffed by volunteers who, in the case of CBOs, tended to support their communities out of necessity rather than as true volunteers. As is the case today, a variety of NPOs scrambled for sought-after funds from individuals, churches, foreign donors and corporates.

The international donor market also went through dramatic shifts at that stage. Up to 1994, donors channelled their funding through NGOs, as a means of bypassing what was then perceived to be an illegitimate government. Relationships tended to exist between individual donors and selected NGOs. After 1994, many donors changed their stance and worked through government bodies. New CSI programmes were made available by foreign countries to our new government. The approach was to intervene in the short term, build capacity and introduce workable models, which could thereafter be sustained by newly developed government structures.

The gradual elevation of CSI as a necessary corporate activity and the concentration of donor funding had an effect on the "professionalism" of giving. Support shifted from what was considered to be pure philanthropy: the latter now came with certain obligations. It was expected that development would address the social shortfalls in the country, and that real developmental returns would be achieved. Giving by implication became more strategic, thereby shifting the environment from a "donation" mind-set to an "investment" approach. While the long-term benefits of such a shift were obvious, the more strategic approach was undoubtedly more complex, and inevitably mistakes were made. This is not to say that corporate giving – pure philanthropy – went into decline. On the contrary, efforts in this regard continued, and in some instances were substantially increased.

Long-term developmental gains are not easy to achieve, and often a lack of familiarity with the sector leads to misjudgements that derail what would otherwise be a credible effort. For instance, a donor might unilaterally decide on a facility that a community needs, and by failing to engage or consult the community end up having its support rejected; or, perhaps, provide only part of a solution by dumping used computers at a school without maintenance support or guidance on how to use them. The consequences of such errors lead to wasted resources, frustrated donors and disgruntled communities.

Setbacks experienced in the 1980s and early 1990s were mostly a consequence of too many independent donors supporting a fragmented developmental industry. The result was a lack of critical mass, too much spent on administration, insufficient monitoring of progress, poor measurement of outcomes, and an ongoing process of corrective action.

In summary, prior to 1994 the South African experience of global and local CSI was essentially one of investment through the NGO and CBO communities, as well as via a number of important initiatives such as the Urban Foundation and the African Children's Feeding Scheme. Government lacked legitimacy and was not much interested in delivery to the disenfranchised black, Indian and coloured communities. Despite sanctions, a number of local families and companies continued to give money to important causes, either through individual resolve or through the NGO sector. Government was largely disconnected from the process, as its policy was mostly to reach the poor via the apartheid-styled homeland governments. This differentiated South Africa from other countries whose governments were responsible for delivering social infrastructure, and significantly shaped thinking on CSI post-1994, when democracy made all South Africans equal for the first time.

Donor money now became strategically directed at enabling government structures to deliver on their responsibilities. The international donor community was first to recognise this, and moved quickly from "plugging a hole" through the NGO and CBO community to supporting capacity-building within government. The corporate donor community followed suit with a more strategic focus aimed at building capacity through public/private partnerships, while justifying its involvement to its various stakeholders.

Simultaneously, there were a number of circumstances in South Africa that impacted negatively on CSI. First, the new government inherited significant debt, which put pressure on the private sector to make up the shortfall in the provision of both physical and financial resources; second, the new government had to take account of 44 million people, as opposed to the previous government's focus on five million white people; and third, the tax base was too narrow, moving over ten years from two million people (paying R100 billion in 1994) to five million people (paying R284 billion in 2003). (At the same time, tax rates for both individuals and companies were reduced.) Fourth, while rapidly building capacity to deliver on roads, housing, water and electricity, government has had to struggle with the issues of job creation, poverty alleviation, ill-health and education.

The miracle of South Africa will only be sustainable if these challenges can be overcome.

GLOBAL THINKING

In an expansive article in the *Harvard Business Review*[2] of December 2002, Michael Porter and Mark Kramer examine the changing nature of corporate philanthropy. Much of what they say is reflected in the changes in thinking that have taken place in South Africa. More then ever before, corporations are feeling the pressure of being caught between critics who demand ever higher levels of corporate social responsibility and investors who apply relentless pressure in order to maximise short-term profits. These conflicting demands, combined with the new "triple bottom line" requirements of corporate governance, have necessitated a long, hard think about where and how to be philanthropic. Philanthropy has had to move from being an "art" to becoming a "science", from being emotionally heart-driven to becoming logically head-focused. Quite simply, organisations have had to become more strategic in their philanthropy; they had to align goodwill with commercial logic.

Some basic questions require answers: Should corporations engage in philanthropy at all? Should local and international corporations treat South Africa as a special case? And should corporations use their charitable efforts to improve their competitive positions as well as the quality of the business environment in which they operate? In recent years, a handful of companies have begun to use context-focused philanthropy for the purpose of achieving both social and economic gains. This is not to suggest that every corporate expenditure will bring a social benefit, or that every social benefit will improve competitiveness. However, there are conditions, such as a lack of government delivery, that can be crucial to competitiveness, and therefore assisting delivery through corporate philanthropy can bring enormous social gains to poorer nations, as well as significantly

---

[2] "Competitive advantage of Corporate Philanthropy", Michael E Porter and Mark R Kramer, *Havard Business Review* (2002).

improve regional economies. This will allow constituent firms to be more productive, make innovation easier, and foster the formation of new business opportunities. "Philanthropy can often be the most cost-effective way – and sometimes the only way – to improve competitive context," say Porter and Kramer. They then go on to list four ways in which companies can create social value, by:
- Selecting the best grantees
- Signalling to other funders
- Improving the performance of grant recipients
- Advancing knowledge and practice in the field.

"These efforts build on one another: increasingly greater value is generated as the donor moves up the ladder, from selecting the right grantees to advancing knowledge. The same principles apply to corporate-giving, pointing the way to how corporate philanthropy can be most effective in enhancing competitive context."

When corporations support the right causes in the right ways – when they get the "where" and the "how" right – they set in motion a virtuous cycle.

Porter and Kramer conclude, "To some corporate leaders, this new approach might seem to be self-serving. They might argue that philanthropy is purely a matter of conscience and should not be adulterated by business objectives; context-focused philanthropy does not just address a company's self-interest, it benefits many through broad social change. If a company's philanthropy only involved its own interests it would not qualify as a charitable deduction, and it might well threaten the company's reputation.

There is no inherent contradiction between improving competitive context and making a sincere commitment to bettering society. Indeed, as we have seen, the more closely a company's philanthropy is linked to its competitive context, the greater its contribution to society will be. If systematically pursued in a way that maximises the value created, context-focused philanthropy can offer companies a new set of competitive tools that justifies the investment of resources. At the same time, it can unlock a vastly more powerful way to make the world a better place."

South Africa is rising to the challenge set out by Porter and Kramer. We are not unique – but many of our social and economic infrastructure challenges mirror the relationship between the developed and the developing world. For this reason, South Africa is – for many people who are interested in international affairs – the most fascinating country in the world. It also provides evidence that CSI initiatives can be highly effective and will pay handsome dividends in the future.

THE CSI LANDSCAPE IN SOUTH AFRICA

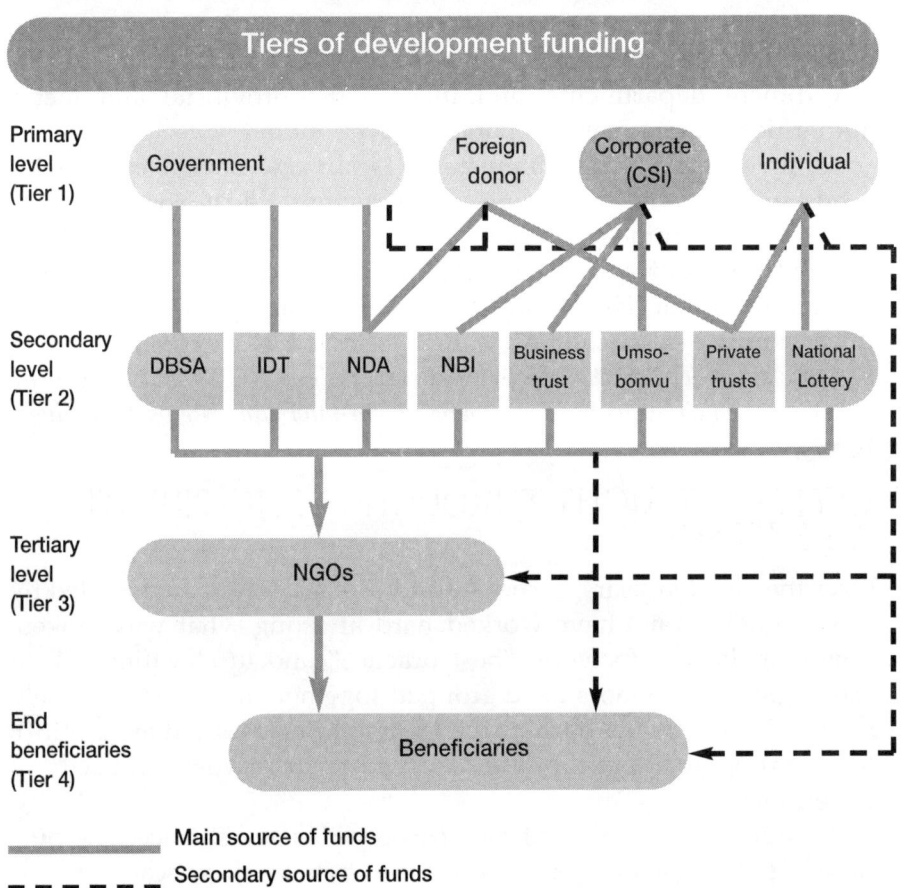

Source: *CSI Handbook*, 6th Edition (2003)

The diagram above illustrates how CSI has evolved in South Africa over the past ten years. There are now four clearly defined tiers that interconnect donors, delivery units and beneficiaries. As can be seen, the emphasis is now on fixing what used to be an indifferent and skewed system and enabling government to deliver. This is what makes the South African situation so different and for that matter so fascinating – its challenge of bringing government and the private sector together in order to build capacity.

To begin with, the new government, realising that there were significant expectations within the new electorate, initiated the Reconstruction and Development Programme (RDP), with a budget of R3.5 billion. Significantly, it was just as quick to realise that administering this programme centrally was impractical. Quite soon the money was brought back into the treasury and allocated to various government departments, and then to the provincial and metro authorities. In summary, at national level, money was set aside for social investment, to be administered locally and not mixed up with funds allocated to improving infrastructure. Most commentators agree that government's performance in this regard has been patchy: some of the monies have been misallocated and some have gone to communities that do not have the skills to manage the projects. Yet this is a universal phenomenon. *It is our view that governments cannot be expected to develop the requisite skills as well as NGOs and the private sector can, which opens the door, therefore, for public/private partnerships.*

GETTING IT RIGHT THROUGH PUBLIC/PRIVATE PARTNERSHIPS

Over the past ten years, corporate and foreign donors (mostly led by civic organisations) have worked hard at fixing what was broken. There has been a focus on "best practice" and in elevating CSI to "strategic CSI". Donors have grouped together, and worked closely with collective bodies such as the National Business Initiative (NBI), to take projects to appropriate scale and to improve the capacity of government.

Resources are scarce both in terms of skills and finance. The purpose of public/private partnerships is to harness these scarcities and to bring parties together in an optimal manner. This requires a national strategy, which will delineate the government's and private sector's roles and indicate where there are joint responsibilities. Former US president Bill Clinton emphasised the importance of this strategic approach at the World Economic Forum in 2004.

Corporate funders and large donor agencies have been through a steep learning curve in moving from a philanthropic stance to one that focuses on investment. While marginal gains (or even outright failures) are still evident, pockets of excellence have emerged and real progress has been achieved. Donors as well as leading NGOs have become experts in their chosen areas of intervention.

In the corporate sector, it is often easier to leverage the expertise that resides within the business. There are many good examples: MTN and MultiChoice have worked within their field of competence to support distance education; Standard Bank has made useful contributions in the field of adult financial literacy, as has Tiger Brands with its Unite Against Hunger campaign and the PG Glass Group with its Field Band campaign. The latter has trained young people to participate in bands modelled on the American-styled college band. As its organising chairman says, "There is no greater joy than to feel that you have helped someone better their life."

The formation of collective business partnerships has enabled projects to be scaled up to achieve nationwide impact. Such large collaborative efforts require accountability for funds spent and agreed measurable deliverables. An early example was the Joint Education Trust (JET) of the early 1990s which, after disbursing over R500 million to more than 400 NGOs, applied its expertise to developing management services in education. The Business Trust is another joint initiative, raising nearly R1 billion from the private sector, and applying these funds to a range of national projects in education, job creation and tourism.

Large public/private partnership-based interventions, driven by corporations and others and involving a mix of players, are starting to make a real impact. A leading example is the Mindset Network, which combines the resources of leading companies in order to deliver educational content directly to schools. The expertise of each contributing partner ensures a collective whole that is far greater than the sum of its parts. The project was initiated by the Liberty Foundation, which has since drawn in the support of Standard Bank and a raft of other companies that provide vital links in the chain. PanAmSat, for instance, provides access to a transponder, MultiChoice Africa the uplink facilities via its DSTV technology, and Sentech the wireless connectivity. In addition, the *Sunday Times* carries educational material in print supplements while the SABC offers electronic media coverage. In total, corporate support for this project is valued at R225 million.

Individual initiatives have also continued with similar enthusiasm, but with a more strategic focus. CIDA City Campus, started by Taddy Blecher, is a prime example. This corporate-supported and subsidised city university rose to prominence when Investec Bank made its old head office available. Other lead sponsors followed, with First National Bank providing additional facilities and bursaries for students, Dimension Data providing IT infrastructure, South Africa's top auditing firms providing lecturers and DaimlerChrysler providing vehicles for transport. The CIDA City Campus now educates 1800 business students from the most disadvantaged communities. Today, its pass rate reaches 75 per cent. The cost of tuition during the first year, including board and accommodation, is R380 per head. Students of high-calibre are already emerging from CIDA.

Starfish, begun by two young South Africans living in London, now supports 3000 AIDS orphans. By organising 10 000 fundraising "Dinners of Hope" among SA expatriates all over the world on Freedom Day (27 April), they have collected as much as $350,000 in donations. With this money, Star Centres were set up to care for orphans, in partnership with existing organisations. It is estimated that there are over 3000 such initiatives focusing on the AIDS-orphan crisis.

The list goes on. A further example is the establishment of TIKKUN ("Transformation") led by the Jewish community, who realised that, after 1994, they needed to look beyond their own people and work with disadvantaged black communities. Their work, in some instances, is now being done in conjunction with other faith-based groups in South Africa. With Nelson Mandela as its patron, TIKKUN is successfully serving previously disadvantaged communities by setting up a range of social investment schemes that are guided by a tight set of "ten commandments" and adhere to the principle of helping those who can and want to help themselves. For the "commandments" to be met, the following questions have to be answered satisfactorily:

1. Is this project what the chosen community needs?
2. Is the money allocated to those recipients that are in need of help?
3. Is the money being productively and usefully spent?
4. Are all the issues of governance and leadership consistent with best practice?
5. Is the organisation equipped with the skills to ensure that the funds are properly allocated?

6. Is the cost/admin ratio acceptable (set at 15 per cent)?
7. Are the accounts of the beneficiary properly kept and audited?
8. Is the donor advised on how the money is allocated?
9. Does the programme have sustainability and continuity into the future with adequate succession planning?
10. Can the project be independently and objectively verified as providing "best practice"?

An independent authority is called upon to decide whether these "commandments" are being met, and it is encouraging to note that TIKKUN's example is increasingly being followed by other CSI project co-ordinators. These rules of governance can be adopted by any structure – government, company or NGO – as part of its delivery mechanism. To further its programmes in South Africa, TIKKUN has opened offices in London, New York and Sydney to garner international support for its endeavours.

According to the *CSI Handbook*, published by Trialogue, the major areas of CSI focus are: Education, Job Creation, Health, HIV/AIDS, Training, Social Development, Arts and Culture, Community and Rural Development, the Environment, Sports Development, Safety and Security, and Housing.

As its editor Vanessa Rockey says, "Significant recent developments herald a new dawn for CSI in South Africa. The Broad-Based Black Economic Empowerment Bill currently being legislated, industry charters and transformation scorecards in the financial, mining, IT, petroleum and other industry sectors, and the recently launched JSE Socially Responsible Investment Index (SRI) all render CSI part of the broader transformation imperative in South Africa. In so doing, they elevate the importance of CSI to many a boardroom agenda. Such changes require companies and practitioners to respond with greater professionalism and better business alignment for their CSI programmes."

MEASURING RESULTS

Success does not only come from partnerships that scale up the level of intervention. There are many individual programmes that make a considerable difference in the lives of communities. The mining companies are a case in point, with individual mines investing substantial resources in communities that surround their areas of operation. Projects tend to be holistic, covering a range of essential services, such as education, housing, and healthcare.

There are also efforts to decrease dependence on mining by setting up job creation and entrepreneurship projects in order to offset the impact that any eventual closure of mines might have. These initiatives are not part of a mine's core business, yet the existence of a healthy and stable community is clearly desirable for business in general. This is one of many examples of a mutually beneficial arrangement, a critical factor when striving for sustainable development.

On a smaller scale, substantial progress has often been achieved off relatively small budgets. One such example is the Delta Foundation, which works on a replication model. CSI funds are used to set up a pilot project and thereafter to create a blueprint for development which documents the lessons learned and verifies workability. The documented approach is then "marketed" to other developmental agencies, companies and the government, thereby promoting replication and extending the influence of the programme. Thus far, the Delta Foundation has made significant advances in the field of housing development and education.

The true success of a project or programme lies not in the funds spent, but in the outputs achieved. Measures of output might be in the form of an improvement in student results, numbers graduating from an institution such as CIDA, or health statistics in a region where primary healthcare has been upgraded. It is important, if one is investing in development, to be able to calculate a return on one's investment: it is not sufficient to gauge one's impact by reporting on inputs alone. So, while it may be tempting to talk about the money spent, or people trained, it is far more useful to discuss achievements. Leaders in the developmental arena appreciate this, and go to great lengths to measure performance and determine actual impact.

When it comes to context-focused investment, it is increasingly being accepted that spending on development should achieve real results, and that funders should achieve a real benefit in return. The reality, however, is that it is often self-interest that justifies the continued investment.

For local donors, this may mean the stabilisation and upliftment of a community. For foreign donors, the intent may be quite different –

having a foothold in the developing world, stabilising a region, and maybe even improving international relations. Even church groups will seek some self-benefit, usually the opportunity of promoting the views of a particular religion.

Whatever self-interest is sought, successful interventions will make development the primary objective, and treat self-interest as a secondary priority. It is a case of finding the correct balance. Those who spend ten cents in the rand on community work and the rest on publicising their meagre effort run the risk of being exposed and losing credibility. On the other hand, those who do not promote their good work miss an important opportunity. The trend towards "enlightened self-interest" was underlined by Michael Spicer in a report on Anglo American's corporate social investment in South Africa, where he noted that the company had shifted from its previous position of "doing good by stealth". Making a significant contribution to development and balancing self-interest with social needs is becoming standard practice in South Africa.

HOW MUCH IS ENOUGH?

The debate over the right amount to give is never-ending. A church may suggest that its members pay a tenth of their earnings as a tithe, a part of which might be used for support of disadvantaged communities or individuals. Companies, on the other hand, might contribute a percentage of pre- or post-tax profit. The amount spent by foreign donors will vary according to international developments and priorities.

In a study of the non-profit sector[3] in 1998, it was estimated that the sector had an income of R14 billion, of which: 42 per cent or R5.8 billion came from government contributions; nearly R3 billion from the private sector; R4.6 billion from self-generated income; and a maximum of R1 billion from international funding. Another estimate of corporate contributions comes from the annually produced CSI Handbook, which estimated funding of R2.35 billion by companies for the year 2003.

---

[3] "The Size and Scope of the Non-profit Sector in South Africa", Swilling, S & Russell, B (2002).
[4] *The CSI Handbook*, 6th edition – Rockey, V (2003).

It was also suggested that the spending of leading listed corporations amounted to about one per cent of pre-tax profits. South Africa's newly introduced lottery is now making a significant contribution as well.

THE NATIONAL LOTTERY

In the year ended 31 March 2003, our National Lottery dispensed R170 million to 230 art, culture and national heritage foundations; R344 million to 1325 charities; and R211 million to 407 sports and recreation organisations. As the chairman J A Foster says in the fifth annual report, "One of the most identifiable brands in South Africa today is the National Lottery logo. Every effort is made to distribute funds to as many qualifying beneficiaries as possible, especially those in the poorer regions of our country." With an average number of 4.5 million players per week and 7429 terminals, the "Lotto" is a fine example of government's direct involvement in fundraising.

COPING WITH AFRO-PESSIMISM

One of the major challenges facing South African organisations is the climate of "Afro-pessimism" which hampers efforts to engage in social investment projects because of the mind-set that "Africa is a basket case." The question is often asked: So what makes South Africa different? Two local businessmen, overwhelmed by the desire to change these perceptions, have produced two books on the remarkable progress that has taken place in South Africa since 1994, entitled *South Africa – The Good News* and *South Africa – More Good News*. Six of South Africa's top ten companies have also rolled out "good news" programmes as part of their CSI initiatives.

Many significant personalities have contributed to the battle against Afro-pessimism.

- ◆ Former president Nelson Mandela has used his political stature to inspire the nation and improve its social consciousness. His Children's Fund has raised R250 million to assist with poverty relief and the alleviation of child abuse, so much part of the South African malaise.
- ◆ Bill Clinton has used his political stature to raise money for AIDS by inviting pharmaceutical companies to contribute.

- Bill Gates has raised millions of dollars to combat malaria.
- Peggy Delaney, a daughter of the famous Rockefeller family and chair of the Synergos Institute, has spearheaded major initiatives to alleviate poverty and bring hope to Africa.

CONCLUSION

There can be no doubt that the establishment of public/private partnerships, with defined roles for both parties, is vital to the future of South Africa. If the scarce resources of skills and money are to be harnessed – while accepting that the prime responsibility for looking after the poor will *always* be the government's – then a dispensation is required in which government will work with the private sector where there are difficulties in fulfilling a need. New pressures are emerging: improved corporate governance, industry charters and the call for racial transformation of the economy.

Increasingly in South Africa, and globally, there is a new breed of employees who want to work for organisations that enable them to make their skills available to communities in need, as "volunteers". In addition, there is growing agreement that social investment activities now need to be performed by specialists who understand the complexity of context-focused social investment and marry such investment with the organisation's brand.

Corporations in South Africa are now integrating their CSI programmes with their sustainability and transformational goals, in many cases treating CSI as a pillar of their operations. Considerable time is spent on reporting on CSI matters to the investor community. Business is engaged in ongoing discussions at the top level, influencing policy and working in partnership with government on CSI projects. Government is acutely aware of the need to do the right thing in terms of governance and sustainability. There is an implicit and growing understanding that government and the private sector have to work towards the same goal of socioeconomic upliftment and sustainable development.

Nevertheless, the challenges facing South Africa remain daunting: 29 per cent unemployment; 20 per cent of our communities living in abject poverty; 12.5 per cent of the population HIV positive; low skills levels and inadequate educational facilities all mean that there is considerable work to do. Yet South Africa is fulfilling the requirements set out by Porter and Kramer: our thinking is strategic; our structures are aligned; our transparency and accountability compares with the best in the world, and our resolve to help this wonderful land back onto its feet is unparalleled. In corporate social investment, as in many other fields, South Africa could become a role model for Africa and many other parts of the world.

> *The shame of poverty is not with those who live in poverty, it is with us who allow it to exist.*
> – Eli Weisel

Dr Bertie Lubner
O.M.S.S., Director, Plate Glass Holding, South Africa

References
South Africa – More Good News, published and edited by Brett Bowes and Steuart Pennington (2003).
The CSI Handbook, 6th edition, published by Trialogue (2003).

My sincere thanks to Steuart Pennington and Nick Rockey who gave of their time considerably to assist me in the writing and editing of this chapter.

RECOVERING THE SOUL OF THE SOUTH AFRICAN NATION

In the course of an address in February 1998,[1] the then Deputy President Thabo Mbeki, referring to the stories told at the Truth and Reconciliation Commission, and inspired by W B Yeats' "Sailing to Byzantium", remarked:

"The political order that tore our country apart is now no more. Yet it gave us a bitter heritage, which we must strive to overcome.

"Above all else we must create the situation in which the soul can sing and louder sing to restore a social morality which says the pursuit of material gain at all costs is not and cannot be what distinguishes us as South Africans; [we must create] a patriotism which is imbued by love and respect for the fellow citizen, regardless of race, colour, gender or age, and a recognition of our common humanity . . ."

To understand the vision of a "soul [which] can sing and louder sing to restore a social morality", and to grasp its related challenges, it is necessary to take stock of the past decade of democracy, before considering the future.

DEALING WITH THE PAST: THE CONSTITUTION

One of the fascinating, if not miraculous, features of South Africa's transition to democracy is the way in which South Africans have dealt with their past, setting their faces against vengeance and retribution. This feature found expression in the Postscript of the South African Interim Constitution (Act No 200 of 1993) which committed South Africans to the promotion of a "secure foundation for the people of

---

[1] Thabo Mbeki: *Africa: The Time Has Come, Selected Speeches*. Cape Town. Tafelberg/Mafube 1998, p. 259.

South Africa to transcend the divisions and strife of the past, which generated gross violations of human rights, the transgression of humanitarian principles in violent conflicts and the legacy of hatred, fear, guilt and revenge. These can now be addressed on the basis that there is a need for understanding, not vengeance, a need for reparation, not for retaliation, a need for ubuntu, not victimisation".

"Understanding", "reparation" and "ubuntu" were the outcome of a carefully developed consensus – and eventual commitment – over many months of dialogue, which began prior to the unbanning of the ANC and other political parties, as well as the release of Nelson Mandela. This consensus has its roots in 1987, driven by a common and deeply shared love for South Africa and an intuitively accepted common humanity and destiny.

This commitment was embodied in the final constitution of 1996, whose Preamble now stated:

"We, the people of South Africa,
Recognise the injustices of our past;
Honour those who suffered for justice and freedom in our land . . .
We therefore, through our freely elected representatives, adopt this Constitution as the supreme law of the Republic so as to –
Heal the divisions of the past and establish a society based on democratic values, social justice and fundamental human rights;
Lay the foundations for a democratic and open society in which government is based on the will of the people and every citizen is equally protected by law . . ."

There are a number of reasons for this strong constitutional stance. A powerful reason was the nature of apartheid – a system inherently immoral in its core values, giving rise to the violation of fundamental human rights. Apartheid left its marks on three dimensions of the South African political system: its value system, structure and political culture. Its wide-ranging legacy extended well beyond the political domain and into, for instance, the economic order.

Apartheid could not simply be done away with by abolition or by getting rid of its masters and replacing them with others. It could only be abolished by transforming the structure, culture and values it had produced in such a way that a new dispensation with a new structure, culture and values could come into being.

South Africa, as will be argued, is still busy with this process – a process that could be termed, from an ethical point of view, an exercise in restorative justice and reconciliation.

RESTORATIVE JUSTICE AND RECONCILIATION

How to deal with the past in order to recover the soul of the South African nation, was a moral and strategic question of historic magnitude. We are only now beginning to fully understand the values which underpinned and inspired the response.

South Africa opted for what is commonly called restorative justice – explained by Tony Marshall as a "process whereby all parties with a stake in a particular offence come together to resolve collectively how to deal with the aftermath of the offence and its implications for the future"[2]. Restorative justice is a deliberate moral and strategic choice – or, as the Postscript of the Interim Constitution declared: a choice "to transcend the divisions and strife of the past" and to make things right between those who have been locked into an adversarial relationship.

The Truth and Reconciliation Commission was instrumental in this process, giving flesh and blood to confessions of "gross violations of human rights", to acknowledging responsibility, making some form of reparation and fostering reconciliation.

South Africa's commitment to restorative instead of retributive justice or forms of revenge is best explained by the moving testimony of Cynthia Nomveyu Ngewu before the TRC. Her son, Christopher Piet, was one of the Guguletu Seven shot by the police in March 1986. To those seeking revenge or retribution, she replied: "I do not agree with this view. We do not want to see people suffer in the same way that we did suffer, and we did not want our families to have suffered. We do not want to return the suffering that was imposed upon us . . . We would like to see peace in this country . . . We do not want to return the evil that perpetrators committed to the nation. We want to demonstrate humaneness towards them, so that they in turn may restore their own humanity."[47]

---

[2] Jennifer J Llwellyn and Robert Howse: "Restorative Justice – A Conceptual Framework". Unpublished manuscript. Referred to in *Looking back. Reaching forward.* Eds. Charles Villa-Vicencio & Wilhelm Verwoerd. UCT Press, Cape Town, 2000, p. 69.

[3] TRC Report, Vol 5, p. 366.

The spirit of our Constitution's Preamble, and the values imbedded in our democracy's founding document, is given flesh and blood by this statement which reflects the hopes, dreams and commitment of the vast majority of South Africans who have made a choice in favour of understanding, reparation and ubuntu.

This choice is expressed by a word that is the ethical kernel of the process of democratisation and the values inspiring our new democracy: reconciliation. Yet, given its common usage, reconciliation has become potentially bewitching and misleading. (See Ludwig Wittgenstein's analysis of the implicit dangers in language and metaphors: becoming stale gatekeepers to the world of created meanings while ensnaring the users thereof in dogmatic and one-sided interpretations.)

Reconciliation is essentially "a call to action", as Nelson Mandela – the father of South African reconciliation – so aptly stated in Parliament on 25 February 1999, in speaking about the TRC Report. Reconciliation is not a once-off event; a moment of remorse; a minute or two reserved for saying sorry. It's a process – the restoration of destroyed trust; the development of a new relationship of trust; the establishment of visible "deeds of trust"; the removal of conditions undermining relationships of trust, whether of a personal, socioeconomic, political or structural nature.

One of the great achievements of South Africa's young democracy is that the emphasis on restorative justice and reconciliation has been inspired by an overriding ideal: the development of one, unified nation. Put differently: it is to make all citizens aware of their obligations towards each other and towards their country. South Africans have quickly understood that the building of a democratic state requires the development of a responsible, independent and vibrant civil society.

The imperative of "dealing with the past differently" (Charles Villa-Vicencio) through restorative justice and reconciliation helps one to understand another core concept of the moral and strategic fabric of the new dispensation: transformation.

TRANSFORMATION

The word "change" generally functions as an umbrella for two distinct processes, each triggered by human intervention. These processes differ in terms of their objectives and their outcomes. These interventions may be divided into conforming strategies (or strategies for order and continuity), and transforming strategies (or strategies for discontinuity and reconstruction). The processes they entail can be referred to as "first-order" and "second-order" change.

In the case of the former, the system itself – its structure, culture and defining values – does not change. Change within a system is referred to as "adaptation", "renovation", "adjustment", "incremental change" or "piecemeal engineering". The objective is to change behaviour within a prevailing system without affecting its culture, structure and defining values.

Second-order change is of a "form- or frame-breaking"[4] nature. Its primary objective is not to intervene in the operations of an institution, but to transform its structure, culture, defining values and overall form. It goes hand in hand with what is commonly called a paradigm shift or mind-set change. Paradigms reflect our prejudices, our values, our beliefs, our social conditioning, and our way of thinking and looking at the world. Accepting a new paradigm requires a period of transition. It is "seldom completed by a single man and never overnight" (Thomas Kuhn).

In South Africa the need for transformation is linked to environment-specific considerations, the most important of which are moral and strategic.

The moral perspective should be obvious: the necessity of transforming a racially based organisational and economic pattern, a legacy of the past, into a commonly shared, open and nonracial, non-sexist pattern. The main objective of structural change inspired by a moral perspective is to establish legitimacy and moral acceptability. Without legitimacy, no institution can survive.

This is no easy task, given that discriminatory patterns and practices in South Africa are not of a mere coincidental nature but stem from structural conditions. These conditions have created vested interests as well as "entrenched" mind-sets or paradigms on both sides of the racial divide.

One of the issues on the agenda is equitable access to scarce resources, opportunities and skills. Another important issue is the need to establish cross-cultural and cross-racial economic alliances in order to stabilise the country politically and socially. At present,

---

[4] Bake, P: *Strategies for Cultural Change*. London. Butterworth/Heinemann, 1980, p. 16.

affirmative action and black economic empowerment are the procedures used to address these issues, but they do not constitute the full scope of transformational or structural change that is required. In the South African context, in particular, they represent specific aspects of transformation, albeit important moral and political aspects. Transformation entails much more than affirmative action or black economic empowerment, however.

This becomes clear when one analyses the strategic perspective of transformation within the South African context, with its socioeconomic inequalities and extreme levels of poverty. Democratising South Africa and setting up viable structures embodying the vision of a nonracial and non-sexist democracy are laudable strategic objectives, but should be underpinned by strategies aimed at alleviating the plight of the poor, effectively addressing socioeconomic inequalities and establishing a thriving economic environment. In a strategic nutshell: a stable and viable democracy in South Africa is dependent on vigorous (people) development and economic growth. To this end the structural transformation of South Africa is imperative

Much progress has been made in this direction. The policy document on "Growth, Employment and Redistribution" (GEAR), combining economic growth and reconstruction and development strategies, was a major achievement. The outcome of these strategies will have a decisive impact on South Africa's future political and social stability.

The important point here is that the concept "transformation", strategically applied to the South African context, does not refer to the domain of politics only. It would be strategically unwise for the transformation of South Africa to be viewed solely from a restrictive political rather than a holistic perspective.

In this regard, it should also be emphasised that transformation includes much more than the establishment of legitimacy for institutions and organisations. Transformative interventions also have to enhance performance, productivity, efficiency and competitiveness. Transformation is about an improved order of things.

Looking back on the past ten years, and taking stock of how we have fared in recovering the soul of the South African nation, we have reason to be very thankful. However, the most challenging part of our journey on the road to transformation, particularly the building of a workable moral consensus, will be reconciling the expectations of the historically disadvantaged with the vested interests (and rights!) of the historically privileged class. Much has been achieved, but real transformation remains a daunting task.

THE VALUE OF THE TRC PROCESS AND REPORT

On many occasions the hearing of personal accounts of suffering, and the understanding of these accounts as instances of suffering and systemic injustice, triggered moments of truth on the part of listeners. It is during these moments that human beings are motivated to genuinely utter the phrase "it was wrong", and to begin to understand what justice requires from the evil-doings of the past.

An example will illustrate the point. After having acquainted himself with some of the stories told before the TRC, a conservative Afrikaner phoned me and, in a voice conveying his anguish, uttered one sentence only: "Ek skaam my tot in my boude" (I am deeply ashamed of myself). Over the past few years, many Afrikaners have expressed similar feelings in private conversations, and even in the letters pages of Afrikaans newspapers. A number have commented on the powerful impact of Antjie Krog's book on the TRC, *Country of My Skull*. Her extensive use of testimonies from TRC victim hearings and her honest existential struggle, as an Afrikaner, to respond to the many, many victims who testified about violations at the hands of Afrikaners in the security police have moved many people deeply. These responses illustrate the converting potential of the TRC process.

But converting values is of no use without legitimising new values – without positive notions of justice that create new commitments and motivate us to constructively rise above the legacy of the past. Only new and better values can legitimise the process of transformation.

Our constitution is imbued with legitimising values such as "democracy", "nonracial" and "non-sexist". Our constitutionally entrenched Bill of Rights legitimises the values and the conception of justice that underpins the processes of transition and transformation.

But how to get those who profited from the past to realise that an *awareness* of the injustice is but one side of the coin; that the other side demands deliberate *intervention* in order to transform South African society? This is one of the most serious ethical, political and strategic challenges facing our country. What is needed is a national consensus on, and commitment to, a set of legitimising values that will underpin the process of transformation.

Moreover, it needs to be emphasised that transformation will remain an idealistic dream without decisive, visionary and value-driven leadership. Any discussion of transformation without a discussion of leadership – and what transformational leadership entails – is empty. If transformation, for strategic and moral reasons, is South Africa's bridge to the future, it unfortunately also has to be said that too little attention is being devoted to the question of the kind of leadership that is needed to effect the required change.

Accordingly, the debate about apartheid and about transformation will not be over very soon. Yet there can be no enduring reconciliation in this country without the transformation of that which apartheid left in its wake. Indeed the values now entrenched in the constitution of the country – the development of a nonracial, non-sexist democracy on the basis of reconciled relationships – are not possible without such far-reaching transformation.

That is why reconciliation within a country like South Africa is not based simply on confession of guilt and the asking of forgiveness. Acts such as these, painful as they may be for some, are but the first steps on the road to reconciliation.

Reconciliation that can lead to a culture of trust and freedom also requires that structural and other reparations and adjustments take place. Put differently, reconciliation must become flesh and blood through concrete deeds, through the making of sacrifices, through transformation. Reconciliation can therefore never come cheaply; it is a costly process that was bought with blood.

Reconciliation necessarily has as its converse side the fundamental changing of relationships as well as of conditions within which distorted relationships previously existed. Apartheid was, after all, not just an article of faith or an attitude of people. It was a structure, supported by a value system and culture. It was not just something in the heads and hearts of people. It was also a practice that impaired people's humanity and dignity and led to appalling forms of inequality.

Does this mean that the past ten years has not produced a viable and growing moral consensus, a consensus which should energise the recovery of the soul of South Africa?

A NEW MORAL CONSENSUS IS GROWING

South Africa's transformation into a fully-fledged democracy is still in progress. However, it is possible to identify at least two distinct dimensions of the process thus far: political democratisation and the transformation of the state; and the restructuring and transformation of the economy and its integration into a globalising world.

Political democratisation in South Africa since the first democratic elections in 1994 has resulted in a deepening and broadening of democracy over the last ten years, as well as the entrenchment of a number of fundamental rights and values.

Transforming the economy, and integrating it into a globalising world, proved to be a more complex process – a delicate balancing act between the imperatives of the core values of liberty, on the one hand, and equality on the other. The tension between these two values – the former inspiring liberal democratic views and the latter social democratic views – runs deeply through our society.

Despite this tension a convergence of opinion has taken place on what the core values of our democratised society are. The deepening and broadening of this convergence will determine the future strength, stability, vibrancy and sustainability of that society.

Davidson and Rees-Mogg, in their book *The Sovereign Individual*, make a point worth noting: "The most successful periods in the history of societies tend to be those in which the collective morality is shared. Such morality not only performs specific functions such as reducing crime, and helping to support family and social structure, but gives citizens a sense of purpose and direction".[5]

They present an extreme position: "All strong societies have a strong moral basis. Any study of the history of economic development shows the close relationship between moral and economic factors. Countries and groups that achieve successful development do so partly because they have an ethic that encourages the economic virtues of self-reliance, hard work, family and social responsibility, high savings, and honesty".[50]

Davidson and Rees-Mogg go too far in their emphasis on the role

---

[5] J D Davidson and W Rees-Mogg: *The Sovereign Individual*. New York, Simon & Schuster, 1997, p. 359.
[6] Op. cit., p. 351.

of the individual. Their reference to key phrases such as "shared collective morality" and "consensus on morality" is however critical to the question of the recovery of the soul of the South African nation, or, to put it differently, to the sustainability of our democracy.

Despite the legacy of the past, and despite the diversity of the South African nation, an "essential" moral consensus – i.e. agreement on and acceptance of basic core values – has emerged.

In democracies such as ours, the Constitution plays a decisive role in entrenching, institutionalising and internalising such an "essential" moral consensus. In our case the main pillars of this consensus were negotiated and not decreed. These pillars are "nonracialism", "non-sexism" and "human rights" – with the latter a remarkable epitome of a "shared collective morality". Institutions such as the Constitutional Court and the Human Rights Commission have been set up to protect and put into practice this shared collective morality

Have we succeeded in restoring the soul of the South African nation with these and other initiatives? Developing and implementing an "essential" moral consensus is an enduring task, a never-ending innovative and creative process – not a final or static product. If our Constitution could be regarded as the inspiring script, and South African citizens the players, we have succeeded remarkably well in turning the script into an entertaining play called "The New South Africa". Enacting the script is energy-sapping; the theatre is not always well managed and well equipped; some players lack skills and devotion – or prefer participating in sideshows; others don't want to be participants at all. And too many play their own destructive games.

However, those taking part in the drama have made progress. Moreover, they are growing in numbers, because they know that the play they are in is for real.

Willie Esterhuyse
Professor of Business Ethics,
University of Stellenbosch Business School, Bellville

NEW PARTNERSHIP FOR AFRICA'S DEVELOPMENT (NEPAD)

Africa is generally perceived as being underdeveloped, politically unstable and economically volatile – and plagued by ubiquitous poverty. In reality, the continent possesses a massive pool of untapped potential, both for its own development and for the political, economic and cultural development of the global community.

With regard to their own development, African people have to define their own needs and formulate solutions rooted in their own experiences, in partnership with the rest of the world. Important lessons from the past indicate that peace and security, democracy, sound economic management and good corporate governance are prerequisites for sustainable growth and development. With this in mind, NEPAD was conceptualised by visionary African leaders as the route to sustainable development and high economic growth. NEPAD is a vision that inspires and energises the African people to take charge of their own destiny.

The NEPAD vision proclaims that the time has come for African people to take control of their destiny and to take responsibility for freeing themselves from poverty and underdevelopment. The time has come, too, for Africa to assume its rightful and equitable place in the global political economy. The overarching objective of NEPAD is to accelerate poverty eradication and to place African countries, both collectively and individually, on a sustainable path of high economic growth and development, thereby overcoming Africa's continued marginalisation from the global economy.

The alleviation of poverty can be achieved by:
- growth, through improving infrastructure to enable markets to develop;
- job creation, through both internal and external investment;
- competitiveness, through the harmonisation of legal systems and law; and

◆ good governance, through the adoption of sound corporate governance principles (as set out, for instance, in the 2002 King Report on Corporate Governance for South Africa).

From the business viewpoint, some of the principles underpinning NEPAD include good governance, African ownership and leadership, anchoring development on the resources and resourcefulness of Africans, partnerships among African people, the acceleration of regional and continental integration, competitiveness within African countries and the continent as a whole, and partnerships with the industrialised world.

African leaders have recognised that the challenge for African countries is not to obstruct the process of globalisation and liberalisation, but to participate and shape the process to reflect Africa's priorities. NEPAD has enabled these leaders to take responsibility for their own economic development through a commitment to peace, security and good governance, the development of key physical and social infrastructures, the building of institutional capacity and human capital and the implementation of effective strategies for sustainable development. NEPAD aims to address the backlog of poor infrastructure, promote the acceptance of cultural diversity and encourage regional co-operation. It also seeks to identify Africa's comparative advantages and position these as the continent's competitive edge.

NEPAD also calls for support from governments of the developed market economies. To date, the response has been encouraging, especially since many Organisation for Economic Co-operation and Development (OECD) states have committed to providing improved access to their markets, enhancing debt relief and strengthening flows of development assistance and direct investment. If NEPAD's goals are realised, the result will be Africa's effective integration into the global economy and great improvements in the welfare of its people.

NEPAD heralds the new beginning of an emerging partnership among civil society, business and transformed states throughout Africa. These evolving partnerships have no choice but to work if they are to end the pervasive mood of Afro-pessimism. Africa offers much to the world and humanity is obliged to respond to the challenge, as currently defined. NEPAD is about developing the continent as a united economic and trading bloc, thereby increasing its competitiveness. To do so, however, Africa must first put its own house in order, with all countries working together towards common goals and objectives.

The African Peer Review Mechanism will further consolidate the adoption and implementation of comprehensive development plans, encompassing all NEPAD's principles and priority programmes.

COMMITMENT TO NEPAD

African leaders have been engaging business leaders and other civil society institutions in discussions on NEPAD's vision and programme of action. This led to the World Economic Forum (WEF), together with the South African government, organising an Africa Economic Summit in Durban in June 2002 to examine the role of business (the private sector) in NEPAD. In a landmark development, some 150 multinational and national companies doing business in Africa signed the Business Endorsement of NEPAD following the summit, in response to a proposal by the Presidency and the NEPAD Secretariat that business should become a partner in NEPAD. From the outset, the three pillars of support were government – through the department of Trade and Industry in South Africa, the NEPAD Secretariat under Professor Wiseman Nkhuhlu, and business, then as now represented by the NEPAD Business Group. These three partners meet regularly to discuss how best to execute NEPAD's programmes.

The business signatories took the view that NEPAD would be successful only if the partnership between African and OECD governments were extended to include business as well. Although business regarded NEPAD as being ambitious, it also recognised that there was no other option for dealing with the magnitude and severity of the problems of Africa. Since leadership, vision, ambition and courage were required to uplift Africa, it was agreed that the role of the private sector was vital and that business had a responsibility to contribute as effectively as possible.

Companies and service organisations based or doing business in Africa committed specifically to:
- the development of best practice standards of corporate governance throughout Africa, buttressed by proper accounting and audit procedures and the elimination of corrupt practices;

- continuing improvement of the quality and effectiveness of corporate social responsibility programmes and continued transfer to national economies of appropriate skills and technology to help build human capital and productivity; and
- support for African governments in their efforts to achieve best practice standards of economic governance by sharing experiences and seconding skills where appropriate; by enhancing national accounting, corporate law and financial market operations; and by harmonising listing requirements, investment codes and other processes and procedures where the knowledge and skills of private-sector institutions are relevant.

FORMATION OF THE NEPAD BUSINESS GROUP

The NEPAD Business Group was formed to develop effective ways of honouring the commitments made in Durban, to forge a closer working relationship with government and the NEPAD Secretariat and to play a meaningful role in realising NEPAD goals. Member firms and institutions – including the King Commission on Corporate Governance, the JSE Securities Exchange, the South African Chamber of Business, the Industrial Development Corporation and leading accounting and auditing firms (including Deloitte & Touche, Ernst & Young and PricewaterhouseCoopers) – contributed their time and expertise to developing four documents aimed at making the commitments of the signatories more tangible. The four documents, which all have as their objective making Africa more conducive to investment, are:

- the Business Covenant on Corporate Governance;
- the Business Declaration on Corporate Responsibility;
- the Business Covenant on the Elimination of Corruption and Bribery; and
- the Business Declaration on Accounting and Audit Practices.

These documents commit business to the development of best practice standards of corporate governance throughout Africa, to the improvement of corporate social-responsibility programmes, to the assistance of governments in various fields and to the development of a partnership with the NEPAD Secretariat. These covenants and declarations were compiled under the supervision of the NEPAD

Business Group committee, comprising Danisa Baloyi, Colin Beggs, Seshi Chonco, Seán Cleary, Mzolisi Diliza, Peggy Drodskie, Nolitha Fakude, Reuel Khoza, Bruce Koloane, Chris Liebenberg, Russell Loubser, Wendy Luhabe, Patrice Motsepe, David Moshapalo, Andrew Mthembu, Futhi Mtoba, Vassi Naidoo, Clive Smith, Michael Spicer and Leon Vermaak.

The NEPAD Business Group in South Africa also acts as an intermediary between NEPAD, governments and business, and aims to assist both governments and the private sector to take advantage of NEPAD-related opportunities, identify bottlenecks and engage with various role-players. It is committed to the improvement of standards of corporate governance, the enhancement of corporate social responsibility and co-operation with African governments to achieve best-practice standards of economic governance. It is also committed to working with the NEPAD Secretariat and governments to develop effective public-private partnerships, which can be replicated in other African countries. The Business Group has benefited from the active interest of the NEPAD Secretariat, the WEF and WEF-initiated NEPAD Business Groups established in several other African countries. The Business Group's Secretariat in South Africa is run on a voluntary basis by the JSE Securities Exchange and currently comprises Sydney Maree, Geoff Rothschild and Rentia Vendeiro.

PERCEPTIONS OF NEPAD

Prior to the commitment it made in Durban in 2002, business was sceptical about NEPAD, as evidenced in a study conducted by A T Kearney shortly after the launch of the NEPAD Business Group. However, a study commissioned by the WEF Forum prior to the 2003 Africa Economic Summit in Durban revealed a fundamental change in corporate perceptions of and attitudes towards NEPAD. Not only were a large majority of South African corporations aware of NEPAD, they were also favourably disposed towards it.

To investigate more deeply, a survey was commissioned by the NEPAD Business Group in 2003 to measure the attitude of South African business leaders towards NEPAD and to determine the issues of concern to business leaders when conducting business in Africa. The survey was sponsored by Eskom and ABSA and conducted by Bateleur Research Solutions. It identified common frustrations, challenges and attractions that South African companies faced in their involvement in various projects in Africa, particularly in Angola, Botswana, Ghana, Kenya, Mozambique, Namibia, Nigeria, Swaziland, Tanzania, Uganda, Zambia and Zimbabwe.

While almost all respondents indicated that doing business in Africa was not easy, they acknowledged that the potential for good returns outweighed the difficulties of doing business on a continent in transition.

The common frustrations of South African companies operating in the countries mentioned above included a lack of, or poor, infrastructure (particularly in telecommunications and transport); corruption (at both government and private-business levels); high costs (of start-ups, including skills training); high travel costs and irregular flights; difficulty in obtaining visas and expatriate quotas; high corporate taxes; currency fluctuations; language and cultural barriers; government or party-political interference in decision-making; and inconsistent or limited sector-specific policy-making.

The common magnets for South African companies included the growth potential of the countries mentioned above; their large size; their political and economic stability; the emergence of democracy; Afro-optimism; their willingness to embrace new business approaches, and to conduct business with SA companies; their openness to foreign direct investment; and the fact that many global and multinational corporations were already operating there.

Three clear messages came out of the Bateleur survey:

i. the NEPAD Business Initiative needed to change the perceptions of business leaders that it was politically oriented.
ii. the NEPAD Business Initiative needed to include other countries and regions to avoid creating the perception that it is South African-dominated. Business leaders from across Africa have to be involved for the initiative to be successful. The incorporation of other African countries would further enhance the creation and maintenance of stable economies in Africa and encourage African leaders to rise to the challenge of creating economic wealth.
iii. the NEPAD Business Initiative had the potential to unlock the development opportunities that exist in Africa. NEPAD could make this happen by creating actionable agendas that would identify and prioritise NEPAD projects.

DOING THE GROUNDWORK

NEPAD focuses on the establishment of a new partnership between north and south to end the old relationship of dominant northern donors and subservient southern recipients of charity. While the partnership between business and political leadership is pivotal, the NEPAD Business Group also recognises the need for forging partnerships with developed economies. For NEPAD to succeed, it must enjoy the support of developed countries, specifically the Group of Eight (G8). The G8 countries realise that the fight against poverty is in the enlightened self-interest of the economically developed countries. Wealthier countries have to help poorer countries not only to build capacity but also – by opening up their own markets – to trade. Debt relief is imperative for the financial stability of highly indebted countries, as funds spent on debt-servicing could be diverted to infrastructure and poverty alleviation programmes. However, the G8 has to focus on its own responsibilities, particularly the fact that its current policies create and sustain an unequal relationship, which frustrates many African efforts to secure peace, development and democracy.

The NEPAD Business Group has had several sessions with various G8 ambassadors and commercial attachés to identify OECD governments' expectations of NEPAD where corporate business is concerned, and to take account of these in the Business Group's programme of action.

After the delivery of the G8 action plan on Africa in Kananaskis, Canada, African leaders were invited to the June 2003 G8 Summit in Evian, France, to discuss the future of NEPAD. Although matters such as debt relief, farm subsidies maintained by Western countries, access to medicines, water shortage, sanitation and HIV/AIDS were on the agenda, these were hardly discussed. It was agreed, however, that the creation of conditions to attract private-sector capital to African countries should be accelerated. The G8 leaders undertook to encourage their private sectors to invest in Africa to promote recovery, economic growth and sustainable development. African and G8 leaders looked into the future and concluded that NEPAD was a long-term agenda that needed sustained effort to achieve its laudable goals. It was agreed that the current structured engagement and dialogue between G8 Africa Personal Representatives and the NEPAD Steering Committee should continue.

The NEPAD Business Group also ensured that its programme of action was recognised and accepted by the Johannesburg World Summit on Sustainable Development (WSSD) through:
- actively participating via the Business Action for Sustainable Development (BASD), the business arm of the WSSD;
- co-hosting the WSSD via the Business Consultative Forum (a partner of the Johannesburg World Summit Company); and
- ensuring incorporation of the NEPAD Business Group's programme in the WSSD set of resolutions.

This materialised as a result of the indefatigable efforts and patronage of Bertie Lubner, several preparatory sessions with the South African Department of Trade and Industry and by the full support of the WEF leadership.

NEPAD BUSINESS GROUP'S ACTION PLAN

Africa's leaders understand that the continent can benefit tremendously from the experience of some countries in the south, especially since the latter share similar historical experiences, face the same challenges in terms of poverty and underdevelopment and encounter similar obstacles to accessing the benefits of globalisation. Some southern countries have found solutions to many of these challenges, mastered information and communications technology (ICT) and overcome many difficulties in the fields of energy, transport, water and sanitation.

The NEPAD Business Group's action plan identifies sectoral priorities as a means of promoting economic and social development. Sixteen sectors have already been identified: they include energy, water, ICT, infrastructure, transport, accounting and auditing, banking and finance, mining and resources, agriculture, stock exchanges and the environment. Efforts to foster capital-market development and improve accounting and audit practices are also under way. Work has commenced on the energy, water and ICT sectors, to be followed by infrastructure and transport. The accounting and auditing profession and the JSE Securities Exchange have already presented action plans to advance the goals of NEPAD.

The NEPAD Business Group is very active in the development of key aspects of the NEPAD programme, and in identifying investment opportunities and regional infrastructure projects across the continent. A case in point is the optic-fibre submarine cable that connects a number of west African countries to Europe and Asia, launched in May 2003. Planning has started on extending the submarine cable along the east coast from South Africa to Djibouti. The setting up of the e-Africa Commission to drive the implementation of the NEPAD ICT initiative, designed to bridge the digital divide, is another example. Electricity-transmission projects have been identified across the continent and the African Energy Fund set up to operationalise these projects, with the eventual aim of establishing a continental power grid. The identification of regional spatial-development initiatives is on the increase, particularly in southern Africa. The aim of these initiatives is to promote investment in regions that are underdeveloped but have the potential for growth.

A further priority will be the establishment and funding of a NEPAD Business Group office. To date, the work of the Business Group has been done on a voluntary basis. It is now intended to open an office, funded by the business community. The clear lessons to be learned from the work of the South African Business Trust will be heeded and put to good use for the benefit of the continent. The NEPAD Business Group is aware, too, of the activities of the Commonwealth Business Council and the Africa Business Roundtable. As progress is made, the Business Group will integrate its activities with those of other bodies in order not to conflict but to dovetail and find a common course.

INVOLVEMENT IN NEPAD BY THE SOUTH AFRICAN GOVERNMENT

The South African government is active in the NEPAD initiative and constantly reiterates its full support of NEPAD and the NEPAD Secretariat. Its economic strategy has given priority to strengthening and formalising trade and economic links with other countries in Africa. This strategy is based on the following imperatives:
- South Africa's economic development is inextricably linked with the economic development of the continent.
- As one of the leading economies in Africa, South Africa is presented with unique trade and investment opportunities, as well as with the challenge of contributing to the continent's economic revival and development.

- South Africa is increasingly contending with growing competition for markets and projects in Africa as the major developed economies seek an increased presence on the continent through various trade initiatives.

South Africa, through its Department of Trade and Industry, has been active in trade facilitation and export-incentive promotion, establishing business linkages through joint ventures, capacity-building and technical co-operation, government-to-government bilaterals, the establishment of intergovernmental partnership forums, cross-border development projects, economic research analysis and the promotion of a conducive legal and institutional framework.

However, business is not limited to large corporations and multinationals. The benefits of Africa's renewal should not be denied to the small and medium enterprise (SME) sector. SMEs can play a vital role in job creation and strengthening competition in the domestic markets. The challenge is to ensure that individual success at company level contributes towards the competitiveness of the national economy. NEPAD has the potential to turn Africa into a dynamic and economically vibrant continent that could offer the following to the SME sector:

- Through donor assistance, development finance and contributions of national governments, there will be many opportunities in the various areas of infrastructure development, such as building, upgrading and maintaining roads, ports and railway links as well as opportunities in telecommunications, health care, education and training.
- By reducing the risk of doing business in Africa through a concerted effort, NEPAD will create a favourable environment for the private sector to thrive and grow. It will also provide the scope for the establishment of new enterprises that can service the basic needs of people.
- In addressing corruption, NEPAD aims to lower the cost of entry into new markets and to allow for greater access to these markets for SMEs.
- NEPAD also aims to address the problem faced by countries dependent on single commodities, such as oil, minerals, coffee and tobacco, by assisting them to diversify their economies and to develop a stronger industrial and manufacturing base.

◆ By improving the dynamism of the private sector, NEPAD aims to act as a catalyst to attract new large-scale investments. Such investors will rely on small businesses to supply them with quality goods and services at competitive rates.

SOUTH AFRICAN COMPANIES IN THE REST OF AFRICA

As the business drive into Africa gathers momentum, South Africa has become the largest investor in Africa, overtaking the United Kingdom and the United States. South Africa is one of the key drivers of NEPAD, has elevated the developing-country profile at the World Trade Organisation and continually ensures that Africa remains a priority on the agendas of the G8 and the World Economic Forum. Through NEPAD, South African companies are able to take advantage of the benefits and growth opportunities elsewhere in Africa, whether as investors, traders or suppliers. Many South African companies are able to achieve superior returns in Africa, offsetting difficult, overtraded markets at home.

Companies such as Eskom are linked to more than 32 countries on the continent, Telkom and Spoornet are among organisations with significant investments in Africa, and Shoprite Holdings is the continent's largest retailer. MTN has an extensive subscriber base in Uganda, Rwanda, Cameroon, Swaziland and Nigeria, and Vodacom is pushing up its subscriber base substantially in the rest of Africa. The oil and gas sector is also showing significant growth, resulting in Africa becoming of increasing strategic importance as an oil producer. Nigeria pumps more oil than Kuwait, and Angola is producing significant quantities of oil and gas. While corporations such as Unilever and Shell have been active throughout Africa for decades, others such as Sasol and South African Breweries have only been active for five to ten years.

Valuable lessons on how to do business on the African continent can be learned from these organisations. A fine example of regional co-operation is MOTRACO, the co-operative project by South Africa, Swaziland and Mozambique to supply essential electricity to the by now highly successful Mozambique Aluminium Smelter. A similar but larger-scale, long-value, chain project now in progress is the Western Power Corridor Project, involving the Democratic Republic of the Congo (DRC), Angola, Namibia, Botswana and South Africa. This enterprise aims to connect the DRC and South Africa, spanning the five countries in the SADC region and is a bold endeavour to harness Africa's huge energy resources in order to power the continent's economies. Pooling power through integrating the region's electricity sectors will result in a massive market. Because energy in southern Africa is relatively inexpensive, the Western Power Corridor interconnection should attract high power-consuming industries to the region. These projects can be replicated in other regions throughout the continent. But business would be well advised to avoid reinventing the wheel in its zealous quest to implement NEPAD's business programmes.

Fresh lessons can also be learned from the big four accounting and auditing firms, each of which operates in thirty or more African countries according to globally determined standards. All these firms have strong intra-Africa networks that work together on joint projects, exchange staff and share resources. These firms have a record of ongoing participation in nationally and internationally funded projects that involve the development of infrastructure, governance, education, social welfare and financial capacity. Through their intra-Africa linkages, these firms are actively promoting NEPAD's ideals and encouraging local leaders to become involved in their own country's NEPAD activities. The South African Institute of Chartered Accountants, together with other major African institutes, is developing a programme for Africa with the support of the International Federation of Accountants (IFAC) to develop and upgrade auditing institutes and regulation, promote the adoption of international accounting and auditing standards and assist with quality assessment.

To ensure sustainable development in Africa, via NEPAD, South Africa has established four cross-border parks with its neighbours since 1994, with two more in progress.

IMPACT OF THE HIV/AIDS PANDEMIC

In developed countries, medical care for people living with HIV/AIDS is continually improving, yet in Africa people are dying because they cannot afford the health care or medicines that could save their lives. The disease is a heavy burden on Africa, because it weakens and kills adults in the prime of their working lives and consequently lowers productivity and erodes the skills base of African countries.

Improving access to treatment is vital in helping to prevent the spread of the disease. However, many governments in Africa – crippled by an illegitimate debt burden – have been forced to cut health and social services as part of structural adjustment programmes, and do not have the resources to provide the requisite treatment. Combating HIV/AIDS has been the focus of many international meetings in recent years, and is high on the agenda of the G8. Despite acknowledging HIV/AIDS as the biggest development challenge facing the continent, however, the G8 has failed to live up to its political and financial commitments to the HIV-positive and AIDS-infected people of Africa.

The vision of a new Africa arising in the 21st century could be lost if leaders fail to recognise that Africa's children, women and men are its greatest treasure and that the transformation of Africa can take place only if it is driven by its people. There has to be a real partnership to ensure a full engagement between African leaders and African people. This should include more extensive consultations with governments, regional and continental organisations, national representative assemblies and civil societies. Since NEPAD has now moved to centre stage, both in terms of policy and implementation, it is essential that African governments deliberate on the broader aims of NEPAD to deepen understanding among officials and the wider public on NEPAD's underlying vision and principles.

CONCLUSION

Africa is on the move. That the global community realises this is evident from the support for NEPAD at the 2002 G8 Summit in Kananaskis, at the WSSD, and at the plenary session of the United Nations on 16 September 2002.

Africa has embarked on a process of accelerating the bridging of the developmental, trade and digital divide. Rapid progress will be achieved only through increased trade and investment among African countries. Africa stands at the crossroads, with the winds of change blowing once again.

Many fine initiatives have been developed in the past, but have failed owing to timing, a lack of capacity for implementation and a lack of political will. NEPAD is a positive African Road Map that seeks to address many critical economic issues on the continent. Clearly, there are many positives as well as negatives to doing business in Africa. But the outlook is positive, because African countries are seen to be willing to adopt global economic and political practices. And the benefits of doing business in Africa outweigh the challenges and frustrations that are faced.

A great African enlightenment is beginning to unfold on this continent where the first *Homo sapiens* rose, stood erect and populated the world. By concerted effort, Africa can reclaim its past, reverse its marginalisation and make valuable contributions to the advancement of humanity.

The continental challenge is clear. It is this:
- To replace Afro-pessimism with an abiding sense of efficacy and optimism;
- to replace breakdowns with breakthroughs;
- to transform the wars in Angola and the DRC into the fire-power that will energise the African Renaissance;
- to turn the Zimbabwe ruins into icons of hope for Africa's future;
- to harness Nigeria's energy into a force of light and enlightenment;
- to ensure the interconnection of African energy, transport, communications and social networks.

Do these things and the vision of an African Renaissance will become a reality.

Reuel Khoza
Chairperson: NEPAD, Eskom Holdings Limited and AKA Capital (Pty) Ltd

THE NEXT
TEN YEARS

"War is an easy jive!" So said a young man to me in 1986 in Soweto, when I was outlining various futures for South Africa. "Let me take you up North and introduce you to some of the more conservative partners you'll be jiving with," was my response.

In retrospect, the country could have so easily jived into a war – and it didn't. I was, at the time, the co-ordinator of Anglo American's scenario planning function and the team had come up with two scenarios for South Africa: the "High Road" of negotiation leading to a political settlement with the country being accepted back into the international fold, or the "Low Road" of confrontation leading to a civil war and ultimately a wasteland. Were we to become a "winning nation" or a "losing nation" in the global league? We offered South Africans this stark choice and – against all expectations – they took the political High Road. Unequivocally. If you ask me for a simple reason why, it was because we were fortunate enough to have a group of remarkable leaders in command of the contending parties at the time. Their positive chemistry and collective vision bonded them sufficiently for the deliberations never to be in serious danger of being overwhelmed by the usual nasty stuff that precedes breakthroughs of this kind. In the event, the key that unlocked the door to full-scale democracy was the Government of National Unity. The GNU meant that nobody faced an immediate loss of face and power and it allowed the transition to proceed smoothly and over time. One of the "rules of the game" in our scenario study was that neither side would succeed with a "winner takes all" strategy. There had to be compromise. And there was.

So now, ten years on, will the miracle continue? Will we progress down the High Road towards a society that is a model for and the envy of Africa; or will we do a U-turn (slowly or quickly) which brings the Low Road back into play and will cause Afro-pessimists locally and overseas to say "I told you so"? Interestingly, our scenario team developed a model in 1986 which had two forks in the road ahead. The first one was a political fork, where the National Party either negotiated with the real leaders or co-opted a bunch of tame representatives of the majority into the existing government. As I've indicated, the first (and correct) fork was chosen. The second fork was an economic one where, having taken the High Road politically, there was a chance that South Africa could get it wrong economically, which would then impact on the new political dispensation and even reverse the gains made.

The positive economic path called for economic growth in the range of 4 to 6 per cent per annum. This would ensure the formation of a solid black middle class and, more importantly, begin to improve the lives of people who lived in abject poverty. The negative economic path (low, zero or negative growth) would mean growing pressure on government to become more populist in its attempt to retain the support of the squatter townships in urban areas, as well as the marginalised and cashless communities in rural areas. We named the ensuing downside scenario the "Argentinian Tango", where a populist government was replaced by a military regime which reverted back to a populist government and so on. All the while, the country would gradually spiral down towards the wasteland. It was our "cautionary tale".

IN FAIRLY GOOD SHAPE

While, on the one hand, South Africa has never achieved a 4 to 6 per cent annual growth rate since 1994, on the other hand we now have an economy which – on the basis of all the macroeconomic parameters normally used to judge performance, such as low inflation and low government budget/current account deficits – is in pretty good shape. Moreover, none of the nationalisation programmes threatened in the ANC's Freedom Charter, including those for the mines and banks, has taken place. Instead, black economic empowerment is being implemented in both the mining and banking fields via charters approved by both government and the private sector. Black mining magnates have emerged to rival their white counterparts.

Employment equity is now a standard target in all businesses, although for some it is not proceeding as fast as it should at board level. Procurement programmes are increasingly demanding that potential suppliers show progress in both black share-ownership and employment. If one studies the cars on motorways in rush hour in the cities, it appears that the ownership of fashionable makes is definitely becoming nonracial and non-gender-specific. The majority of lower-income commuters still get to work in taxis and trains and then by foot, but it's no different in many other parts of the world.

Residential neighbourhoods in cities and towns are beginning to be more integrated. Ironically, the ones that have shown most progress are some of the more conservative Afrikaans-speaking towns, where properties are more reasonably priced. There too the golf clubs are mixed because the fees are more affordable than those of exclusive courses in the major centres. Generally the local chambers of industry and commerce are merging to create one united business voice, and awards dinners see black and white winners coming up to the podium. Universities really have transformed themselves without dropping standards and so have plenty of formerly white schools. There again transformation has been least in the most exclusive schools, simply because most black parents cannot afford the fees and bursary funds to subsidise black children are still in their infancy.

Obviously the civil service is very different from what it was twenty years ago. People complain about delivery, but there are areas where the quality of service has definitely improved. The South African Revenue Service, for example, is now a world-class tax collection enterprise. Furthermore, the whites who have stayed on from the old days have blended into the new structures and, in my experience of dealing with particular departments, there's plenty of goodwill between old and new team members. An argument is sometimes put forward that affirmative action is just apartheid in reverse – but it isn't. Yes, blacks are replacing whites in the managerial chain and inevitably there are grumbles from reactionary quarters. But there's no way that that the changing of the guard is being driven by the same ideological fervour that underpinned apartheid. The ANC, so far, has lived up to its promise of remaining a nonracial party with a vision of a nonracial society, African in nature but which accommodates the unique history of South Africa and all its peoples. Pragmatism pervades all the governing party's policies in trying to achieve this goal.

Importantly, we have had moments in the new South Africa which are entirely symbolic and yet have powerfully reconciled old adversaries. Nelson Mandela's wearing of a rugby shirt to greet the South African team in the Rugby World Cup of 1995 and Charlize Theron being welcomed by the President when she visited South Africa a week after winning the Oscar for best actress in 2004 are prime examples. These things count because South Africans tend to be great put-downers and do the opposite of counting their blessings. You only have to listen to the talk-radio stations! Occasionally, however, the sun comes out and a great outpouring of national pride takes place. Then it's back to business as usual, the miracle being "usual" when it could have been so much worse.

THE ISSUE OF LAND

Given all this good news about how South Africans are busily adapting to their new circumstances, where is the bad news that can lead to the Argentinian Tango? The answer lies in three areas: land, unemployment and HIV/AIDS. On the issue of land, South Africa has made little headway in redistributing ownership, even with the glaring evidence just north of us of what can happen if the status quo continues for too long. We know that land is a highly emotive issue and, were land invasions to start on a wide scale in South Africa, international confidence would crumble. Probably nothing else could cause a tumble in world economic rankings as quickly as an unauthorised move of this nature.

The lack of progress in agriculture compared to industry is because industry has ownership structures which lend themselves more to transformation than land does. Crucially, ownership and management have been separated in industry, with shareholders owning the company and managers running it. Obviously, there are family businesses where the two are the same and in many companies managers have shares or share options. But the basic business model in industry divorces ownership from management, and black economic empowerment can proceed without too much disruption or resentment. In agriculture, the prevailing model doesn't allow for this type of transformation. Land, on the whole, is individually owned and the individual is the CEO of the farm. Any type of conventional transformation therefore is far more dramatic because it involves the replacement of the individual (and his or her family) as owner and CEO by a new individual (and his or her family).

Somehow or other South Africa is going to have to develop a land ownership model more in keeping with the industry model. One way to do this would be to turn farms into companies, with shares in the company being spread variously among employees, new black shareholding consortiums and the original farm owners. In parallel, and following in the footsteps of industry, employment equity plans could be put in place whereby a highly skilled class of black farm managers will evolve over time. This is not suggesting that plenty of competent black farmers do not already exist. They do, but they don't run the big commercial farms. Whatever model is chosen for the transformation of agriculture in South Africa has to recognise that farming these days is a very risky business. Protection is around no more. Artificially high prices are no longer offered by State boards, and fixed for the season. In a world of globalisation and free markets (where only American and European farmers continue to be subsidised), South Africa needs large, world-class, nonracially owned, professionally managed farms. The current idea of taking unwanted land, dividing it up into small plots and handing it over to black farmers, is doomed to failure. These farmers are being given a licence to lose money. Furthermore, much of South Africa is too fragile ecologically to sustain intensive small-scale farming. Desertification will inevitably follow such a policy.

HOW TO CREATE JOBS

The second issue is the current unemployment rate in South Africa, where the figure oscillates in the 30–40 per cent range. This calls to mind a rule called Karl's rule – as in Marx. If the masses are alienated, expect a revolution. With the level of unemployment where it is, South Africa faces the risk of Karl's rule coming into play. In a book written not too long ago entitled *When Mandela Goes,* Lester Venter posited the scenario of an extreme left-wing movement splintering from the ANC and eventually taking over the reins of government (the populist half of the Argentinian Tango).

The problem of unemployment stems from the fact that the formal sector of our economy is delinked from the informal sector – we are a "two worlds" economy and the two worlds are far apart. Moreover, the formal economy is no longer creating jobs as it used to – neither in the private sector where globalisation has meant business here having to produce more products and services with fewer people, nor in the public sector where constraints on tax increases put a lid on expanding the civil service and instituting public works programmes.

The bottom line is that the vast majority of jobs in the "Miracle Continues" scenario will have to be created in the medium-, small- and micro-enterprise sector, which up to now has been given short shrift in economic policy debates. Essentially we need an affirmative action programme for small business. For a start, an entrepreneur running a business below a certain size should be offered a significant tax holiday to compensate for the risk of setting up a new enterprise (like the first one million rand of profit tax-free). In addition, investors in small business will need to be given tax breaks for the risk they are taking. Perhaps one could even contemplate differential corporate tax rates, depending on the support a company is giving to small business and transformation generally.

The red tape surrounding the establishment and running of small business ought to be simplified to the point where the entrepreneur can do all the accounting and legal work required at a one-stop shop. Mentorship schemes should be encouraged, whereby the experience of retired business people can be tapped to assist first-time entrepreneurs with the formulation of their business plans and their subsequent implementation.

The retail banks in South Africa, as the principal reservoir of capital, will have to rethink their strategy of concentrating on ever higher value-added business to grow their profits, because this usually emanates from large corporate clients and high net worth individuals. How can we assist in banking "the unbankables" without risking the money of our depositors, they should really be asking themselves. How can we play the role in communities, both urban and rural, that we used to play when the bank manager was seen as a key player in sustaining the businesses and farms within that community through hard times? Nowadays, credit requests are normally handled through impersonal computer systems located in the head office which cannot discriminate (like old-fashioned bank managers did) between clients who looked at you with a level gaze as they voiced their requests and those who looked down at their shoes and shifted their eyes! Even if farmers did not have the necessary balance sheet to support the amount being asked for, allowances could be made for their business track records, standing in the community and general demeanour.

That's why human beings are so much better at making these judgements than computers. Dealing with small business is people-intensive and there's no way around that. If the banks in South Africa need motivation, it is simple. Should the country experience a breakdown in the social harmony currently pervading our society and end up in yet another chaotic war of the kind that seems to blight much of the Third World, the banks will go down with the country because none of them has significant overseas business. It's this worst-case scenario they have to guard against (like the farmers with land invasions).

One final avenue to be pursued is the strengthening of links between big business and small business through outsourcing. It's already happening, as many large South African companies entrust non-core activities to outsiders in order to concentrate on their own core skills. While it may be argued that outsourcing is a zero-sum game because outside contractors displace internal employees, it will create jobs in the longer run if the network of businesses acquiring the contracts expands successfully to take on other clients.

HIV/AIDS – THE BIGGEST CHALLENGE

The third issue – HIV/AIDS – is the biggest challenge of all if we are to stay on the High Road. We call it the "second struggle" in South Africa, the first one being the struggle against apartheid. The virus, in many ways, represents a much more formidable foe than human beings, because it is invisible and therefore harder to mobilise the populace against. If we had a human enemy on our border threatening to kill five million South Africans, it would be easy to conscript young soldiers into the war against the enemy. AIDS will have killed five million South Africans by 2010, and we are only beginning to mobilise the country now. Not only is HIV a miniature (and invisible) weapon of mass destruction, it is a long, drawn-out threat. Other viruses which caused epidemics in the past killed those infected within days or weeks. HIV without treatment kills its victim in six to eight years in Africa, ten to twelve years in America and Europe. The pool of infection is therefore larger and the response to the epidemic that much weaker, because we are not very well programmed as human beings to handle gradual threats. We are much better at coping with sudden threats, and there's nothing sudden about this one. HIV is stealthily and silently stalking its victims.

Furthermore, some recently released statistics on total registered deaths in South Africa by age group are truly disturbing. In 2002, the highest number of recorded deaths took place among people in their late twenties and thirties – more than among people in their sixties and seventies. How can one explain this premature hump in deaths? Perhaps better reporting of registered deaths in those age categories might account for some of the hump, but then better recording presumably applies to the older people who die as well – their recorded deaths have gone up too, so that doesn't explain the *difference* between the two in favour of the young. The second cause could be malnutrition or crime, but either affects everybody at any age. All in all, you have to come back to HIV/AIDS as the primary cause of death since it hits the younger generation much harder than the older one. And we are only just beginning to head upwards on the AIDS death curve in 2002 because the latter lags the infection curve by six to eight years. The majority of HIV-positive people were infected from the mid-nineties onwards and are still in a healthy state. Without treatment, the death curve is set to zoom, thereby distorting the total registered deaths curve even more.

The social impact of HIV/AIDS is more devastating than any other calamity that has befallen mankind such as earthquakes, plagues and wars. Earthquakes and plagues wipe out whole families, whereas wars wipe out young men; but the principal victims of HIV/AIDS where it is heterosexually transmitted are young women – the very ones who are going to bring up the children. Consequently, we are observing a dramatic increase in orphans in South Africa, possibly reaching two million or maybe more in 2010. One of the saddest things I have witnessed in this tragic epidemic has been a seventeen-year-old girl, whose parents are dead, trying to bring up seven younger siblings. She gets them up in the morning, feeds them porridge, sends them off to school, cleans their dirty clothes, goes off scavenging for wood for the evening fire, negotiates with the neighbours for the extra food she requires over and above what she buys with her grandmother's pension, cooks the evening meal and puts the children to bed. She repeats the whole process day in, day out, never attending school herself. Can you imagine doing that?

What are the scenarios for the future course of the epidemic? There are essentially four. The first one is called "Mass Medication", where the government rolls out its treatment effectively but the infection rate remains obstinately high. Right now the cost of antiretroviral therapy can be brought down to $1,500 a year – made up of $700 for the pills and $800 for the doctors' and nurses' salaries plus the cost of CD4 count and viral load tests. The price may go even lower but, however small the figure per patient, it will end up as big by South African standards. For example, if five million people are treated at any one time, that totals $7.5 billion per annum at $1,500 per patient (or R60 billion a year). Perhaps we will get some form of international financial assistance to bring this figure down. Apart from being expensive, this scenario is risky in that should the patients not comply with their drug regimens, resistant viruses may develop.

The second scenario is the "Graveyard Shift", where the treatment programme gets stalled and the numbers of AIDS deaths rise to around half a million per annum in three years time and around a million a year after 2010. Certain parts of South Africa such as KwaZulu-Natal will suffer negative population growth.

The third scenario is named "Early Days" as, in parts of South Africa such as the northern part of the Western Cape, infection rates are still very low. These communities are away from the main transport routes and transmission from the outside world is slow.

The last scenario is named after the prevention programme "ABC", which has been so effective in Uganda. "A" stands for "Abstain". If you can't abstain, "B – Be faithful" and if you can't be faithful, "C – use a Condom". The alternative as some say is "D – Death". The teenage prevalence rate in Uganda has fallen sharply as a result of this campaign. It has pushed the date of first sexual experience up to the mid- to late teens and reduced the number of partners per sexually active nineteen-year-old. We must follow Uganda's example for the High Road to continue.

CONCLUSION

So can we do it – remain on the High Road, that is? South Africa has had a ten-year honeymoon. For the marriage to continue without a messy and angry divorce, we have to face down the three challenges I've mentioned – land, unemployment and HIV/AIDS. On balance, I believe the "High Road" scenario can continue because this country is full of adaptable and resourceful people who will find ways of meeting these three challenges. But we do need help from the international community in achieving our goals. The stakes are high. If South Africa starts descending into a "Low Road" morass, the future of the African continent becomes enshrouded in doubt. The splendid NEPAD initiative will be irreparably harmed. While the focus of the West will clearly be to win the war against global terrorism, South Africa remains of the utmost strategic importance in the bid to spread democracy, freedom and prosperity simultaneously throughout the continent.

Clem Sunter
Chairman, Anglo American Chairman's Fund

INDEX

Please note: Page numbers in italics refer to figures and tables.

Aardklop festival 140
ABSA 201
Accelerating Access Initiative 103
advertising, magazine 150
AECI 32
affirmative action 192, 216
Africa Business Roundtable 205
Africa Competitiveness Report 21
Africa Economic Summit 21, 199, 201
Africa Global Information Infrastructure Project (AGIIP) 118
Africa Enterprise 38
African Advisory Group on ICT 113
African Children's Feeding Scheme 174
African Connection and Ministerial Oversight Committee 113
African Dream Project (ADP) 132
African Energy Fund 205
African Growth and Opportunity Act (AGOA) 12
African National Congress (ANC) 18, 19, 164
 business initiative 34
 Dakar meeting 33–34
 Freedom Charter 212
 Harare meeting 35, 36
 unbanning of 35–36
 women's role 85
African Nations Cup 153
African Peer Review Mechanism 199
African Road Map 210
Afrikaanse Handelsinstituut 36
Afrikaner Weerstandsbeweging (AWB) 36, 40
"Afro-pessimism" 66, 184, 198, 211–212
AIDS
 orphans 180
 pharmaceutical companies 184
 see also HIV/AIDS
Alberts, Louw 37
Alberts, Renee 44
All Africa Games 153
AmBev 66
Anglo American 32, 59
 Chairman's Fund 101
 corporate social investment 183
Anglo Executive Committee 102
AngloGold 100
Anglovaal 41
Anheuser-Busch 64, 66, 67
antiretroviral therapy (ART) 100, 101, 102, 219
Appletiser 61

Armscor 46–47
Arthur (singer) 156
Arts Federation 139
asymmetrical digital subscriber line (ADSL) 144
ATMs 131
Audit Bureau of Circulation (ABC) 149
Awesome Africa Music Festival 140
Azanian People's Organisation (AZAPO) 36

Ball, Chris 32
Bam, Brigalia 37
Bantu education 73
Bantu Men's Social Centre 152
Bateleur Research Solutions 201–202
Bayete 157
beer markets
 brands 69–70
 largest 65
 world's top 10 66
Big Business working group 80
Biko, Steve 16
Bill of Rights, South Africa's 86, 193–194
Binger Film Institute 163
Bisho shootings 40
Black Business working group 80
Black Economic Empowerment (BEE) 72–74, 192, 212
Black Economic Empowerment Commission (BEECom) 75–80
Black Management Forum 36
Blecher, Taddy 180
"Bluetooth" 124
Bond Exchange of South Africa 56
Boom Shaka 156
Boraine, Alex 33
Braithwaite, Loraine 43
Brink, Dr Brian 100
Broad-Based Black Economic Empowerment Bill 181
Broederstroom 34
Budweiser 64
Bureau for Economic Research (BER) 105
business
 duty of 16
 HIV/AIDS challenge 97–98
 initiative 34
Business Action for Sustainable Development (BASD) 204
Business Consultative Forum 204
Business Covenant on Corporate Governance 200
Business Covenant on the Elimination of Corruption and Bribery 200
Business Declaration on Accounting and Audit Practices 200
Business Declaration on Corporate Responsibility 200
Business Endorsement of NEPAD 199
Business Trust 179
Buthelezi, Chief Mangosuthu 19, 41, 42
 Davos 29
 Geneva conferences 30
 Harare meeting 36

Cachalia, Azhar 32, 34
Cannes Film Festival 141
Canca, Nomhle 87
Cape Film Commission 151, 162
Carlton Conference 36–37
Carrington, Lord Peter 41

Cassidy, Michael 33, 38
Castel group 62–63
Castle Lager 60, 61, 62
Cell C 108, 144
cellular technology 109–110
Centre for Educational Technology and Distance Education 118–119
Chaka Chaka, Yvonne 156
Chapman, Neal 19, 32, 35, 39–40
Charter Council 82
charters for empowerment 81–82
Chidzero, Bernard 18
Chikane, Frank 16, 37, 38
Children's Fund 184
China Resources Breweries (CBR) 63
church
 groups 183
 leaders 37
 women as 92
CIDA City Campus 180, 182
Citizen, The 164
City Press 168
Clegg, Johnny 152
Clinton, Bill 178, 184
Coca-Cola 64
CODESA 1 39–42
CODESA 2 39–42
Coetzee, Basil Manenberg 157
Cohen, Leon 35
Coleman, Colin 42, 44
Commonwealth Business Council 205
Communist Party, SA 35–36, 165
community-based organisation (CBO) 172–175
Competition Act 47–48
Confederation of South African Trade Unions (COSATU) 19, 34, 37
Conservative Party 19, 36
Constitution 15, 85, 154, 196
 Interim 189
 Preamble to 188, 190
Constitutional Court 196
constitutional negotiations 39–42
Consultative Business Movement (CBM) 30, 34, 35
consumer price index (CPIX) 53, 54
Contemporary African Music and Arts (CAMA) 132–133
Coors brewers 67
corporate social investment (CSI) 172–175, 183
 landscape in SA 177
Cricket World Cup 153
cultural diversity 137–138
Culture Africa Network (CAN) 133

Da Gama Textiles 61
Daily Dispatch 164
Daily Sun 168
DaimlerChrysler 180
Dakar conference 33–34
Danny K 156
Davos conference 31
De Beer, Zach 16, 32
De Klerk, F W 16, 18, 42
 Davos 29
 Nobel Peace Prize 15
Delaney, Peggy 185
Delmas treason trialists 34
Deloitte & Touche 200
Delta Foundation 182
Department of Trade and Industry (DTI) 109–110, 119, 120, 204, 206
Diageo 66
Digital Partnership 118, 122

digital radio mondiale (DRM) systems 145
digital satellite television (DSTV) 114, 143, 167, 179
digital video discs (DVDs) 145, 151
Dimension Data 107–109, 180
Dinners of Hope 180
Doha Development Round 12
Du Plessis, Barend 30
Durban Film Office 162
Dutch Reformed Church 37
Dyani, Johnny 157

e-Africa Commission 205
e-commerce 130
Ecumenical Assistance Trust 43
e-development 132–133
Edgars 61
e-government 115–117, 121
e-learning 131–132
election (1994) 39–42, 43
electricity-transmission projects 205
Electronic Communications and Transactions (ECT) Bill (2002) 111–112
Eloff, Theuns 33, 36, 37, 39, 41, 44
Employees Pension Fund 77
employment equity 212–213
entertainment industry 141–153
entrepreneurship 134, 182, 216
Ernst & Young 200
Eskom 201, 207
e-training 130–131
e-tv 140, 142, 167
Evans, Leo 'Rusty' 17
Exchange Control Authorities 48
exchange controls, removal of 48, 49

Fassie, Brenda 156
Federal Communications Commission (FCC) (US) 144
Feinstein, Andrew 44
Field Band campaign 179
FIFA's 2010 Soccer World Cup 153
film industry 159–163
Film Resources Unit 162
Films and Publication Act (1996) 141
financial sector 55–56
Financial Sector Black Economic Empowerment Charter 56
First National Bank (FNB) 32, 157, 180
fiscal policy 49–52
Foreign Affairs 17
Foster, J A 184
Fraser-Moleketi, Geraldine 117
Freedom Charter 85
Fresco, Maurice 158
FTSE 100 64

Gallo, Eric 152
Gates, Bill 185
Gauteng Film Office 151, 162
Gencor (now BHP Billiton) 17, 59
gender equality 90
General Agreement on Traffic and Trade (GATT) 47
General Export Incentive Scheme (GEIS) 47
Geographic Information Systems (GIS) 132
Gildenhuys, Antonie 39
Global Council on HIV/AIDS 99
Global Fund to fight AIDS, TB and Malaria 104
global integration 46–49
globalisation 198, 215–216

Global System for Mobile communications (GSM) services 107, 108, 109
Godsell, Bobby 38
Goedehoop colliery 103
Gordon, Donald 17
Government Employees Pension Fund 77
Government Gateway project 117
Government Information Technology Officers (GITO) Council 116
Government of National Unity (GNU) 211
Grameen Phone experiment 129–130
Grealy, Rosemary 35
Greenside Colliery 100
Group of Eight Africa (G8) 203
 agenda 207
 HIV/AIDS 209
 Plan of Action 112–113
 Summit 203
Growth, Employment and Redistribution (GEAR) 74, 192
Guguletu Seven 189
Gumede, Sipho 157
Gwangwa, Jonas 157

Hall, John 29, 37, 38, 39
Harris, Miranda 32–33
Harris, Roger 32–33
Heineken 66
Henry J Kaiser Foundation 104
Heyns, Johan 37
Heyns, Katinka 161
HIV/AIDS 203, 214, 217–219
 and the arts 157, 163
 education and prevention 98–100
 pandemic 208–209
 scenarios for future 218–219
 tests in mine sites 97
 women 89
HIV-positive employees 100–101
Hofmeyr, Murray 35, 37, 42
Human Rights Commission 196

2004 IDC Black Book 114
IBLF, see International Business Leaders Forum
Ibrahim, Abdullah 155, 157
Independent Communications Authority of South Africa (ICASA) 141, 144, 147
Independent Democratic Association of South Africa (IDASA) 33
Independent Electoral Commission 43
Independent Producers' Organisation 161
Industrial Development Corporation (IDC) 151, 200
Industrial Development Zones 78
information and communications technology (ICT) 123–130, 204
 Charter working group 120
 in flux 107–109
 legislation 110–111, 121
 open standards 116
Inkatha Freedom Party (IFP) 15, 37, 41
Interbrew 66
International Business Leaders Forum (IBLF) 118
International Federation of Accountants (IFAC) 208
International Monetary Fund (IMF) Article IV Report 13

internet 110, 123
Internet Solutions 108
Investec Bank 180
"Investment for Growth" accord 77
Irdeto system 143
iscathamiya entertainers 152, 157
Isolezwe daily 148

Jansen, Robbie 157
jazz 151–152, 157
Jensen, Mike 108
Jimmy B 156
job creation projects 182, 215–217
Johannesburg Securities Exchange (JSE) 55, 56, 61, 63, 75, 87, 200, 201, 204
Johannesburg World Summit Company 204
Joint Education Trust (JET) 179
Jordan, Dr Pallo 146
JSE Socially Responsible Investment Index (SRI) 181
Juluka 152
Jury, Brendan 156
justice and reconciliation 189–190

Kearney, A T 201
Kente, Gibson 158
Key Points Act 170
Khoza, Reuel 21
King II Report 133
King Commission on Corporate Governance 200
King, Mervyn (Tradego) 32
Kissinger, Henry 41
Klaaste, Aggrey 38
Klein Karoo Nasionale Kunstefees 140
Klotz, Phyllis 157
Kora Music Awards 140
Kriel project 99
Krog, Antjie 193
kwaito music 156
KwaZulu-Natal Film Commission 162

Ladysmith Black Mambazo 152, 156, 157
land issue 214–215
Land Act (1913) 72
Landau, Basil 17
Legal Aid Board 152
Lekoto, Patrick 34
Liberty Life 17
Lion King, Disney's 156
Lion Match Company 61
liquidity crisis 45–46
local area networks (LANs) 143
London School of Hygiene and Tropical Medicine 103
London Stock Exchange 63
Loring, Richard 158
lottery, national 184
loveLife, SA NGO 104
Lubner, Bertie 18, 204
Luhabe, Wendy 87
Lukhosi, Pathekile 157

Madiba, see Mandela, Nelson Rolihlahla
Maffin, Bongo 156
magazines 149–150
Magubane, Mfiliseni 157
Mahlasela, Vusi 155, 156
Makeba, Miriam 152
Mandela Foundation 104
Mandela, Nelson Rolihlahla 16, 25–27, 42, 97, 104, 153, 188
 Carlton Conference 37

Index 223

Children's Fund 184
Davos 29
  Nobel Peace Prize 15
  reconciliation 190
  sport 152–153, 214
  TIKKUN patron 180
Mandela, Winnie 33
Manhatten Brothers 157
Manuel, Trevor 18, 20, 31
Market Theatre 157
Marsden, Debra 36, 44
Marshall, Tony 189
Masekela, Hugh 152, 155, 157
Mashiyane, Spokes 157
maskandi music 157
Matamele, David 158–159
Matsepe-Casaburri, Dr Ivy 112, 113
Mattera, Don 158
mbaqanga music 157
Mbeki, Thabo 15, 16, 18, 97, 154–155, 187
  Dakar conference 34
  Geneva conferences 30
  Harare meeting 35
Mbeki, Zanele 88
Mboweni, Tito 18, 20, 31
  Dakar conference 34
  Geneva conferences 30
  Harare 35
Mbuli, Letta 152, 156
McCauley, Ray 37
Mchunu, Sipho 152
Mda, Jakes 158
Mdlalose, Frank 15, 16
MDM (Mass Democratic Movement) 34
M'du (singer) 156
media landscape 167–168
Media Development and Diversity Agency (MDDA) 149
Medium-Term Expenditure Framework 51
Menell, Clive (Anglovaal) 41
Menuhin, Yehudi 139
Mercosur 12
Metropolitan Life 75, 105–106
Meyer, Roelf 15, 16, 36, 41
Mgcina, Sophie 155
Mhlongo, Busi 155, 156
Millennium Declaration (UN) 117–119
Millennium Development Goals (MDGs) 98, 117–119, 127
Miller brewers
  acquisition 66–68
  major brands 67
  US market 67
Miller Brewing Company 64, 67
Miller Genuine Draft 60, 62
Mindset Network 179
Mini, Vuyisele 155
M, Lebo 156
M-Net 140
mobile data communication 135
mobile phone (cellular) industry 144–145
Modise, Tim 146
Moeketsi, Kippie 139
Mogoba, Stanley 38
Mojela, Louisa 87
Molefe, Popo 30, 34
Molobi, Eric 30
Mona, Vusi 168
Mondi Forests programmes 99
monetary policy 52–54
Moosa, Valli 33
Morobi, Murphy 32–33
Morris, Philip 67, 68
Mostert, Anton 32

MOTRACO 207
Motsepe, Patrice 22
movie industry 150–151
Mozambique Aluminium Smelter 207
Mphai, Vincent 166
MTN 108, 144, 179, 207
Mtwa, Percy 157
Mufamadi, Sydney 34
Mugabe, Robert 18, 20
MultiChoice 114, 140, 179
MultiChoice Africa 179
music industry 151–152
Myeni, Musa 41
MyWireless 144

Naidoo, Jay 29, 34, 38
Namalwa Sands operation 100
Natal Witness 164
National African Chamber of Commerce 36
National Arts Festival 140
National Association of Broadcasters (NAB) 146
National Black Economic Empowerment Act 79
National Business Initiative (NBI) 178
National Empowerment Fund 78
National Empowerment Funding Agency 79
National Film & Video Foundation (NFVF) 150–151, 160–161, 163
National Party 32, 164
National Peace Accord 38–39
National Peace Process 37
National Science Foundation (USA) 108
Naudé, Beyers 37, 43
Nel, Christo 32, 33, 35, 44
NEPAD Business Group 21, 199, 203, 204
  Action Plan 204–205
  committee 200–201
  formation of 200–201
  Secretariat 201
  Steering Committee 203
NEPAD Business Initiative 202
net open position in foreign reserves (NOFP) 53, 54
New Partnership for Africa's Development (NEPAD) 13, 197–200
  e-Africa Commission 113
  ICT programme 112–115
  government and 205–207
  perceptions about 201–202
  technological development 137–138
Newspaper Association of South Africa (NASA) 148–149
newspapers 147–148, 164–166
  circulation 169
Ngcaba, Dr Andile 118
Ngema, Mbongeni 155, 157, 158
Ngewu, Cynthia Nomveyu 189
Ngoasheng, Moss 30
Nkhuhlu, Wiseman 199
Nkosi Sikilel'i Africa (God Bless Africa) 152
Nobel Peace Prize 15
non-governmental organisations (NGOs) 118, 172–175
non-profit sector 183
not-for-profit organisation (NPO) 172–175
Nujoma, Sam 18
Nyandeni, Thembi 158

Office of Communications (Ofcom) (UK) 144
Office of the Government Chief Information Officer (OGCIO) 115–116
Ohlsson's 61
oil and gas sector 207
Okumu, Washington 41, 42
Old Mutual 59
online banking initiatives 108
Oppikoppie festival 140
optic-fibre submarine cable 205
O'Reilly, Tony 42, 164
Organisation for Economic Co-operation and Development (OECD) 198, 199, 203
Orlin, Robyn 157
Oude Libertas Festival 140
Owen, Ken 38

Pahad, Aziz 35
Pahad, Essop 35
Pan African Congress (PAC) 35–36, 164, 165
PanAmSat 179
Peace Accord 38–39
Peace Committee 29, 38–39
Peace Parks Foundation 132
Peace Secretariat 39
Peng, Li (Chinese premier) 20, 29–30
Perlman, John 146
Peroni 60, 62
PG Glass Group 179
Phuzekhemisi 157
PG Bison 35
Pienaar, Francois 153
Piliso, Ntemi 157
Pilsner Urquell 60, 62, 68, 69
Planact 36
Plate Glass 61
Plzensky Prazdroj (Czech brewers) 62
poverty 192
  alleviation 197
  and HIV/AIDS 97–98
PowerBelt project 99
Presidential National Commission on Information Society and Development 115
PricewaterhouseCoopers 200
Private Equity Fund for Women 92
protest music 155–157
protest theatre 157–158
Public Finance Management Act 51
public/private partnerships 178–181
Pukwana, Dudu 157

radio 145–147
Radegast (Czech brewers) 62
Radmark 146
Rainbow Nation 155
Rakusin, Debbie 158–159
Ramaphosa, Cyril 15, 19, 41, 42
Rathebe, Dolly 155
reconciliation 190, 193–195
Reconstruction and Development Programme (RDP) 74–75, 80, 119, 178
Record Industry of South Africa (RISA) 152
Record of Understanding 41
Relly, Gavin 32, 37
Rembrant/Richemont 59
restorative justice 189
retail banks 216
Robertson, Bruce 44
Roodt, Darrell James 161
Rugby World Cup 153, 214
Rustenburg church leaders' committee 37

SABMiller 59–64
    acquisition 66–68
    future 70–71
    international premier brands 60
SA Media Facts 2003 169
SA Music Week 140
Sander, Mike 32, 35
Sanlam 75
Sasol 46–47, 207
satellite radio 147
SchoolNet SA 118–119, 122
Schwab, Klaus 16, 19, 21, 29, 30
Scott, Tony 139
Scotts Stores Group 61
second network operator (SNO) 144
Semenya, Caiphus 156
Sentech 144, 179
Serobe, Gloria 87
Shante, Aba 156
Shaw Wallace Breweries Ltd 63
Shell 207
Shoprite Holdings 207
short message service (SMS) 110, 145
Sibikwa Players 157–158
Sicre, Frédéric 30
Simon, Paul 152, 156
Singh, Anant 161
Sisulu, Albertina 33
Sisulu, Max 18
Skylarks 157
Slovo, Joe 41
small and medium enterprise (SME)
    e-commerce 130
    sector 206–207, 216
    skills development 78
Soccer Laduma 148
Soccer World Cup (2010) 153
Socially Responsible Investment Index (SRI), JSE 181
Soros, George 165
South Africa Free Elections Fund (SAFE) 42, 43
South African Breweries 59, 70–71, 207
    global consolidation 64–66
    global expansion 62–63
    growth through divesitfication 61
    London listing 64
    people culture 68–69
South African Broadcasting Corporation (SABC) 140, 141–142, 146, 163, 179
South African Business Coalition on HIV and AIDS 105
South African Business Trust 205
South African Chamber of Business 200
South African Chamber of Commerce 36
South African Chamber of Mines 97
South African Communist Party 19
South African Council of Churches 37, 38
South African Federation Against Copyright Theft (SAFACT) 152
South African Institute of Chartered Accountants 208
South African Interim Constitution (1993) 187–188, 189
South African Music Rights Organisation (SAMRO) 152
South African National Editors' Forum (SANEF) 141, 170
South African Post Office 117

South African Reserve Bank 46, 53
South African Revenue Service (SARS) 117, 213
South African Scriptwriters Association (SASWA) 162–163
South African Technology Vanguard (SAVANT) 109
Southern African Development Co-ordination Conference (SADCC) 18
Southern Africa Summit 20
Southern Life 32
Sowetan 38, 164
    Sunday World 148
special purpose vehicles (SPVs) 75
Spicer, Michael 42, 183
Spier Festival 140
Spokes, H 156
Spoornet 207
sport 152–153
Stable Theatre 157
Standard Bank 179
Standish-White, John 100
Starfish 180
Star, The 165, 166, 167
State Information Technology Agency (SITA) 116
STD treatment 99, 104
Steyn, Judge Jan
    Geneva conferences 30
Stimela 157
"stokvels" 92–93
Suidooster festival 140
Sunday Sun 148
Sunday Times 38, 148, 166, 168, 179
Sunter, Clem 101
Sun, The 166
sustainable development
    framework 125–126
    strategies for 198
Synergos Institute 185

Tambo, Oliver 40
tax 50–51, 174
TB management 99, 100
technology
    corporate governance 133–134
    and development 124–126
    and economy 127–128
Telecomminications Act (1996) 111
television 141–143, 167
Telkom 144, 207
Terre'Blanche, Eugene 36, 40
Theron, Charlize 151, 214
Third-generation (3G) high-speed networks 135
Tiger Brands 179
TIKKUN ("transformation") 180
Tradego 32
trade
    reform 47
    relations liberation 49–50
    transformation 190–193
Trust Bank 32
Truth and Reconciliation Commission 161, 189–190
    process and report 193–194
Tsedu, Mathatha 170
Tshwete, Steve 34
Tutu, Archbishop Desmond 15, 16, 155
    Peace Committee 38, 39
Twala, Dan 152
Twala, Todd 158
Tyske Gronie 63

unemployment 214, 215
Unilever 207

Union of Southern African Artists 139
Unite Against Hunger campaign 179
United Breweries 61
United Nations plenary session 209
Urban Foundation 36, 174
USAID Leland Initiative 118, 122
Uys, Pieter-Dirk 157

Van der Merwe, Koos 19
Van Wyk, Chris (Trust Bank) 32
Van Zyl Slabbert 33
Venter, Lester 215
Verwoerd, Betsie 15–16
Video Resource Centre 162
Videovision Entertainment 162
Viljoen, Constand 15, 36, 40
village pay phones (VPP) 129–130
Vita Dance Umbrella 157
Vodacom 108, 144, 207
Vodacom International 114
Voice over Internet Protocol (VoIP) 112
Voluntary Counselling and Testing (VTC) programme 104, 105–106
Von Memerty, Ian 158
Vorster, John 16
Vosloo, Arnold 161
voter education 42–43
Vrye Weekblad 159
Vundla, Mfundi 161

Weekly Mail 159, 164
Western Power Corridor Project 207–208
Whiteside, Alan 101
Wiphold Trust 87
wireless
    industry 136–137
    technology 123
wireless application protocol (WAP) 145
wireless application service providers (WASPs) 145
women
    access to facilities 88–91
    boardroom 86–87
    church ordination 89
    economic empowerment 87–88
    government 86
    role of 91–93
    statistics on 95–96
Women Investment Portfolio Holdings (Wiphold) 87
Women's Development Bank 87–88
Women's League 85
Working Group on e-Government in the Developing World 115
World Bank 94
World Development Report (2000) 94
World Economic Forum (WEF) 16, 44, 178, 199, 201, 207
    Davos 29
World Summit on Information Society (WSIS) 118
World Summit on Sustainable Development (WSSD) 204
Worldspace Southern Africa 147
World Trade Centre 40
World Trade Organisation (WTO) 47, 207
    Doha Development Round 12
Wrighton, Peter 19, 35

Zuma, Jacob 15, 16
Zwelithini, King Goodwill 38